What a Body Knows

Finding Wisdom in Desire

First published by O Books, 2009
O Books is an imprint of John Hunt Publishing Ltd., The Bothy, Deershot Lodge, Park Lane, Ropley, Hants, SO24 0BE, UK
office1@o-books.net
www.o-books.net

Distribution in:

UK and Europe
Orca Book Services
orders@orcabookservices.co.uk
Tel: 01202 665432 Fax: 01202 666219
Int. code (44)

USA and Canada
NBN
custserv@nbnbooks.com
Tel: 1 800 462 6420 Fax: 1 800 338 4550

Australia and New Zealand
Brumby Books
sales@brumbybooks.com.au
Tel: 61 3 9761 5535 Fax: 61 3 9761 7095

Far East (offices in Singapore, Thailand, Hong Kong, Taiwan)
Pansing Distribution Pte Ltd
kemal@pansing.com
Tel: 65 6319 9939 Fax: 65 6462 5761

South Africa
Alternative Books
altbook@peterhyde.co.za
Tel: 021 555 4027 Fax: 021 447 1430

Text copyright Kimerer L. LaMothe 2008

Design: Stuart Davies

ISBN: 978 1 84694 188 7

Printed by Digital Book Print

What a Body Knows

Finding Wisdom in Desire

Kimerer L. LaMothe, Ph.D.

BOOKS

Winchester, UK
Washington, USA

Also by Kimerer L. LaMothe

Nietzsche's Dancers: Isadora Duncan, Martha Graham, and the Revaluation of Christian Values

Between Dancing and Writing: The Practice of Religious Studies

For more information about Kimerer and her work, please visit:

VITAL ARTS
www.vitalartsmedia.com

CONTENTS

Preface

Wisdom in Desire?

There is wisdom in desire.

It sounds too good to be true. Too self-serving and too easy. It isn't.

Desire wells in us as a felt sense of yearning for something we lack. It fills our hearts and minds and bodies to the point of overwhelming other concerns, impelling us towards whatever we believe will grant us the pleasure we seek. We want to move with it.

Yet nearly every aspect of our lives in modern western culture teaches us to distrust our desires. Desires, we learn, are unruly forces — animal instincts and unknowing urges — driving us to act against our better judgment in ways that threaten the very happiness we seek. Simply by participating in our social, economic, and religious systems, we learn to think and feel and act *as if* we were minds living in and over bodies whose responsibility it is to bring our desires in line with what our minds know to be right. The more thoroughly we absorb this education, the more we actively override *what our bodies know*.

There *is* wisdom in desire. It is wisdom guiding us to move in ways that will grant us health, pleasure, and well being. Nevertheless, if we are to find this wisdom, we must learn to experience our bodies differently. Our bodies are not material vessels in which we dwell. They are *movement* – the dynamic and self-creating source of our ability to think and feel and act at all. Once we cultivate a sensory awareness of our bodies as *the movement that is making us*, we have what we need to find, trust, and move with the wisdom in our desires.

ℭ℟

What a Body Knows inspires readers to this task by focusing on the wisdom in three desires that are fundamental to human living—our desires for food, for sex, and for spirit. We desire food—the calories, vitamins, and minerals we need to build our bodies. We desire sex—a life enabling physical intimacy. We desire spirit—the sense of vitality, direction, and belonging that allows us to affirm our lives as worthwhile.

Not only are these desires basic to human life, they are each under fire in contemporary culture for causing or contributing to a societal crisis—obesity, divorce, and depression, respectively. In each case the controversies over diagnosis and cure provide us with a ready grasp of the attitudes towards desire that we have imbibed. In the salvos launched daily in these debates, we find dramas writ large that play out to a greater or lesser extent in our personal lives. If we can understand why the proposed strategies for handling these crises are not proving as effective as predicted, we have what we need to realize why our best move as individuals is to find wisdom in the very desires we are taught to blame for our social and psychological ills.

What a Body Knows begins its discussion of each desire by laying out the contemporary case against it. The arguments are familiar to all. As social scientists, media outlets, and cultural authorities tell us, our desire for food is making us fat: two-thirds of all Americans are overweight, half of those are obese, and the numbers, especially among children, are rising. Our desire for sex is wrecking havoc on our marriages: nearly half of all marriages end in divorce and the number of married couples is at an all time low. Our desire for spirit is weighing us down: levels of depression, suicide, and social disorders are high, among young adults in particular. The message across the board is clear: we are not getting what we want, and our desires are to blame. We want too much.

2

After surveying this landscape, *What a Body Knows* proceeds to interrogate the most highly promoted solutions. Our best recourse, as we are advised in all realms, is to establish a surer mastery over our desire. The controversies that rage over each crisis concern the manner of establishing that mastery. Should we exercise greater will power by going on a diet, sticking to our vows, or choosing a self-help program? Or should we rely on external and expert means, such as surgery or drugs, religious traditions or changes in public policy, to bolster the control over our behavior that we cannot ourselves muster? Despite the intensity of the debates, little progress has yet been made in any realm to reverse the societal trends.

Analyzing this situation, *What a Body Knows* makes its case. Desire is not the problem. The problem is that we make desire the problem. In doing so we perpetuate the cause of the issues we are trying to address. We are so thoroughly trained to think and feel and act as if we were minds over bodies that we have lost the ability to know what our living breathing bodies need in order to thrive. Our attempts as individuals and communities to override our desires for food, sex, and spirit are perpetuating our dissatisfaction.

Although it might not appear so at first, this knot of insights carries threads of hope. For once we grasp it, we can also sense possibilities for response. New ideas are not enough. What we need is to dislodge the sense of ourselves as minds over bodies, and cultivate an alternative. We need to learn how to discern what our living breathing bodies know.

Here *What a Body Knows* makes its unique and most important contribution: it fleshes out such an alternative. We can cultivate a *sensory awareness of our bodies as the movement that is making us.* When we do, we learn to pay attention to what we are sensing—whether boundless hunger, chronic cravings, or sinking depression—and welcome what we are sensing as vital information about how to move in ways that will not recreate

3

these same feelings of discomfort. We learn to find the wisdom in our desires for food, sex, and spirit.

For each desire, this book describes what this wisdom is, how to find it, and why it works. We learn that our desire for food is guiding us *to follow the arc of eating pleasure to a sense of enough.* Our desire for sex is guiding us *to ask our partners for what we need in order to give and receive a life enabling touch.* And our desire for spirit is guiding us in how *to name and make real the network of relations that will support us in becoming who we are.*

Our sensations of disappointed desire are not problems to numb, override, or cover up. Our desires and disappointments are who we are. They are what our ways of living are creating in us. To find their wisdom, we must unlearn, in each realm of desire, our tendency to think and feel and act as if we were minds over bodies. We must cultivate a sensory awareness of ourselves as bodies whose movements are making us. When we do, we find *play* in the moment—the freedom to move differently, and the creativity to discern how.

ʘ

Doing so is as easy, and as difficult, as remembering to breathe.

Breathing. A rhythm of two movements. Inhaling. Exhaling. The diaphragm presses down, creating a vacuum. Air rushes in, filling our lungs. The diaphragm releases and bounds back, expelling air, returning the pressure inside the body to equilibrium with the pressure outside the body. The wave begins again. In and out, empty and full. We are never not inhaling, exhaling, or pivoting in between. We breathe to move and move to breathe, over and again.

Inhale, exhale. As air rushes in, our bodies sift what we need to build tissue and bone, emotion and idea. As air rushes out, our bodies release what we don't need back to the earth, waste and excess, tension and stress. In every moment of our lives, the

4

breathing movements we are making are making us. Our breathing is creating us; it is enabling us to sense, feel, think, and act — to be and become who we are. With every breath, we make it so. We make us so.

Inhaling, exhaling. Every breath we take in passes through the heart. The oxygen absorbed through our lungs into our blood flows first into the chambers of our heart, where it is pumped in rhythmic time to the far reaches of our sensory awareness and deep into the tissues of the heart itself. We breathe to beat and beat to breath. The heart-propelled stream carries earth, warmth, and water too — the elements comprising every cell of our bodies. Its cadences sound out our ongoing connection with the wider universe in which we swim.

Trained as we are to think and feel and act as if we were minds over bodies, we forget that we are breathing. We take breathing for granted as what our bodies do without our conscious involvement.

When we forget to breathe, we forget to feel. When we forget to feel, our inner sense of self pales. Without this internal bodily sense, we fall prey more easily to the barrage of stimuli and boisterous voices telling us who we are, what we should do, and how we should manage our desires. We experience our own bodies as objects whose logic is foreign to us.

We can remember to breathe. When we breathe we sense. When we sense we know. We open up a space of sensory awareness inside ourselves, and in this space, we can greet our desires, turn them over and inside out. We are able to recognize our desires as shapes of our own making, and to learn from them about potentials for our pleasure — our own health and well being — that we have yet to discover.

∞

We cannot change ourselves. The notion that we can change ourselves is a product of our mind over body training: apply five principles, follow ten steps, practice four exercises, and achieve the success, wealth, figure, sex, or happiness you deserve. *Presto!*

Nevertheless, once we cultivate a sensory awareness of the movement making us, we also realize that we are never *not* changing at every level of our being. For every movement we make — every thought, feeling, and action — is changing us, making us into the person who made that thought, had that feeling, or accomplished that action. Every movement we make educates our senses in one direction and not another. We are constantly creating the patterns of sensation and response that become us — that characterize our being in the world. Even though we can't change ourselves we can learn to participate more or less consciously in the rhythms of our own bodily becoming.

This book is designed to support this process — not to tell you how you should change but to help you become more aware of life enabling trajectories in your own living that are already happening in you, in the *movement* of your desires.

There is no formula for living life well that works for everyone. There is only a process of learning to discern, trust, and move with the wisdom of our desires. There is only the work of learning to participate in our bodily becoming with greater degrees of sensory awareness.

All we have to offer the world is the work that the satisfaction of our desires demands.

CR

I wrote this book on a farm. I moved here with my partner Geoff, and our children, Jordan, Jessica, and Kyra (then aged nine, seven, and three), in July 2005. I was nine months pregnant with our son Kai. Our plan was to create a center for arts and ideas, a place where Geoff could make his music and I could dance and write, in closer contact with the natural world. After fifteen years in the academic world, as a graduate student and then professor, I was eager to take what I had learned from my studies of religion and philosophy and apply it to a study of contemporary culture.

I have always been interested in how the big questions of who we humans are get worked out in the small decisions we make day in and day out regarding the most basic elements of our lives. As Nietzsche says, it is "precisely here one must begin to *relearn*."

Moving, I had this book in mind, and our experiences of finding our way in this new place provided me, again and again, with the opportunities I needed to learn what I needed to *relearn* to write the book I wanted to write. Stories of these experiences and others before them weave through this book as what has enabled it to be. I share my own process of finding, trusting, and moving with the wisdom in desire, not as proof of the theories offered, nor as examples of how to do it right. Rather, I seek to portray as honestly as possible the complex process of working with ideas and experiences that has given rise to this book in me. Writing is a bodily process. It can never not be so.

Here at Hebron Hollow Farm, we now have a duck, a rooster, two cats, three cows, four hens, four children, and a horse named Marvin. We are in cooperative ventures with local farmers to hay our fields, tap our maple trees, and raise bees for honey. Our center, Vital Arts Media (www.vitalartsmedia.com) is coming to life, as the fruit of our efforts to live in ways that remain faithful to the earth in us and around us.

While our path is not for everyone, my hope is that sharing it will inspire others to carry out similar explorations in their own lives. Perhaps others will discover in their own way what is also true for me: *It is time to move.*

CR

An
Experience
Shift

CR

1

A Walk

'The sedentary life is the very sin against the Holy Spirit.
Only thoughts reached by walking have value.'
Nietzsche — *Twilight of Idols*, 471

I am having a lovely morning. Our son Jordan, home sick from school, is not too sick, and I am enjoying my time with him. I allow him to watch a movie. Kai falls asleep. I sit down to write. Reading back over the previous day's catch, I make corrections, clarify some rough passages, and print out the pages. I draft some new ideas. Kai wakes up. Jordan returns from screen land. I feel play in the moment, loving work, loving family, in a mutually enabling spiral.

A few hours later, everything starts to feel less fun. I am no longer moved as I had been just an hour before by the intricate web of vessels visible beneath my infant's tender skin, or by the half-smile of a child finding comfort in my embrace. My senses are withering. My ideas stop flowing. I want sugar, caffeine — something sharp. I want adult company, some spark or spur. I want some vital touch. Life weighs heavily.

I have been here before. I know what I need. *To move.* I need to feed my body, stir up my sensory awareness, replenish love. *A walk, the easiest thing.* Of course, I do not want to go for a walk. I want to stuff myself into forgetful oblivion and lose consciousness of this dragging dullness. But I must. My desires, tousled, knotted, and confused, are pointing the way.

Geoff comes home and takes over. I bundle up. My mind is complaining bitterly. It is cold and snowy. Kai will need to nurse.

The kitchen is a mess. There are other things I should be doing. Carrying my screaming mind out through the door, my body propels me forward.

I walk vigorously, pumping my arms and legs, sending blood rushing through my limbs, feeling the pull of air into my lungs. My head lightens and begins to clear. I feel brightness opening.

I walk hard and start to feel again. Hunger stabs. I want to turn back and eat. But then the hunger slips sideways. I know that the energy I want is not of the caloric kind. I feel a deep gnawing ache for the return of my senses, for *what my body knows*. This hunger is the first sign that it is beginning to return.

I trudge up the mountain. Crunch, crunch, crunch. Each step plunges through a crusty surface into powdery fluff. I follow tracks I left earlier in the week, sometimes sticking my foot into an old hole and sometimes stepping sideways, taking cues from the past and honoring my new gait. My hands start to warm up.

I begin to notice things. There are prints in the tracks I made two days ago. Deer hooves. I follow the deer, who followed me. Perhaps I saved the deer some wear and tear on its shins. A thrill passes lightly through me at the thought of our meeting this way.

I keep walking, puffing, crunching up the hill, up and around the field. Ten then twenty minutes pass, half an hour. Gold and silver sparks of snow catch my eye. The rhythmic breaking of the snow echoes in my chest. A pale sun peeps through the soft splotchy clouds. Down by the pond I find the tracks of a snow mobile. An intruder. Anger and dismay rush through. I place a branch across the tracks. *Keep out*. Will they even notice?

Keep walking. My body propels me along, beside the pond and up to the crest of the hill where we first stood in awe of this beautiful land. I feel an impulse to run, to empty myself into space. A surge of energy wells, lifting my arms to the horizons, breathing me deeply. *I want, I want, I want… to play*. I run down the hill on the other side, pulling my legs straight out of each crusty hole so as not to fall. I laugh with my awkward strides. My left leg plunges thigh-deep into a gulley and I tumble to the ground. Without hesitating, I start to get up. *Time to move.*

Then I lie back. *Wait. What can I see from here?* What is it that this fall is enabling me to see?

I watch the clouds, drifting wisps of white and blue and gray. Their mottled layers pass through one another, thinning into translucent floss. I feel the icy cold of the snow seeping through my jacket and snow pants, cooling my lower back where an echo of an old back pain lingers, offering a healing touch. *What do I look like splayed out here on the snow. Would someone find me if I couldn't move?*

I see the stalks of dead flowers and grasses poking up around me. *I want to make something. An ornament.* An angel from Hebron Hollow. A beating sound interrupts the thought. A crow. *Will he see me and think I am food?* A pressure squeezes my heart. Sadness seeps out. *My friend. Her baby girl. It was Downs. She ended the pregnancy.* The pain, a month later, is palpable. Breathing empties the sensation into the colors of the clouds, the cold of the snow, the still silence of the land. I see the beauty unfolding around me.

I sit up. My body sits up, stands, moves forward. I feel softened, revived. I breathe and plunge on.

Before me is Moon Rock. Around the shoulder and up the face I hike. I want to feel alive. An impulse to run surges again — something pressing forward and in and out and through me, a desire to touch what is. I run. Blood screams through my limbs. The horizon, the edge, opens before me. I rise to meet it, wider than before. It occurs to me: *I need this place, this walk, to walk in this place. I need this land to open me to my self, my life, again and again and again.* I see dry plants for my ornament. I pick them. Buttons. Milkweed. Thistles.

I plow my way back to Moon Rock and lean into its arc. I feel its weight, and my weight on it. In the meeting of the two, I sink into myself where I am alive, becoming more body. Tremors of love vibrate through me. It is time to go. The sun, a soft yellow ball, sits atop the tree tufts. The snow glitters blue and gold. Sparkles of light beckon. Again I follow the deer who followed me. Thoughts skitter through. I will need to write about this walk. To reflect on it, remember it, press it through my thinking so that it rearranges my ideas and holds them accountable to this experience of moving, to what is, here and now.

My movements, walking, breathing, feeling, thinking, are making me. My movements are opening me to sense and respond, making me into someone who witnesses this beauty. Someone who is sensing, who can sense, who wants to sense this wakeful vitality. This is who I am.

I enter the house. My dead bouquet is large. I lay it on a newspaper. Needs press in. I am hungry and tired. I need to eat, to write, to make something, to connect with Geoff, to nurse Kai. The kids are home from school. It is dinnertime. I breathe into the sensory spaces opened by my walking. Happy and elastic, I find play in the moment. Grabbing a snack, I nurse my son, hear stories of the day, and then dump my thoughts onto the page. After dinner I help Jessica and Kyra make milkweed angels. They are beautiful. Bits of Hebron Hollow come to life. Like me.

$$\infty$$

A simple walk, but as I write it down, as I know I must, I find it has all the elements of the experience shift that enables us to find wisdom in our desires for food, sex, and spirit. If we can name such an experience shift, recognize it in ourselves, and cultivate it in our thinking and feeling and acting, then we can develop a powerful resource for participating consciously in becoming the people we are and want to be.

What is this shift in our experience of our own bodies?

For one, it involves opening our *sensory awareness*. The walk did not just give me an idea *about* myself, it enabled a lived *experience of* myself, of my bodily immersion in this particular time and place. It was not an awareness that I have a body or that

14

I live inside a body, but that I *am* a body, actively alive in my senses, ever engaged in the world.

Further, it was a sensory awareness that this body that I am is *movement*. I am ceaseless movement — beating, breathing, flowing, and crackling— even in moments of greatest stillness. Simply sensing, I move — an eye scans, a finger brushes, thoughts dart. Responding I move — turning toward and away, moving with and against what appears to me. And on that walk I experienced how this sensing and responding that my body is always doing is what was generating my thoughts and feelings, desires and actions. I knew in my body, from my body, on my walk: *my movement is making me.* "I" was not making the movement as much as the action of my walking was making me into a person who walks, who thinks those thoughts and feels those feelings while walking, and who relies on walking to help unfold her sensory awareness of the bodily movement she is.

This *sensory awareness of the movement that is making me* is an awareness of a process that is always at work in every instant of our lives. Whether we are conscious of it or not, every movement we make represents a *pattern* whose shape is given by the parts of ourselves we mobilize in order to make that movement. Each pattern requires a particular articulation of our senses and a unique expression of our ability to respond. As a result, every movement we make *creates* in us *the pattern of sensation and response* that making that movement entails. Over time, the patterns of sensing and responding we mobilize most frequently *become* us. These patterns come to define our way of being in the world, what we notice and how we react, on any and every register of our awareness — physical, emotional, intellectual, and spiritual.

This process of creating and becoming patterns of sensation and response is what I call the *rhythm of bodily becoming*. Once we develop a sensory awareness of ourselves as this rhythmic process of creating and becoming ourselves, we have what we need to discern the wisdom of our desires. We can sense that and how every desire itself is a movement we are making that is making us. Every desire represents particular patterns of sensation and response that we have learned to make. When our experience shifts in this way, we can begin to welcome our knots of frustration, disappointment, and despair—the tangled shapes of our desires—as guiding us to move in ways that will not recreate those knots, but instead, promote healing, freedom, and pleasure.

This is what happened to me on my walk. I left the house stuck in patterns of thinking and feeling and acting that were dividing me against myself, mind over body. The signs were clear: dwindling sensations and flagging energy; gentle depression and longing for a quick fix.

I knew I couldn't mentally will myself out of the moment. It wasn't a matter of copping a good attitude, or reframing my perspective. I needed to move (my body) differently — to invite an experience shift from a mind over body sense of self to a *sensory awareness of the bodily movements that were making me*. I needed to find wisdom in my feelings of discomfort—impulses to move in ways that would not recreate these sensations. So it was. My walking recreated me into a person able to sense and respond to myself and others from a growing reservoir of self-respecting love.

ʘ

How can this sensory awareness help us find wisdom in our desires for food, sex, and spirit?

To understand, we need another example.

Take the case of learning to ride a bike. I learn to ride as I learn to coordinate my arms and legs in the patterns of sensation and response needed to hold, propel, and steer the bicycle. Each time I animate this coordination of nerves, muscles, and limbs, the patterns of riding grow stronger, clearer, and more precise in me. I change; the body I am changes. I become someone who can pedal, steer, and balance, and not only that. I also grow more able to sense and respond to nuances in the movement of my body and the bicycle. I sense the tilt of a tight turn and respond with a shift in weight that allows me to stay upright. I anticipate the slowing action of pulling on the brake by sinking back into my seat and holding on tightly. In this way, the movements I make in learning to ride make me into a bike rider. I become someone who can bike, who is apt to notice bikes, and who can respond to any object that appears as like-a-bike by straddling it, whether horse or motorcycle. I become someone who feels the feelings and thinks the thoughts that riding a bicycle stirs in me — the spike of fear, the press of determination, and the release of relief that accompanies a sweep through a turn. Every bike-riding movement I make, then, makes me into someone who can respond to challenges that feel similar by animating these patterns.

Of course, I can engage in this process of becoming a bike rider without cultivating a sensory awareness of what is happening, just as I can go on a walk without even noticing the experience shift whose effects I enjoy.

However, when I tune in to how my movements are making me, something shifts. I become aware of any pain or discomfort that my movements are creating. Sometimes how I am riding is creating a pinched feeling in my neck, or a tension in my shoulder. As I become aware of this connection, the pain itself suggests to me a possibility for moving differently. My body spontaneously adjusts, and I find myself making micro-movements on all registers of awareness. My right shoulder twists, my chin stretches forward, my lower back softens, and the thought of last week's embarrassment lets go. Of course, "I" am making these movements, but in another sense, these movements are making me. I am merely inviting their possibility by attending respectfully to my sensations of displeasure. As I do, I find myself riding with greater ease and strength, in ways that are freer, faster, and more precise. It is intoxicating.

This is what I mean by the *wisdom in our desires.* The wisdom is this knowledge of how to move in ways that coordinate our pleasure, our health and well being, and the context within which we find ourselves. Such wisdom emerges in the moment, for the moment, as an impulse to move through the moment. It appears in the form of *play.* We find the *freedom* not to react through patterns of sensation and response forged in the past; we find the *creativity* to make new patterns, and re-create ourselves. Often, once we develop our sensory awareness, we find our bodily selves spontaneously adjusting, generating the thought, feeling, or physical gesture that coordinates our pleasure and our health in that moment. Yet this wisdom cannot and will not dawn in us if we are not both in touch with our discomfort *and* willing to trust and move with our body's response.

It can happen when we ride a bicycle. It happened when I was walking in the fields. It happens when we cultivate a sensory awareness of our desires for food, sex, and spirit. As we do, we learn more and more to experience these desires as *expressions* of movements we ourselves are making. We begin to notice that our sensations of frustration, disappointment, and despair are more often than not *caused* by our attempts *to think and feel and act as if we were minds over bodies.* We see how our mind over body movements are *making* us into people who feel our desire as a problem.

In this discovery, lies hope. For once we see *that* our movements make us, and *how* our mind over body movements are making us, we can interpret the shapes of our dissatisfaction as calling us to move in ways that will *not* recreate this mind over body sense of ourselves.

The implication: if we can find ways to move that honor our bodily movement, we will draw closer to the nourishment, touch, and affirmation we seek.

CR

The challenge of taking this path is not insignificant. What I am describing runs counter to nearly everything we learn about desires and bodies from our participation in modern culture. The scope of this relentless education is worth pondering.

Think of our systems of mandatory education. Remember back to days in elementary school. From a young age, you were asked to sit for hours each day, holding a pencil, pen, or crayon, making marks on a book or piece of paper. Ostensibly you were learning to read, write, and compute — tasks we all must master in order to function as citizens. Really you were learning to sit, and not only sit. You were learning to sit *in order to think*; you were training your thinking movements away from your bodily sensations. It is likely that you regularly practiced deferring hunger and thirst, ignoring aches and pains, and channeling restlessness into mental gymnastics in order to think. You were rewarded for the effort. Even the short blocks of "physical" education you enjoyed reinforced the idea that the rest of school was about the more important "mental" education that would predict your chances for achievement. Those who had trouble learning to stay still were labeled as problems. They required special education, even drugs, to help them fit and sit.

Thus you learned to drive a wedge between your sense of yourself as a thinking, computing mind, or "I," and your sense of yourself as a "body" whose desires your "I" could and should override as the condition for your satisfaction, maturity, and success within contemporary society. You exercised repeatedly, over long periods of time, a pattern of sensing and responding to yourself as if you were a mind acting in and over a body. Your teachers reveled in the power of it, and eventually you did too.

This mind over body training extends beyond the classroom. It is ubiquitous in contemporary culture. Think about the movements we make to live through an ordinary day. We wake up in a bed lifted off the floor, and roll out, literally, without needing to bend our knees. We stand up in the shower or while brushing and grooming. We sit to eat, to commute to work; we stand to ride escalators and elevators; we sit in an office, at a desk, before a computer. When our energy flags, we go for a cup of coffee, doughnut, or candy bar. After work, we feel tired and want to be entertained, some stimulant to compensate for the day. We sit some more to eat, watch television, talk. We stand to wash dishes, fold laundry, and get ready for bed.

Sitting and standing all the day long, we are rarely called to mobilize a full range of bodily movement. We have little need to engage the core muscles of our backs and bellies. Our labor saving devices and technologies, our furniture and media, our modes of travel, entertainment, and work, all encourage us to think and feel and act as if the movements of our bodies were irrelevant to the thoughts we think, the problems we solve, the care and attention we have to offer our friends and family. Even when we engage in work that requires us to move constantly, in the trades, childcare, or on the hospital floor, we treat our bodies like machines, relying on them to get the job done without breaking down. Nor do we seriously challenge this sense of ourselves when we manage to get up out of our chairs and go to the gym to "work out." At the health club we fit our bodies to machines. We pedal, row, or stride while reading a magazine or watching the news. On the road, we use tunes to distance us from our own exertion.

Given how pervasive this mind over body training is it is not surprising that when it comes to dealing with sensations of discomfort — whether physical pain or frustrated desires — our first response is to mobilize the mind over body sense of ourselves we have been practicing. It is who we think we are. It is who we think we should be. It is the resource we imagine is our strongest.

Think about the last time you felt the pressure of a building headache. You are sitting at a desk or in a car, in front of some kind of machine. A pain throbs behind your temples. You try to ignore it. You don't want to stop what you are doing. It is important. You hope the pain will just go away. People are depending upon you, your corporation, co-workers, bosses, partner, or children.

When denial fails you look for a distraction. A burst of comfort. You surf the web, glance through a paper. You look for a quick fix. *Who has some painkillers?* You ask a colleague or friend, or stop by the local store. At home you turn on the computer, a movie, or the evening news. When it is time for bed, you finally feel better, and don't want to go. You stay up later than you should before giving yourself a dose of something to help you sleep. The next morning, eyelids heavy, you down a cup of coffee. Later your headache returns. The cycle begins again.

Deny. Distract. Isolate. Anesthetize. Whether the trigger is fear or doubt, anxiety or sadness, a jilted romance or a family crisis, we rely on our most familiar patterns of sensation and response as our first line of defense. We do not *intentionally* ignore our bodies. It is not our goal to do so. We just want to make the pain stop.

What happens then, when faced with the troubling realities of an expanding waistline, a rocky relationship, or a spirit-sucking depression? The cultural messages echoing through us, and rehearsed in chapters to come, are not surprising. We mobilize the sense of ourselves we have been practicing. We vow to rid ourselves of our pesky desires and their insatiable dissatisfaction so that we can live in a place of constant peace and contentment. It never arrives.

We have come to a point in history where the strategies and technologies we have invented for enhancing our lives are compromising our health. Despite awesome advances in science and knowledge, the movements we are making in our daily lives, as we think and feel and act as if we were minds over bodies, are making us sick, frustrated, and unhappy. Our attempts to alleviate our dissatisfaction are perpetuating its causes.

It is time to find other ways to move.

ଔ

I am sitting at the kitchen table. We have been here at the farm for almost six months. We are remembering our friends in Boston.

Kyra, now four, pipes up. "My mind is a world."

"Oh?" I respond.

"Boston is in my mind," she continues. "But there is a piece of the puzzle that is missing, that is not attached to my mind. And that is me, my self. My self is not in my mind. My self is outside my mind." I gasp as the foundations of western philosophy crumble before me.

"What happens when you are in Boston?" I ask.

"Then my mind is here," Kyra replies. "I miss both places."

I ponder her words. She has not yet learned to sit and read and write. She has not yet learned to identify her "self" with what goes on between her ears. And for her, her self is *not* in her mind, but outside her mind. *Her self is her body.* Her self is the body that she can see, touch, feel and feel with. What goes on inside her mind strikes her as something else, somewhere else, looking forward or back to what was or may be. Boston or New York. But not *her*.

ଔ

We *can* imagine it both ways. We can identify our "self" with our bodies or with the pictures in our minds. We can also identify our "self" with the rhythms of bodily becoming that give rise to a sense of ourselves as one or the other. We can, and, if we are to find the wisdom in our desires, we must.

Cycle of Breaths

'Lead back to the earth the virtue that flew away, as I do—back to the body, back to life, that it may give the earth a meaning, a human meaning.'

– *Zarathustra*, 188

It seems mysterious. Even if we are willing to consider that there is wisdom in our desires, even if we are ready for a shift in our experience that will help us find it, what can we do to make it happen?

Nothing, really. We can't *make* it happen.

We can, however, *invite* it to happen by moving in ways that open our senses and draw our awareness into our bodies. We can bring our senses to life.

While there may be infinite ways to invite such a shift, I offer one simple exercise that weaves through this book—*a cycle of breaths*.

When we practice the cycle of breaths, we attend to a movement that is making us — the movement of our breathing. As we move through the four moments of the cycle, we open four distinct sensory perspectives on our breathing movement: we experience our breathing as connecting us with the elements of earth, air, fire, and water. The process inevitably shifts our sense of breathing. Regardless of where we are or what we are doing, we find ourselves breathing differently, with greater ease, depth, and pleasure, more in sync with the challenges and opportunities at hand. Patterns of tightness and tension appear and fall away. It is as if the opened span of sensory awareness releases the potential of our breathing for supporting our health and well being.

In this way, by inviting a fourfold sensory awareness of a movement we are always making that is always making us, the cycle of breaths helps us discover what is true for us in every moment of our lives. We can then use this sensory awareness to find life enabling, life-enhancing ways to move whatever we are feeling, wherever we find ourselves. We can learn to discern the wisdom in our desires.

CR

I am swimming in a mountain lake. It is green and sweet, shallow enough to warm quickly in the summer sun, and deep enough to hide the sandy depths. There is not too much vegetation to snarl ankles and wrists, and the bottom drops quickly enough that its squishy texture is soon left behind. Then there is nothing to do but swim for miles, in clear open water ringed with mountains. Dazzled blue air floats overhead. The wind picks up in the afternoons, but mornings, when I swim, the mirror surface is glassy flat.

There is a small island not far from shore. I swim around it. Coming around the far bend, I am swimming well, hard, and my thoughts ride up and down in the currents of my stirred energy. I am thinking loosely about being in this water and its magic, about our connection to the earth.

Why is swimming in this gorgeous eye-of-the-soul-opening lake any different than swimming anywhere else? It is. *It is.*

I am doing the crawl. I breathe in, and as I exhale, I allow my moving body to drop into the water. I release the tension of effort and exertion, still moving, but without the force of added will. I breathe out through the length of my body into the water, allowing it to support me. The water is holding me up, as solid as the earth, carrying my weight. Every increment of skin is touched and held, gently. I feel my shoulders release and my arms reach forward a bit further. My neck unfolds. I move my head side to side. My back lengthens and my hips spread outwards. My kick intensifies.

The thought enters my mind. What if I allowed each breath to relate me to an element? What if I breathed each breath using that breath to explore my relationship to that element as it exists in me and in the world around me?

Air, I need *air*. I turn my head to breathe and imagine the waves of air breaking into my body. It is never so delicious as when it is needed. The air is light, it makes me feel light. I find myself filling with light—a light that releases again into the supportive weight of the water. I experiment with this breath some more. My arms seem to float up and around my head. I can feel an added stretch through my lower back, all the way down to the source of my energy, the fire in my belly.

Fire. I breathe again, this time sending the breath to that fire. I contract the muscles of my lower abdomen — squeezing up from the pelvic floor, pressing in with the lower belly. Hollowing out. I am hollow. Empty. Dissolved into the pure flame of my efforts.

As I pull at my center, my body lengthens again. The top of my head presses forward, my toes reach back, my lower back opens a notch more. I gather strength, preparing to launch myself forward. My shoulders round to protect the flickering. I am about to burst.

I breathe again. *Water* I think, *water*. The flames in my belly turn liquid and flow out through my churning limbs. *Power*. I feel *power*. My body surges. I am moving faster, gliding on top of the water. I chuckle. I must be leaving a wake.

I can't hold the sensation for long. I fall back again into a slightly disorganized paddling. Why don't I start back at the beginning?

I try again. With one breath I release my body into the earth weight of the waves. With the next I fill my body with airy light.

With the next I squeeze sensation into the cauldron at the base of my spine. With the next I allow that kindled flame to flow, as molten lava, rolling out through my torso, back, arms, legs, and head. Again I find that moment of extended release and joy shimmers through me.

My heart is full. I never knew I could swim this way, with this sensory awareness, with this level of engagement.

What a gift. *Oh, this lake.*

Breathing to swim, swimming to breathe, my movement is making me — the universe is creating itself — a cycle of breaths.

☙

To begin, don't do anything. Just breathe. Allow yourself to be in your senses. Notice what is going on. Pay attention to the air entering through your nostrils. Feel the air pass through the back of your mouth, stream down your throat, and into your expanding chest. Every breath enters your heart, passes through your heart, and picks up whatever is there on the way to the rest of your body. Our sensations and desires, our feelings about them and attitudes to them.

Sense your ribs lift and lower, your belly softly open and release. Notice that as you pay attention to your breathing, it changes. Your body changes. Your exhalations grow longer, trailing into infinity. Your forehead releases, shoulders drop, chest opens, even as you continue reading. (And even as I am writing.) Your legs relax, your lower back eases, currents of air swirl around you, through you.

☙ *Earth breath* ☙

Breathe in. Breath out.

Take another breath into your bright white heart, and as you release the air out again, open your sensory awareness to notice the points where your body is connecting with the earth, or at least with the chair or bed or floor that is between you and the earth. Where do you touch down?

As you follow the movement of the air through your heart and into your body down to your points of contact with the ground, rest your consciousness around those sites.

If you are sitting, feel your sit bones pressing on the chair. Feel the chair pressing back. Feel your feet on the floor, or tucked under you. Feel one leg pressing across the other. Feel the small of your back against the chair. Scan through your body, as you breathe, and allow the breath to swirl around and settle into those points of contact.

Take a breath into your heart, and again, as you exhale, send the breath down to the ground. Feel the points of contact together, all at once, as an image of your connection to the earth— as a picture of your dependence upon the earth, a picture of the earth supporting you. As you breathe into this matrix of points, allow yourself to melt into it. Feel how the earth presses up to keep you up. Surrender.

ભ

There is not a moment in our lives when the body of the earth is not supporting us, holding us up, enabling us to stand and walk and breathe and be. There is not one moment where the earth is not there for us as a constant source of stability. The ground may shudder in an earthquake. It may fall away beneath us in quicksand. We may launch ourselves into the water; or propel ourselves high above the ground in an elevator or airplane. But even when mediated through water or air, there is some point of contact where the forces of gravity pin us to the earth. Hold us up by holding us down.

ભ

Keep breathing. Stop holding your self up. Allow the flesh to fold around you, to hang loosely on your bones like soft drapes. Empty your thinking, feeling, and sensing, your hopes, fears, and expectations, your wanting, judging, and yearning into the ground. Give it up. Feel the earth as your strength.

Feel the earth in you as your strength. Feel this pattern of sensing and responding in you as your strength, enabling you to become who you are.

Breathing again, shift from side to side, rearrange your legs and back. Put your book into a new position. Shake your head and tilt it in another direction. Notice how the earth comes with you, meets you wherever you go, comes alive in you again, as your rock. Feel this movement of the earth in relation to you.

As you empty all of your efforts to launch yourself up and out of your body into the sky-high world of numbers and letters, know this: you are creating yourself into someone who can find an enabling ground in his or her desires.

CR *Air breath* CR

Are you still aware of your breathing?

Breathe in. Follow your breath in through your heart and allow your heart to open, unfold, expand in space. White light.

Now breathe again. Sense air, streaming into the nose and mouth, throat, and chest. As you exhale, feel the surface where you meet the outside world. Invite a sensory awareness of your connection to air — of all the places where your skin touches air. Allow these air-touched surfaces to float lightly, buoyed by the currents of breathing.

Breathing, feel your skin as porous mesh, a translucent web of tissue lightly touching and touched by what surrounds you. Imagine each cell filling with light, spilling over with light, dissolving into light. Breathe air into radiant rings of light, moving in ever-expanding circles around the heart.

At the end of each exhalation, remember your connection to the ground. Keep releasing into the earth. Trust it to support the vulnerable expanse of skin. And as you release your weight into the earth, fill your sense of your body's shape with emptiness.

ဢ

I am walking on the hill behind our farm. The sky is bright blue. A few lone clouds graze on the horizon. The air blows. A wind from the north, a local farmer said. The air does not seem cold. It is sun-filled. Compared to winter squalls, it feels balmy. I walk up to the crest of the hill. The wind blows freely here, whipping around my head, blowing off my hat. I close my eyes.

A felt sense of the wind appears — a buffeting against my cheeks, a pull on my hair, tendrils of air weaving through my fingers. I didn't even notice these sensations when my eyes were open. I follow the currents of air along the surfaces of my skin, around to the other side. I block the wind, but it circles me and continues.

I practice an air breath, breathing myself light. I imagine the wind blowing right through and emptying me out. My face dissolves; arms, torso, legs dissolve. All that exists are the soles of my feet, pressing down against the ground, and up against the light.

My thoughts clear. An impulse to run grabs my heart. I lift my arms to the sky and allow the wind to blow me. I run. I turn and plow into the wind, air roaring in my ears. My self is streamlined by the current. Buoyed in blue, I fly.

Sensing and responding to wind in these ways, another sensation sweeps through me: freedom. I taste and touch, hear and smell this freedom as my movements create me wind-blown, wind-strewn, wind-gathered. I am the air that is breathing me, blowing right through my bright heart and back into the world. Breathing, I am creating myself as someone who can find this soft in-spiring freedom in her desires.

29

✺ *Fire breath* ✺

Are you breathing? Follow that breath into your heart, and through your heart to the places where you are touching the ground, to the surfaces where your skin dissolves into air. Feel your weight against the earth, your light oneness with space.

Now as you exhale, release all of the air out of your body. Empty yourself down to the very bottom of your belly. Push the air out for a second more. Wait in the emptiness until the urge to breathe opens you again.

Breathe all the way in and exhale again. This time, follow the breath out even further, sinking your awareness deeper into your internal cavity, the bowl of your pelvis. At that moment of greatest emptiness, push your diaphragm down and squeeze the muscles along the bottom of your pelvic floor up. In this pulled circle of muscular sensation, light a fire.

Release the effort. Take another breath in through your heart. As you exhale, activate that same muscular sphere, sending fuel to the burning fire. And again. Feel the fire blaze. Feel its vitality, your vitality, coming to life.

✺

At the root of our spines, in the cradle of our bellies, is the source of our life energy. It is where the pulse of living ignites. This fire not only warms our skin and soul; it radiates through our pores and projects. Yet even more than that, the fire, if strong enough, provides us with a center or core of our being that can support an ever-expanding array of sensory creativity.

✺

You want to hike up a mountain. It will be a challenge, but you have confidence that you can do it. As you begin, your mind starts to wander through all of the things you left behind at work, to the plight of a family member, or the state of the world. Your leg hurts. You notice and honor the complex texture of sensation and coax your body forward. You breathe and feel tightness in your chest. You plow on. Movement will help.

For a while you have some energy to burn, congested though it is. Then it runs out. You feel tired and want to sit down. You notice what weighs so heavily — a comment someone made to you last week. You focus on your breathing. You breathe deeper, reigniting the fires in your belly. Burn that thought there. Let it go.

You continue. Your mind still wanders and your limbs still ache, but your core — your breathing belly core — is now aglow. You feel its pulse within you, propelling you up the mountain. You feel yourself coming alive. Your mind darts to and fro, but spontaneously returns to your movement which is now as compelling as any other phenomenon. The force of the energy through you is aligning your faculties — thinking, feeling, sensing — in a singular arc. You move more easily and gracefully, your cells falling in line with your desire — that it be good.

ର

When we move we burn. In every cell, we are aflame. Our ongoing fires feast on the fuel we provide — oxygen and calories. But if our cells are not being exercised to their potential, these fires smolder. Our energy pathways grow cloudy and clogged. We move less, need less, consume less. Our temperature cools. Our ardor wanes. We are less able to mobilize ourselves in the pursuit of any goal or the satisfaction of any desire.

When a fire-breathing breath bursts alive in us, it burns away materials we don't need. It restores our sensitivity, and opens us to farther reaches of our mobility. We not only spend energy, we create it. We find freedom in the possibilities for movement we unfold in ourselves.

CR

Inhale, and breathe into this cleansing, creating fire in the cradle of your belly. As you exhale, allow the muscles contracted around it to explode. Feel the warmth in this opened region of sensation.

Breathe in again. This time, without contracting any muscles, activate a sense of them. Feel the strength and the length of the lower abdomen, its width and breadth and depth. Feel that fiery core rooted into the ground and warming the airy volume of your physical space. Breathing, know that you are becoming someone who can find this enlivening fire in her desires.

CR *Water breath* CR

Earth, air, fire, we are also water. Mostly water. Lapping around our island eyes, beneath our lips, everywhere under our skin, in our blood, our lymph system, our flesh. We are like sponges. Squeezed out, all that would be left is a small pile of dust.

The water we are is warm water. Water warmed in the fires of our cells and center. It is this water that washes through our bodies, streaming through shapes of sensation. It is this sense of our watery selves we seek to awaken through the last of the cycle of breaths.

Breathe in through your open heart. See the air, feel the air, streaming in, and illuminating the heart. Exhale, sending air down through your points of contact with the earth; out through the surface of your skin, and deep into the fiery hold of your pelvis.

Now breathe in again and as you exhale imagine the glimmering warmth from the fire in your belly caught in waves of fluid. Imagine this light-flecked fluid flowing thickly from your center through your arms, your legs, and out the top of your head.

Breathe in again, filling your heart and awakening your sensations of ground, skin, and core, and then breathe out, spilling the fire of your desire through your extended self. Feel the flowing, warm, air-suffused water moving through you, moving you.

Whatever you are doing in the moment will flow. Even if you are sitting and reading a book, your spine will straighten, your eyes open, your attention clear. You will sense yourself creating yourself as an open conduit for the forces of bodily creativity — of sensing and responding — coursing through you.

Allow this luminous breathing to open you to yourself. Trust yourself. Trust what you sense as a guide to your own unfolding.

ଔ

Practicing the cycle of breaths in stillness is a good way to begin. Try it when you are alone in a quiet place. Standing, sitting, or lying down. Allow yourself to stay on each breath until you begin to feel a shift in your bodily awareness. Explore it, then move to another breath. Go back and forth among the breaths, doing one and then another. Allow the sensations opened in one to enter into the experience of another.

After a while, try to cultivate an awareness of all sensations in the rhythm of one breath. Inhale through your heart, and as you exhale, focus on your connection to the earth for two counts, the light buoyancy of air in you for two counts, the fire in your belly for two counts, the flooding flow through you in the last counts. One day you may feel like practicing one kind of breath for a long time. Do.

When you are familiar with the cycle of breaths, you are ready for a further step: to practice the cycle of breaths while engaging in some form of rhythmic bodily movement. As you move through the cycle of breaths while doing this activity, each breath will call your attention to different aspects of that same movement. With each breath, you will find yourself making that movement slightly differently. You will sense possibilities for adjusting the movement — the wisdom in your desire to do.

ଔ

Pick some movement activity that is familiar to you, one that you do regularly and easily, like walking, running, biking, or swimming; doing yoga or shoveling snow. Remind yourself of what the doing of the movement usually feels like. How do you feel as you begin? What happens when you are moving? What do you notice? How does the session end? How do you feel when you are done?

The next time you begin your chosen activity use the cycle of breaths to help you find play in the movements you are making.

Take for example, going for a run. As you settle into the rhythm of running, breathe in through your heart and out through your points of contact with the *earth*. Feel the line of energy connecting heel, ankle, knee, hip, and shoulder. Feel your toes pressing against rubber, pressing against the ground. With each stride, feel the earth pressing up against you, holding up your weight, supporting you in space. Breathe in through your heart and as you exhale, collapse all of your efforts, all of your tension into those points of contact that are holding you up. Keep running. Notice what sensations open for you as your legs propel you forward in space.

As your tension drains into the earth (stride stride), take an *air breath* in through your heart and send it out through your skin in all directions. Breathe in and as you exhale, dissolve the entire substance of your body into white light. Feel your lightness suspended, floating above the earth. Feel the wind pass right through your body (stride, stride). Notice differences in the sensation of striding. Feel bursts of energy, the ease of a rotation, a release of shoulders and wrists. Your neck relaxes forward and your eyes rise to see the road.

When you feel as if you are white light, take another breath in through your heart and send it right down to the base of your spine. Kindle a *fire*. Squeeze your pelvic muscles, warming and waking your sensation (stride, stride). Press down into your pelvic cup with your diaphragm. Breathe in again, streaming through your heart, feeding the flame. Feel your energy drive inward and push you forward (stride, stride). Feel the weight of effort settle in the cradle of your power.

Then breathe in through your heart a streaming blue streak, send it down through the fire, and breathe liquid, air-filled and warm, through your limbs.

Follow the currents through your body, down into your toes and out through the top of your head, reaching forward through the gaze of your eyes, the propulsion of your heart. Repeat this breath until the fiery liquid energy rearranges your cells and releases you to move even more. Then begin again. Want more.

ॐ

As you mobilize the cycle of breaths in an activity you know well, you will find that your experience of that activity shifts. The cycle of breaths provides you with an opportunity to experience the familiar movement from four different perspectives, with each perspective representing a different sensory map of your body and its relatedness to what is. Each time you shift your focus from one element to another, you will be creating a moving image of yourself — as releasing into the earth, softening into light, kindling into blaze, or spilling into the world — that you are enacting.

In this way, the cycle of breaths invites a sensory awareness of the play in the moment. You are *free* to make movements that vary in intensity, quality, effort, and intent. You are able to *create* and *become* new patterns of movement. The cycle of breaths invites this sensory awareness by exercising it—by exercising the rhythm of bodily becoming.

As you move through these sensory perspectives, moreover, you will find that habitual patterns of effort loosen their grip. As sensations of soreness, stiffness, or stuckness, come into focus, the cycle of breaths provides you with a space to receive them, circle them, explore them, and deepen your experience of them. You can develop a sensory awareness of how the patterns of coordinating muscle, attention, and effort that you are making are making you into someone who feels this discomfort.

As you become aware of the movements making you, you will find that each cycle of your breathing invites your bodily movement to reorganize itself in line with the featured element.

The earth breath invites you to release your tension into the earth and locate your ground in a stronger support. The air breath invites you to open points of tight pain, and find play in your movements. The fire breath invites you to connect your efforts with the fire in your core. And the water breath invites you to sense a released, air-infused, ionized flow coordinating your movements in a fluid whole.

Moving through the cycle of breaths, then, helps you discover your ability to create patterns of sensation and response that move you with greater ease and effect. You will find yourself *wanting* to move in ways that *enhance* your health for the *pleasure* of it.

When such wisdom is released in you, it feels like a blast of oxygen. You are flooded with feelings of generosity and courage. You feel expansive, in love with the world. You taste a pleasure you want to experience again and again. It is the pleasure of participating in the rhythms of your own bodily becoming. It is the pleasure of discerning, trusting, and moving with the wisdom in your desires. It is the pleasure of unfolding who you are and what you have to give and giving it.

As we practice the cycle of breaths in this way, we are creating ourselves into persons who *want* to sense and respond to all things with love, who *can* sense and respond to all things with love, who *know* ourselves as sensing and responding to all things with love, and who willingly practice doing so for the *pleasure* of it.

☙

We are always breathing. We are always experiencing through the enabling rhythms of our breathing. As we practice the cycle of breaths, we open the possibility for living every moment of our lives through the sensory awareness this practice opens in us. Regardless of what we are doing we can practice the cycle of breaths, whether we are taking a shower, driving in a car, or sitting at a desk. Regardless of what we are doing or feeling or even thinking, we can do so from a place within ourselves where we are aware, at a sensory level, of how our movement is making us.

We can find wisdom in our desires.

☙

It is Saturday morning. I am decidedly uninspired. Lethargic. The list of ten-minute projects stretches into infinity. Starting any one of them seems daunting. My throat is thick; my head is heavy. I move a dish from here to there.

I could stay in this place and get some satisfaction from doing chores and checking things off my list. At the end of the day I might look around and see a neater house, but I wouldn't feel great. A day would have gone by leaving me restless in its wake. I would have never come alive, never felt the flow of life coursing through me.

I sigh. It seems easier *not* to be born to life on any given day. It seems easier to fit myself into what I think others expect of me. Hard as I try, I can never escape the dissatisfaction, sometimes acute, often vague and lingering, that reminds me once again. *It is not so easy.*

Move. "I" need to give my "body" a chance to *move me* in line with its — that is my — capacities for creativity, freedom, and love.

Dance. I lure myself gently, prodding my recalcitrant will. A sip of coffee. A bite of ice cream. *I'm coming. I'm coming.*

I make my way into the living room and lie down on my back. Pulling my knees to my chest, I begin the cycle of breaths. My back is a block. I'm stiff and groggy, scattered and numb. I breathe an earth breath, pressing all air out, opening a cavity in my chest, and allowing it to fill again. I still don't feel my points of connection to the earth, so I do it once more.

Unexpectedly my right hip drops to the floor and my right leg floats loosely in my hand. It is as if a fist in my lower back lets go. I can feel a sensation inside my hip where I couldn't a moment before. An air breath. My internal gaze shifts and bends. My jaw releases, humming. My spine settles along the floor, beads of white light.

As I press my right heel to the sky, a fire breathe plunges deep into my belly. Currents of energy ignite upward and outward, along trajectories my limbs are tracing. A sense of connection and connectedness surfaces.

Suddenly it is as if I am tumbling into my body, shifting sideways and down. New depths and angles of sensation dawn. The pleasure. I attune fiercely to it, following its guide.

I begin a new series of movements on my back, lowering my lifted legs to one side and then the other, breathing into and through my heart. I pass through the cycle of breaths again. A sensation in my hip prompts me to stretch up through my lower back, turning a bit farther than I have before, digging deeper with the opposite shoulder.

Earth, air, fire, water. A gasp of a release. Something surges. I ride it through my fingertips.

Lovely.

I stand up. I feel completely different. My head floats. My breathing glides in and out. My sense of weight gathers in my lower abdomen, off my back and thighs, freeing my torso, shoulders, and arms, while rooting me in the earth. My legs sing with anticipation of more movement to come.

The thought confounds me. I could have gone the whole day living out of a small span of my sensory capacity, using my mind to propel me around without ever tapping into this creative energy that now bubbles through me. It is delightful.

It is also maddening. I didn't *do* anything to awaken this sensory awareness. I desired it, yes. I invited it by breathing to move, moving to breathe, and attending to my sensations. But then all "I" could do was wait. "I" had to wait, vulnerable in my desire for change, and ready to notice it. I had to be honest about how numb I was and stay with it. I had to trust that my body— the lump of material I perceived it to be at that moment—really was alive, really knew what to do, and really would move me, if given the chance. It did. It moved. "I" moved.

I grin. Yes, it would be so much easier if I could *will* this awakening with my mind (*Hey! Wake up!*) or manipulate my body deliberately, or inject some stimulant. But none of these mind over body approaches would bring about what I want: the sensation of how my bodily movement is making me. The pleasure of participating in the flow of bodily becoming. The pleasure of making the patterns of sensation and response that make me.

A near miss. People live day in and day out, not knowing that there is more of them, more *in* them — more movement, more vitality, more wisdom.

I come to the end of my dance time. Limbs tremble slightly. Every breath washes through me, cleaning bright. Pockets of strength break open and courage streams out. Thoughts crackle in the horizon of awareness, snapping with intention and understanding.

I greet my vivid self with relief. Joy. I know what I want to do. It is time to write.

ભ

Desire
For
Food

ભ

3

An Elephant in the Room

'Nothing can be explained, while everything may be confused,
by the popular and thoroughly false contrast of soul and body.'
— *Birth of Tragedy*, 129

I wake up starving and head for the kitchen. A banana, a handful
of raisins. Instant sugar suffuses the bloodstream. Light bright
energy. My eyelids crack open. My face softens into mobility.
Limbs stretch and release. Morning dawns.

Kyra wakes up early and hungry like me. I fix her what she
wants, warm cocoa and soft chex. Jordan will follow soon
enough, sights set on a bagel.

I retreat into my study. Mornings are my time to work.

An hour later, the school bus is due to arrive. Through the wall
I hear Geoff in the fray, brushing hair, packing lunches, and
zippering coats. I know I will want to pop out in a moment to say
goodbye. So I glance through the headlines of my online *New York
Times*, ever on the lookout for articles relevant to my project.
There is always one.

Sure enough, there it is: "Two Approaches to the Nation's
Obesity Epidemic Coming Up for Review" (*NYT*, Jan 17, 2006).

Those two "approaches" are both drugs, each vying to be the
"magic pill" that will address this "epidemic" and reap their
respective companies billions of dollars in profits. For as the
article confirms, according to standards set by the Center for
Disease Control and Prevention, two-thirds of all Americans are
"overweight," with half of those falling into the category of
"obese." Even among adults not classified as overweight,

researchers claim that most wish they could lighten a bit, if only by five or ten pounds. We are not satisfied with what we eat, or with what it does to us when we do.

In the text of the article, "obesity epidemic" is highlighted. I click on the link and a long list of related articles appears. The titles map the debates over this contemporary concern. For one, most experts seem to agree that the rising tide of obesity is an "epidemic" — that is, a widespread *disease*, or, if not itself a disease, then at least the cause of numerous other diseases, and one that is growing at a rapid pace with life-threatening consequences. The National Institutes of Health, the Center for Disease Control and Prevention, and the American Heart Association, all weigh in, predicting that the increasing numbers of overweight and obese persons will cost Americans alone billions of dollars in health care. Not only are two-thirds of all Americans overweight, but even more alarming, a greater percentage of children are overweight than ever before. The life span of our children may be shorter than ours. Nor is this "epidemic" unique to the United States. It is spreading around the globe as other nations embrace styles of eating popularized in modern America and made available through forces of global capitalism. According to estimates by the United Nations, there are more people overweight than undernourished in the world today.

The facts I see before me are neither surprising nor new; I find them everywhere I turn. Magazines, medical bulletins, radio shows, and all manner of television programs sound the alarm. The problem is dire, and something must be done. Now.

Despite this general consensus about the issue, there is far less agreement on what should be done. Sure, people are consuming more energy than they are expending, and their bodies are storing the excess energy as fat, but when it comes to identifying the *causes* of the energy/expenditure imbalance and proposing a *solution*, there are multiple and contradictory theories. Experts argue with and against each other, citing hard facts based on scientific or social scientific research to defend their claims. It is no wonder. Millions of lives and billions of dollars hang in the balance.

As I skim through the articles, a range of possible explanations comes into view. I learn that people in the United States have a higher chance of being overweight if they watch television, are low income urban dwellers, eat fast food, live a sedentary life, don't get enough sleep, or have overweight parents. I learn that people have a lower chance of being overweight if they eat breakfast, live in the upper middle class, are breastfed until the age of six months, eat fruits and vegetables, eat dinner with their families, exercise regularly, or fidget constantly. Even so, every explanation raises as many questions as it answers. For every study and its facts, there are exceptions. There are people who exercise regularly and are overweight, or people who do not exercise, eat constantly, and are slim. Most of the data presented in these articles identifies correlations, probabilities, and anecdotes, but not strict *causality*.

Among the few success stories, no golden key appears. Usually something clicks and a person is suddenly willing and able to make radical changes in the way she lives in relationship to herself.

Given this crush of explanations, it is not surprising that the proposals for addressing the epidemic are myriad. Nevertheless, as I take a closer look, I am reminded that the proposals fan out in a spectrum that characterizes the debates, with entries clustered at each end.

At one end, experts claim that responsibility for the problem and for the solution lies with individual will power. In order to stem the obesity tide, individual persons must choose a diet, go on it, stick to it, and keep off the weight they lose. They must learn about food—what to eat, how much, when, and why. And it helps, most experts agree, if those persons also exercise.

At this end of the spectrum, a billion dollar diet industry thrives, publishing books, workshops, diet plans, and fitness programs designed to tell people what they should eat to alter their energy/expenditure balance.

On the other end of the spectrum, however, experts maintain that will power alone, even when educated, is inadequate to the task for the odds are hopelessly stacked against individuals by an array of physiological and cultural factors. During our thousands of years as hunter-gatherers, the human metabolism and digestive system evolved into a highly efficient food processor, able to glean necessary vitamins and minerals, proteins, fats, and carbohydrates from small amounts of berries, seeds, fruits, grains, and an occasional animal. Humans evolved to store whatever was left over as fat. Dwelling now in environments that offer high-calorie, heavily processed food 24/7, we are limited in our ability to resist our biological cues. We need external help, experts concur, from some collective authority — medical, scientific, social or political — that has the power to impose limits upon our desire for food. We need to alter our digestive systems (through drugs or surgery) or orchestrate changes in our lived environments, by passing laws banning soda or whole milk from schools, pressuring food companies and fast food chains to make and market different foods, or regulating and labeling supermarket offerings, in order to bring body and environment into harmony with one another. Without such collective interventions, experts contend, individuals will not succeed in reversing the trend toward obesity.

Moving through the last of the article list, I sort the proposals along the spectrum. While there are some participants in the conversation who work the problem from both ends, the media is ever ready to stage a dramatic battle between warring powers. Which is it? Will power or higher power? Individual mind or collective expertise? Which force will emerge as the hero in our struggle to control our desire for food? To date, the answer is unclear. Despite the time, money, and energy that Americans of all walks are devoting to this issue, the march towards obesity continues. Why? Why aren't we making the progress we desire?

CR

I am out of my study, waving goodbye to the kids, when Kai's happy coos devolve into grunts and groans. He wants breakfast too, which means Mommy. I sit down to nurse him and watch as he latches on, closes his eyes, cups his hands around my breast, and draws sweet milk into his body. His relation to food is as pure as can be. He feels hunger. He cries. He nurses until he is full. He stops and often, falls asleep. Content.

As I watch him drink himself into a dream, I think about his desire for food. As pure as it is, there is no moment in his rhythms of hunger and nourishment that his desire is ever separated from his relationship to someone else. Kai cannot feed himself. He is wholly dependent upon another human to bring the source of nourishment to him, whether bottle or breast, and provide him with the amount he needs to thrive. He is born knowing how to latch on, suck, swallow, and stop. These patterns of sensation and response guide him in discerning what he needs to take in to his body. Yet he cannot eat without a set of arms to hold him. He cannot eat without smelling, touching, hearing, tasting another body — the body of a person who is also, usually, a primary source of affection. He is nurtured and nourished at once, nourished by being nurtured, nurtured by being nourished. My body meets him in his vulnerability, holding him gently, making as much milk day in and out as his body and belly desire. *Ask and ye shall have*. It is nursing logic.

CR

47

It occurs to me. There is an elephant in the room.

If, in the war against obesity, we pretend that "we" can simply decide to restrict what our "bodies" eat by whatever means, whether will power or higher authority, we gloss over a basic fact of human existence. *Nourish and nurture are forever entwined.*

Every time we move something towards our mouth and take it in, taste, chew, and swallow it, we activate patterns of sensation and response formed years before we learned to identify ourselves with the movement between our ears. Even as we grow capable of feeding ourselves, our desire for food is never merely a desire for the energy and nutrients we need to thrive. We can't help but seek an experience of being nurtured, an experience of nourishing ourselves. Sure, we can pretend that such patterns of sensation and response don't exist. We can imagine that our desire for food is simply material. But when we do, we also teach ourselves to forget what Kai knows: how to *recognize* what is good for him, how to *ask* for what he needs, how to *feel his fullness*, and how to *stop* when he has had *enough*.

What is missing from debates over the obesity crisis is *the body*. What is missing is a sense that our desire for food, *because* it is a desire for *more* than just fuel, can provide us with the guidance we need to eat in ways that coordinate our pleasure and our health.

೧೩

Obesity. Perhaps it is the problem. Or perhaps it is a symptom of a larger and deeper issue — the extent to which we learn to think and feel and act as if we were minds over bodies. If this is so, then the strategies we are mounting to address the problem are perpetuating the cause of the problem in the first place.

Is this true? Why don't diets work?

4

Cereal Box Logic

'All our senses have in fact become somewhat dulled because we always inquire after the reason … Joy is transferred to the brain.'
–Human All Too Human, #217, 130

The bus is long gone. Kai has finished nursing. I walk into the kitchen for something to drink. Boxes of cereal are still on the table. I usually try to stick the boxes back into the cabinet as soon as the cereal is poured. The kids are too fascinated by the funny pictures on the back, cartoon images of people exercising, walking, and gardening.

Jessica in particular imbibes the nutritional advice. *It is bad to eat sugars,* she reads emphatically. I want her to learn to trust her body to tell her what to eat. Not a box.

I remember the morning she studied the grapenuts box. Blazoned across the front in blue were the words: *LOSE 10 lbs.*

With some trepidation she asks, "Will you lose 10 pounds if you eat that cereal?" as if by taking a bite she would be instantly transformed.

I look at the box through her eyes. "No. The cereal company just wants you to buy the cereal and thinks that making such a promise is the way to do it."

I stop there. Yet I have read the fine print. More is being sold by that box than cereal or a diet. The box is selling us a way of *thinking* and *feeling* and *acting* in relation to ourselves, in relation to our desire for food. It is leading us to believe that "we" are at war against our bodily fat, and that the best attitude we can assume in the fight is to enlist the power of our minds. Desire is the problem.

Yet, in pointing us so, the box is setting us up to fail. For we come to depend on a diet plan for the control over our desire for food that we are supposed to have. It is a *cereal box logic* shared by nearly every diet on the planet.

ભ

Take a look. The back of the box elaborates the banner's promise announcing "3 simple steps" to losing 10 pounds: *Replace, Focus, Add*. In each step the audience is clear. The "step" is addressed to someone who *wants* to be operating in control of his body, weight, diet, and life. In each step this "I" must do something differently with or to his body for reasons that are rational and objective, scientific even. *It is good for you*. In other words, the steps are *simple* for a self who has already attained some measure of control over his desire for food.

This appeal assumes that personal power, the seat of the will, lies in my "I" and that my desire for food is a physical force, a desire for calories and nutrients whose messages "I" can intentionally override.

The desire is not trustworthy. I know better.

The stress on "simple" further implies that if "I" can't decide to replace, focus, and add and stick to it, then there must be something wrong with me. But I know, as the box assures me, that there is nothing wrong with me — only my body. So, since nothing is wrong with me — only my body — I should be able to replace, focus and add, just like the box says. As the slogan reads: *It's just this easy*.

But is it?

Look at the first step: "Replace" two meals a day with a serving of "your favorite Post Healthy Classics cereal." While the box gives you a choice of three such cereals, the asterisk reveals that to

50

lose ten pounds, participants in their scientific study ate two cereal meals a day for twelve weeks. That is a lot of cereal, a fact not lost on the manufacturer. Two servings a day for twelve weeks equals about thirteen boxes, assuming that a person only eats one serving at a sitting, and it is likely that she will eat more. Even I, daily consumer of grapenuts for nearly twenty years, would tire of all three cereals quickly at that rate. Nor would I feel full with the combination of cereal, fruit, and milk they suggest.

The thought of such a diet makes me hungry.

The second step is even less simple. "Focus on portion control at mealtimes, as part of a reduced calorie diet." The soft pitch. They are not saying *control* portions, just *focus* on controlling them. *Try* to control them. The implicit message: while focusing may be easy, control is elusive. *Beware.*

The word "mealtimes" is also confusing. Aren't we supposed to eat just one meal a day? Then the second clause: "as part of a reduced calorie diet."

The truth comes out. Really, it is not the cereal that is responsible for the weight loss at all. It is the act of reducing calories. The cereal eating is a trick to help control portion sizes for two meals a day, and not merely *focus* on that control. It is a trick designed not only to help us avoid making decisions about what to eat, but also to help us ignore or override our desire for food. *You, dear eater, need help!* But why do we need such help? A shadow crosses. Perhaps our minds are not as capable of controlling our desire for food as we would like to believe. We are not making good choices; we are not happy with the results. That is why we need a plan, numbers, goals, and lots of encouragement in order to succeed. Two meals, three cereals, three steps, ten pounds, twelve weeks will save us from the whims of our desire. *Yes you can!*

I am starving just thinking of it.

The third step: "Add more physical activities to your day." A soft pitch once more, not exercise, just more physical activity. Yet there is no connection made here between the focus on portion control at mealtimes and the increased energy expended. How will that discrepancy feel?

The thought makes me tired.

Then the asterisk again: *It really works!* The small print below tells the story. In a scientific study run by a "leading cardiologist," people lost ten pounds by following these three simple steps. *Science says.* But are the results of the study evidence that the diet works? Surely the participants knew that they were participating in a study and that it was a reputable study led by a heart doctor. Why else would they agree to eat thirteen boxes of cereal in twelve weeks? Each also knew he or she was part of a larger group of individuals; competition and peer pressure enter the game. Perhaps they were paid, maybe with boxes of cereal, or lured by hopes of cereal box fame. It is highly likely that the "proof" of pounds lost has less to do with the simplicity of the diet's steps than with the motivational support provided to participants by the structure of the study itself, its perks and pressures. The small print reveals that even then, at most only *half* of the participants in this study succeeded in losing ten pounds, the *average* weight loss was ten pounds. *Easy?* When the motivational pressure of the study waned, how many of those individuals kept the weight off? Statistics show that the percentages of people who do are small.

ଔ

The message on the box is not as straightforward as its attention-arresting banners and bold print want us to believe. The box represents itself as an ally in the path towards health and well being. It promises results. Yet it does so by giving us a picture of ourselves as minds over bodies — minds who can control their desire for food and stick to the plan — while acknowledging at the same time that such control over desire is elusive and perhaps even impossible.

The promise is that the diet plan will help us bridge this gap between ideal and actual. But can it? Will it? Will spending twelve weeks eating cereal twice a day teach us what we need to know in order to master our desire for food?

Look further. The box does not only admit that we may not be able to master our desire on our own, it appeals to our desire for food itself. The box actually feeds our desire for food—our desire to derive pleasure from food—even while admonishing us to override it.

The most prominent example of this contradiction is captured succinctly in the pun: *Eat 2 lose*. The sound of the message — *eat* **to** *lose weight* — brings joy to our hearts. *You, dear eater, can* **eat** *in order to lose weight*. We love it.

Yet this meaning of the phrase is belied by its expression on the box — *eat* **2** *lose weight*. *You, dear eater, must eat 2 and only 2 cereal meals a day*. By combining these two messages in one phrase, the box implies that you, dear eater, will find the satisfaction your desire for food craves. The box surreptitiously acknowledges that it is our desire for food that has been driving us all along. Our desire for food is more powerful than the mind we prop up to control it. We want so much for the sound of the phrase to be true that we glaze over the written form. *It's just so easy*.

In the end, this contradiction reveals even more: it reveals how the problem (extra weight) and the proposed cure (a diet) share the same mind over body sense of ourselves. The cereal box is playing the obesity epidemic both ways—promoting food reduction even as it works to sell more food. And the box *can* play the obesity epidemic both ways because both messages reinforce the same assumption we want to believe is true about ourselves: that we *can* and *should* override our desire for food.

We override our desire for food if we focus on controlling portion size *or* if we help ourselves to more cereal than we would otherwise choose. We override our desire for food when we stick to a diet plan *or* when we stuff ourselves past a point of comfort.

Both messages promise us that we will get the satisfaction we most desire when we override our desire. After all, we are minds over bodies. Aren't we?

ᘓ

This cereal box is not an isolated phenomenon. The same kind of analysis could be done for nearly every diet plan on the market, and we would find a common *cereal box logic*.

The nutshell is this. "We" are *minds* over bodies. Our *desire* for food is making us fat. "We" need help in corralling this desire, and we can get that help by *buying* consumer products like the ones in and on the box. When we purchase the right plan and follow its simple steps, we will win over our desire to eat *by* consuming more delicious food than we otherwise would. Eat to/2 lose. Satisfaction guaranteed. *It's just this easy.*

Using this logic, diet plans snag our attention by appealing to the very desire for pleasure they are supposed to help us control. They lure us in with candy bars and shakes; they ply us with the promise that we can eat all we want of foods x or y, or eat all we want between these hours of the day, or eat all we want at this one meal. They promise us that we won't be hungry eating what they recommend. They thus reinforce our desire to get pleasure from food even as they direct our sensory awareness away from the lived experience of eating. They appeal to our desire for pleasure, even as they prop us up to override it.

When we decide to go on a diet, then, we are not just investing in a particular set of books, workshops, and products. The movements we make in doing so are making us into people who relate to food through their minds, and who experience their desire for food as an unruly urge for pleasure that they should but cannot completely control.

As we count calories, chart glycemic indices, measure grams of carbohydrates, fats, and proteins, we train ourselves to believe that food is a matter of its chemical and physical make up. As we count the number of meals, the minutes between meals, the spacing between each bite, the time before and after exercise, the time elapsed while chewing, we convince ourselves that our bodies need schedules. As we monitor the number of steps we take, the number of minutes and days we exercise, the weights and distances we push, we teach ourselves that our health is a matter of bending our bodies to concrete goals.

Through it all we learn to find the pleasure we desire from food in abstractions—the numbers on a scale, the image in a mirror, the quantity of calories. We glean whatever satisfaction we can from knowing we have eaten the right kind of food, in correct portions, at the designated time of day. We train ourselves to obey the scientific and nutritional experts to tell us what, when, and how to eat.

When the diet grows dull, and the pleasure of being "good" fades, we are left with few internal resources for making decisions for ourselves about what to eat. We have forgotten what our bodies know. We have lost the ability to discern wisdom in our desire for food. So we fall back on what is familiar and what is available, believing that we are setting our desire for food "free." Are we really surprised when the weight bounces back?

As it does, we turn again to what we want to believe is true about us. We want to believe that losing weight is a matter of a small correction in calories. We want to believe that we are the minds over bodies we are training ourselves to be. We go looking for another diet on which to pin our hopes.

In this way, every diet we try works, even and especially when it doesn't: every diet works to addict us more firmly to the *idea* of a diet—to the idea of finding the *right* diet. So we keep looking to the marketplace for the diet that will give us the pleasure we seek from food by helping us override our desire for it. It is cereal box logic.

When we buy it, we don't know when to stop.

CR

We stand in line at the grocery store, and gaze hungrily at the magazines arrayed before us at eye level. *Lose five pounds fast. Diet tips from the experts.* Smiling faces of famous, rich, beautiful people stare back at us. Slender, buff bodies. We wait to check out, our cart loaded. We buy the images, dazzle ourselves with figures we long to achieve, and then stuff ourselves with food to prove we can indeed override our sense of enough. It will be *just this easy.* Tomorrow.

CR

Diets don't work. The evidence is growing and the reasons given are many. Diets don't work because our bodies adjust to the decreased energy intake, slowing our metabolism so that we use fewer calories. Diets don't work because we suffer feelings of deprivation and eat more to compensate for the lack. Diets don't work because we go on and off them, shedding fat-burning muscle mass from our bodies. Diets don't work because we return to past patterns of eating. Even diets that do seem to work at first are discovered to have unintended consequences — such as when a popular and lucrative high protein diet is linked to increased risk of heart disease.

Yet all of these reasons miss the cereal box logic at the heart of the matter. Diets don't work because they both stimulate and fail to satisfy our desire for food. Going on a diet, we devote ourselves to food while training ourselves away from our physical sensations of it. We pit ourselves against ourselves: mind over body. *It feels horrible.* We don't want to be policing ourselves even for a short period of time. Even for a good reason. We want to nurture ourselves. We are bound to rebel, if not today, then tomorrow.

ભ

If diets don't work and individual will power cannot succeed even when fortified by an array of props and plans, then it is tempting to hope that the experts will be able to invent something to fix the problem we have created. Won't they?

As noted, no ready alternative to dieting has emerged. A pill that would enable people to lose weight is proving elusive. The human body seems infinitely capable of creating detours around attempts to derail the fat storage process. Most drugs that have made it to market as beacons of promise have remained only briefly before being found to have harmful "side" effects. Forms of surgery for weight control available in the United States — stapling the stomach or removing pieces of stomach and intestine — are costly and complications are common (four in ten patients suffer from complications, according to a 2006 report by the federal government).

Where school districts limit fat and calories in school lunches, the effect on student weight has been negligible. Kids buy candy bars on their way home. When people switch to lower calorie foods, they end up eating more of them.

Yet even if some company did succeed in discovering a magic pill, and even if that pill did provide relief to some individuals, it would not solve the problem. Why not? For the same reason that diets don't work. It is cereal box logic. Such external adjustments do not teach us what we need to know to experience the pleasure we want from food.

If we try to reduce our desire for food to a material register that "we" can manipulate, we create in ourselves a dissatisfaction that impels us to eat more, in search of what we are missing. We cannot buy the pleasure we seek from food. We have to educate ourselves to it. We have to bring our senses to life.

ભ

The two ends of the obesity debates are not far apart. Both ends participate in the same mind over body logic. Even experts who insist that individual minds may not be strong enough to wield control over biological bodies, still propose that we rely on a *collective* mind — the experts in health and medicine who can tell us what to eat, or the public health officials who can legislate what we encounter in the marketplace.

Regardless of whether the proposed solution is stricter dieting or environmental management by those in the know, the cast and intensity of the debates reinforce the idea that humans *are* and *should be* minds operating in and over bodies, managing if not mastering their insatiable desires for food. All positions on the spectrum train our desire for food away from the lived experience of eating, leading us to believe that our bodies do not and cannot know what is good for us to eat.

The implication is clear: the solutions towards which we yearn are failing because they are reinforcing the sense of ourselves that encourages us to eat more and other than we want or need in the first place for our own pleasure. *We can override our desire for food and so we should.* In pursuing these strategies, we make ourselves into dissatisfied eaters who perceive their desire for food as a temptation, and are constantly in need of props and products, programs and pills, to maintain their front against it.

ଔ

Is there any hope for finding a way to our health? Is the trend towards obesity destined to continue unabated?

Yes and no. In fact, once we understand that the mind over body movements we are making in response to this "crisis" are making us into people who are incapable of finding the pleasure we seek from food, then we have the crucial information we need to move differently in response.

We realize, first of all, that if we don't want to produce the same patterns of dissatisfaction, we need to be sure to make movements in relation to our desire for food—in relation to ourselves—that do not reinforce a mind over body sense of who we are.

Second, we realize that such movements will necessarily express the sensory awareness that has enabled us to acknowledge our dissatisfied desire and shift our experience of it. That dissatisfaction is guiding us to move in relation to food with the same care and attention to our sensations that cultivating an awareness of the movements making us requires.

We need to ask ourselves again: what is it we desire when we desire *food*? What is it that will provide us with the *pleasure* we seek?

◈

Lying on the floor writing again, my breathing belly supported by a soft rug, I remember back to my own breakfast. A piece of fruit and some raisins. Oatmeal and grapenuts, topped with low-fat cottage cheese and milk. Just thinking of it, I breathe easily.

Why do I eat it? I eat it because I want to. I like it. But why do I like it? I like it because I like how it makes me feel. The meal is heavy enough to quell my hunger, light enough not to weigh me down, slow enough to stabilize any erratic morning energy, and nourishing enough to vitalize my active core. It is quiet food. It sits calmly, allowing my attention to float away to other activities. It is familiar food, offering comfort in the face of daunting tasks. It encourages me to breathe, down into my body, into the earth, open into the sources of my own freedom and creativity. Eating this food builds my confidence that I will be able to flow with what I want to do on a given day, writing and dancing, for I know that I can provide myself with what I need.

Eating, I feel the pleasure of making the movements that make me into someone who knows: *I am nourished. I can be nourished. I can nourish myself.*

Who talks about desire for food in these ways?

5

A Sense of Enough

'It is not fat but the greatest possible suppleness and strength
that a good dancer desires from his nourishment.'
– *Gay Science*, #381, 346

Growing up, we always had at least one black Labrador retriever.
Friendly and enthusiastic, these dogs were members of the
family, and they loved to eat. As soon as the food bowl was placed
on the floor, its contents were gone. When we returned to the
house, it was often to find upturned garbage cans, torn bread
packages, and vanished leftovers. These beautiful dogs would eat
themselves silly. They depended on us, people, higher minds, to
provide them with a sense of enough.

Compare these dogs with the cats we now have. Selective and
spare, these cats live alongside a bowl of food that is constantly
full without eating more than they need. They don't rely on
people to tell them what (not) to eat.

Cat and dog. Both domesticated as pets, useful and
affectionate companions to human beings. Yet dogs have lost
something that the cats have not — *a sense of enough*. The wilder
ones know when to stop.

ക

I decide to do an experiment. As Geoff is away, I am doing
the weekly grocery shopping. I forget grapenuts and cottage
cheese. I can't stand the thought of going all the way back to the
store, so I set myself the test: eat something else. My mind

screams that this is a terrible idea. *I won't be able to know when I have had enough!* Really? I take a breath. Yes, it is risky, but it will provide me with some valuable information. Why does what we eat matter?

The next morning comes. I try a different breakfast. The familiar weight in my stomach that signals the end of the meal never arrives. So I keep eating different foods, trying to recreate that recognizable feeling of enough.

It occurs to me: *I can't stand this feeling of not having enough. It is intolerable.*

Why? Because it feels as if I will never have enough. Never get what I most want and need. Ever. It triggers a primal fear.

All from a piece of toast? I ignore the sensation and go to work. It is hard to settle. I flail a bit, and push myself to get focused. But I keep wandering in a fog of restlessness, as if searching for that missing bowl of oatmeal.

As the day unfolds, a pattern of self-incrimination takes hold. I didn't give myself what I wanted, and suddenly I can't. A rigid self-control I practiced for many years slides back into place. By lunch I am eating part of my usual meal. By dinner I am so hungry that I overeat myself into a place of severe discomfort in a vain effort to rebel against my own sense of constraint. *I can't stop!* So much for my experiment. The voices are fierce and blaring. *What is the matter with me? Why am I so vulnerable? Aren't "I" in control?*

No. The answer lands with a belly bottom thud, grounding me in my senses.

ભ

I pause from writing and pop a coffee candy in my mouth. The sweetness seeps out around the edges of my tongue. I press up on the firm disk, sucking hard. It resists and gives, holding its shape in rivulets of sweetness. Waters stream forth from inside my cheeks, around my gums, top and bottom. Flowing flavor. I swallow, and the fountains begin again, soothing and thirst-quenching. I fight the urge to bite down on the disk. I don't want a quick end to this moment. I want to draw it out as long as I can, and allow the comfort to flow through my imagination, sugar to ink.

ʘʘ

No. How do I interpret this "no"? Do I lack will power? Perhaps my reason is forever corrupted by emotional and physical biases. Perhaps I am out of control and will never succeed.

I have heard such voices for years, rehearsed by family members, amplified by dispatches from icons of entertainment, articulated by philosophers and teachers of Christian religion, and ensconced in ideals of love, beauty, and goodness proffered to me in all these contexts. Will power over desire is the path to bliss. *Phew.*

It isn't true. I breathe deeply, release into the ground, and drop into a sensory awareness of the *movements that are making me.*

As I breathe open the knots of dissatisfaction and judgment, I see. The seemingly insatiable desire is what I have been creating in myself as a result of how I have been thinking and acting towards food. My movements are making me *dissatisfied.* I hadn't gotten what I wanted, but no amount of food was going to help. I was already full.

So why wasn't I satisfied? What did I want that I hadn't gotten?

As my breathing opens and softens, the pulse of my desire surfaces through the feelings of dissatisfaction themselves. *It isn't the food.* I am dissatisfied because I want *more,* and the more I want is a *sense that I have had enough.* I want the *pleasure* of being nourished, the pleasure of nourishing myself. A sense of enough, not a knowledge that I have eaten the right thing or a good thing, but a felt comfort in my belly. *It is OK to stop.*

Given my experiment, I realize, I had little chance of arriving at such a felt sense of enough. The instruction to eat toast came from my mind, armored with all kinds of good reasons, and bowled over my sense of what I really wanted. But again, it wasn't just that I preferred oatmeal to toast, as if the oatmeal itself could give me the satisfaction I desired. It was that, in deciding to eat the toast, I was splitting my desire between what I wanted to eat and what I thought I should eat. Pitted against myself in this way, I created myself into someone who could not find her way to a sense of enough, regardless of what she was eating.

As I continue to follow this line of thought, breathing it through, the call of my persistent yearning for more food rings loud and clear. Even though it feels like it, I really do not want to eat more, I just want to feel like I have had enough.

My dissatisfaction is calling me to remember that my desire for food will not and cannot be satisfied by food alone. If I try to master my desire for food by overriding my sense of what I want, I make myself into a mind over body who can't find the pleasure she seeks. *I can't stop!*

If I breathe open to welcome my desire for food and learn to discern its wisdom, I make myself into someone who can know that she has had enough, that she is enough, and that she will be enough.

ଅଛ

A sense of enough. Could it be true? Do we have one? Is finding it for ourselves really what we *desire*?

It seems unlikely, trained as we are to think and feel and act as if we were minds over bodies. We are biologically hardwired, aren't we, to want more food, always more? The failures of our massive efforts in dieting away the pounds or designing an effective drug are proof. Aren't they? Look again. If anything, the human digestive system is designed to maximize our ability to move, not our ability to take in food.

Think about it. Humans stand upright. As a result of our upright posture, we have a mobility that is rare among animals. We do not hibernate. Our transformation from infant to adult does not involve a cocoon or chrysalis stage. We are constantly moving. We are not the fastest or strongest. We are not the most agile or deft. What characterizes our movement is its novelty: we are constantly learning to make new movements, new patterns of sensing and responding that guide us in thinking, feeling, and acting. As a result of this ability, we have proven ourselves capable of finding food and making ourselves at home in nearly every climate on earth.

At every point, our digestive system *enables* us in making these movements. Our manner of processing what we consume provides us with a steady stream of energy so that we can keep moving. We do not eat one meal a week and sleep it off like other carnivores. Nor do we spend a third of every day grazing like the large herbivores. Instead we move through recurring cycles of hunger and fullness over a 24-hour period. We stomach small, dense meals, mostly cooked, preferably several a day. These rhythms of digestion allow us time between meals to hunt, gather, and grow food, while still providing us with the steady stream of nourishment we need in order to do so. Even when we are in a position to eat more energy than we are burning, we store it all over the body, in patterns that, until we are extremely obese, maximize our ability to keep moving. We eat to keep moving so that we can eat to keep moving from environment to environment, season to season, continent to continent, meal to meal. And in order to move, we must stop eating.

Further, in making the food-finding movements that our digestive system enables and requires, we have evolved to rely on our sensory awareness as a primary guide. Unlike many of our animal siblings, we can catch and cook, chew and digest almost anything. Our food needs are not determined by instinct or climate. We *have* to make choices about what to eat, how to acquire it, and when and how to eat it. We have no choice but to choose. While culture and tradition and habit do constrain these choices, the surest guide we ever have is *our senses*. We are creatures who can and must use all of our senses — taste, smell, touch, sight, hearing — to guide us in identifying, pursuing, and securing what will nourish us and rejecting what will not. The foods we are primed to sense as pleasurable, then, are those that support us in the ongoing project of moving, sensing, and responding to food. Our survival depends upon it.

Gathering the pieces together, this picture is suggestive. The pleasure we derive from food does not come from the quantities of vitamins and minerals, or the salts or sugars present in a chemical substance. *The pleasure we seek comes from participating in the process of learning how, when, what, and why to eat so that we can keep moving.* The pleasure we seek comes from the experience of finding our way to a sense of enough so that we can stop eating, as we must, and keep making the movements of sensing and responding that enable us to live.

C&R

Our most powerful resource in meeting our desire for food is not a mental capacity to impose our will upon "it." Our most powerful resource lies in our desire for food itself. Any dissatisfaction we experience, whether an insatiable hunger even when we are full, or a craving for foods that make us queasy, or an inability to eat when we know we should, or a displeasure with the size and shape of our bodies, is calling to us to look again at the movements we are making in relation to food. This dissatisfaction is what we are creating.

We are eating in ways that are cutting us off from our sensory selves, from the sources and sites of our own pleasure, and from the wisdom in our desire. We are not eating what will keep our bodies moving, sensing, and responding to what we eat. And we are not eating in movement-enabling ways because we are no longer listening to our desires—not because we are enslaved by them. We feel it.

The problem is not that our desires run rampant in the field of abundance; the problem is that we have lost touch with the desires that are and remain our best guide *wherever* we are. Our dissatisfaction is calling us to tune into our sensory awareness, and to find our way to a sense of enough.

Are we repeatedly overriding our sense of enough in search of more pleasure? Or are we eating in ways that keep our senses tuned, active, and alive to the rhythms of our ever-evolving desire for food?

At stake is far more than our health. At stake is our relationship to ourselves. For the kind of attention that allows us to discern wisdom in our desires is best described as love. *Nourish and nurture are forever entwined.*

☙

Jordan wakes up raring to go. The blush of dawn on his cheeks, he is affectionate, ever ready for a morning hug. Many days he finds Jessica and the two of them disappear into one of their imaginary realms.

One morning, I hear a squeal — Jessica sounds as if she has been bitten. Jordan appears, his face darkened, contorted. She complains. I scold him.

"I am dumb," he responds, and begins to plummet, spiraling deeper into an intense frustrated, self-hatred, one I recognize all too well. I try to talk him out of it.

"It's OK, Jordan. You didn't mean it like that. Just say you're sorry. It's OK. You are not bad or dumb or anything of the sort. She hurt your feelings and you lashed out. I know you can make other choices."

It does little to help. He plunges deeper. I give up and order him to the breakfast table. "Drink this juice." No discussion allowed. I offer him his favorite bagel.

Minutes later, his face begins to lighten. His head lifts. His forehead clears.

"Mom," he opens, "did you know that the milk from Jersey cows has a higher fat content than milk from Holsteins?"

I look at him, bewildered. He is a completely different person. He is speaking with a clear and even tone. He smiles readily, head held high.

"You needed something to eat!" I reply.

❦

Jordan needed something to eat, but not just because his blood sugar was low. Jordan, wrapped in play, was overriding his desire for food. In response, his body shut down a whole bank of emotional registers. When he is in such a place he loses access to these emotional resources. He soon feels frustrated and irritable, and takes out his frustration on his sister, his pencil, his drawing, or himself. He acts in ways that bring him the attention he knows at some level that he needs, but the attention is negative, and he hates himself for that. Caught in a downward spiral, he falls, feeling powerless to act otherwise. Not eating, he makes himself into someone who has turned against himself, and takes it out on others.

There was a time when I would get sucked into Jordan's emotional whirlpool and be cross with him for responding so poorly. I made it worse. He was already bent against himself. He didn't need me to join in. Then I realized. In such moments Jordan does need to eat, but not just for the calories. He needs to eat because, in the act of eating, he is relating to himself, to his own desires, in a way that honors them, honors him, as worthy of such care and attention. He is nourishing himself. His movements make him into someone who is giving himself the experience of having and being enough. And from that nourishing, nourished place, he is able, once more, to open to the extraordinary range of emotional maturity Geoff and I have witnessed in him since he could talk. He can sense and respond in ways that were, moments before, impossible, and he knows it.

Jordan's post-breakfast words and actions did not only express a full belly. They recreated, in acts of generosity, empathy, and humor, the *pleasure* he felt in honoring and finding his own sense of enough. He had had enough. He was enough. He could succeed in giving himself enough. And feeling that pleasure, he grew stronger in his desire to be the person that he senses he is, *Jordan, a river of compassion.*

CR

If what we desire from food is this experience of nourishing and nurturing ourselves, this experience of finding our way to a sense of enough, then how do we get it?

6

Eating Pleasure

'A breeding of feelings and thoughts alone is almost nothing...
one must first persuade the *body*.'
— *Twilight of Idols*, 552

It begins with our senses, and not just the sense of taste, nor the combination of taste and smell. We *see* our food, its shape, texture, and color. The air pockets opening in bread, the drizzling of frosting on a bun, the red and white of a bitten apple. We *hear* our food. It crunches and crumbles, bubbles and drips; it resists the knife, squeezes against the edge of a fork, or eludes the scraping spoon. We *feel* our food with our fingers, our lips, our tongue, the insides of our mouth, our esophagus, our stomach.

It is impossible to eat without seeing, hearing, and touching, even when thickly congested to the point where we cannot smell or taste. We rely on our sensory experience of food to welcome it into our bodies. And the more open our senses in the moment of eating, the more pleasure we are primed to receive.

So too the sensory experience of eating does not stop with the usual five. There is also a sense of *movement* at work, a kinetic sense. I stretch my arm and reach my hand toward food. My fingers grasp a morsel, close around it, and draw it near. In a returning arc I circle on myself. I use my hands together to pry the meat from the bone, the skin from a grape, the seeds from the orange. I lift the cone of ice cream to my lips. I open and shut my mouth to cut and bite and tear and grind. I close my eyes, jaw lifting and lowering, making soft mush.

I swallow, moving the pressure down along the inside of my chest to a quiet thud in my belly. I touch myself.

There is also a sense of *time* and timing. Our desire for food is rhythmic. A bite that pleases in one moment will not give the same sensation in the next. Our pleasure oscillates between eating and not eating, sitting and moving, forming arcs of anticipation and gratification. Past and future wind through the present, heightening each bend of the wave.

As I sense food in these ways, moving to move substances to me and into me, those substances become me, and not only chemically. While the food particles do dissolve into elements that nourish every cell, what becomes me are the patterns of sensing and responding that acquiring and ingesting those substances require. Eating, I am creating and becoming patterns of sensation and response that accompany me — that *are* me — wherever I go. I *am* these ever evolving shapes and nuances in my relationship to myself.

Nourishing myself, I open pathways to my earliest movements of surrender in the arms of those who were feeding me. I continue their work.

It is only human.

❧

When we operate with a mind over body sense of ourselves, we imagine that eating is a chemical exchange or a strictly physical pleasure. By contrast, when we invite a sensory awareness of the movements making us, we begin to sense how the movements we make in eating are making us into people who can or cannot find their way to a sense of enough. We begin to feel the pain of falling away from the arc of our pleasure, and the delight of aligning ourselves with it. We start to feel that pain or dissatisfaction, in other words, as wisdom—as an impulse to move in ways that will return us to our senses, and unfold our capacity for pleasure and health.

The wisdom in our desire for food is guiding us to follow the arc of our pleasure to a sense of enough.

ભ

I get up, walk around, pick up Kai who has just woken up, feed Kyra some pretzels, give Kai a toy, get myself some pretzels, and settle back down in my chair. The movement always does me good. I see the big picture again. A burst of carbohydrates sends me along.

What we desire from food is an experience of being nourished, the pleasure of finding our way to a sense of enough. Good.

But I know too, it is not enough to admit that we desire this, or that our desire is good and worthy. It is not enough to acknowledge that we have a right and even a responsibility to pursue this desire. On top of all of this, we must still *do the work that the satisfaction of this desire requires.* We cannot just talk about eating, learn about eating, theorize about eating, or wax poetic about how eating can be an expression of love. We must actually eat. We must find and follow the arc of our pleasure to a sense of enough. Several times a day. So how? How do we follow the arc of our pleasure to a sense of enough? *What should we eat?*

I write down these questions and hit a wall. What can I say? What can I say that does not imply that "we" can or should change in a way that involves exerting our will power over our tyrannical desiring bodies? What can I say that will not imply either that there is one right way to eat or that anything goes?

What to say indeed. All I want to do is to eat. Lunchtime is not for another hour or so. I am not ready for it anyway. I'm not hungry. If I eat now, I know I won't feel satisfied, only heavy, bogged down, and depressed. I don't want to feel depressed. I want to work, but I can't. I am stuck. Frustrated.

I have to move. The impulse pops into my mind. *Go for a walk.* Yes, I will breathe open a body-enabled mind space and catch the ₒₜₛ that bubble up. I strap Kai in the backpack, click Kyra in the stroller, and set off down the road.

My energy stirs and rises. My breath dives and surfaces, bringing with it a flood of thoughts that I have had so many times before—thoughts that seem to slip from my mind whenever I sit to write.

What should I eat?

Move. It is not really an answer. It is indirect at best. But it is the only kind possible. There is no one recipe for the foods that will make your body lean and strong, or give you the pleasure and nourishment you desire. None. That is the point. Any diet recommendations can give you information that can help you conduct your own experiments, but in the end, the only answer that will work for you is one that aligns with your felt sense of desire for nourishment in the time and place you are.

Move. The answer stresses the physical. *Do something.* It doesn't have to be a walk. It can be any activity that requires you, or rather *allows* you, to exert yourself in some way, to breathe open your body, and move through the cycle of breaths. A rhythmic movement, that requires you to extend your attention along the trajectories of your bodily self, and feel how the movements you are making are making you.

When a space of sensory awareness opens in you, you can release your hunger into it. Let it roam. Breathe through it, into it, around it. Where is it coming from? Where is the play in this desire? What is it that you really want?

Move. While physical, such movement is never merely physical. In making a choice to move as a path to discerning the wisdom in your desire, you are not just moving your bodily self. Your movement is creating you as someone who welcomes her desires with *practices* that enhance her ability to listen to them. You are breathing yourself open. You are paying attention. You are creating a relationship to yourself, in sensing and honoring your desires for food, that is characterized by an *intention* to nurture and nourish. You are practicing *love*. Whatever you say or do will express this love for the ever-becoming movement you are.

Move. Move to breathe. Breathe to move. Breathe your tension down into the earth. Breathe yourself open into air. Breathe to ignite the fire of your own desire. Breathe to let it flow. *Find out what your body knows.*

I return home from my walk, winded and full. It is a beautiful day. I got what I wanted, that sense of my own sensing. I am making the movement that is making me. I am someone who moves to discern the wisdom in her patterns of frustrated desire. *I am alive.*

I unload Kyra and set the sleeping Kai gently on the couch. Ah, now I can feel the arc of my hunger, sharp and clear. I know what I want. Lunch, anyone?

ॐ

What is your sensory experience of eating? What foods give you the most pleasure? Why? What qualities do they have? Are they heavy or light, noisy or quiet, safe or risky, settling or quickening? Are they creamy or juicy, chewy or dry? Do they stick to the roof of your mouth, or land softly in your belly? What color are they? What consistency? Do they have a strong smell, a loud crunch, or a mouth-filling resilience?

What makes the foods you most like to eat good for you?

When during the day do you eat them to get the most pleasure?

How do the sensory experiences of different foods compare? What does an apple do in your mouth? What does a candy bar do on your tongue? What happens to a carrot in your throat? How do pretzels settle in your stomach? How different do you feel after you eat a piece of cake versus a bowl of oatmeal? A cookie versus a chunk of tofu? Ten minutes later? An hour later? What do you do when you feel a pang of hunger? What crosses your mind? What is your experience of it? How do you respond?

How often do you look down at your plate and realize with surprise that you have eaten everything on it? How often do you polish the crumbs before realizing that you have eaten more than your stomach can comfortably churn? How often while eating that handful of chips do you ignore a sensation of discomfort? How often, in reaching for that last brownie, do you override your own desire *to stop*?

How often, when you are eating, are you aware of your breathing?

CR

It has to crunch. If a meal goes by without the opportunity to crunch, no matter how mouth-watering it is in other respects, no matter how filling, I will keep eating, in search of that crunch. I will feel cheated — full without having had the pleasure of becoming full. I'll buy a pack of pretzels after a gourmet lunch.

I know this. So I avoid milkshakes, soup, instant breakfast, or chocolate milk. I don't choose to eat cakes, cookies, or muffins unless there are nuts, chips, or other teeth-resisting ingredients, and not because my mind is in control over my hard-wired bodily cravings for sugar and salt. I don't *want* to eat such foods (unless I am ravenous and there are no other options) because I know that they will not give me the experience of nourishment I want. It has to crunch.

CR

"Why do you like crunchy food?" Jessica asks. She has noticed. I am not surprised. Even at two, rather than moan of hunger, she would ask: "Can I please have a piece of havarti cheese?" More recently, she generalizes by type. "I need something juicy. Do you have something juicy to eat?" She prefers what she calls "juicy foods" — milk, ice cream, and apple sauce; oranges, grapes, cantaloupe, and watermelon, corn and peas. She tolerates dry foods, like bread and cereal, but only as delivery mechanisms for her butter and jelly. Even then she rejects the crusts and crispy edges. Of course she noticed.

She is looking at me intently.

"Well," I reply, trying to figure it out myself, "the crunch sends little ripples through my whole body that are relaxing. Pleasing. When I crunch, it is as if I am getting a massage, inside myself. The crunching loosens the tension in my jaw. I like the rhythm of it. It wakes me up and soothes me." I pause. "Why do you like juicy foods?"

"Because they are soft in my mouth," she says.

As I know from experience, she is serious about this. She will reject many of the options available to her. It is not worth it to her to eat anything. She is not looking for calories or even taste but an experience that will let her know and enable her to feel that she is being nourished. That she has had enough. That she can stop. Soft and juicy it is.

❧

Crunch is part of what I need to bite down, sink in, and make myself at home in food. I also need a balance between foods that *settle* and foods that *quicken*. Something has to ground me, to land warm in the belly and lend a weight to it. Something that rests and radiates a gentle hum. Earth foods. I gravitate towards whole grains and legumes, oatmeal and beans, complex carbohydrates grown close to the ground.

Nevertheless, a meal of warm mush even if punctuated by a toasted crunch, will still leave me feeling hungry if there is not a quickening element, something that pricks my senses and opens me up. Often it is some spice, mustard or hot pepper, salad dressing or salsa. Sometimes it is honey, a handful of raisins, a tang of salt. A small amount forms a sensory bridge between the time settling foods land and the time that they become energy for use. The spark charges a wider spectrum of sensory responses than the settling and crunchy foods, producing a halo effect. In search of such warming sparks, I am careful. Balance is key. Too much quickening food and I am scattered and tense, ungrounded and unable, despite my flightiness, to move.

More important than the crunching, settling, and quickening types, is a pair of categories that cuts across them all. There are *quiet* foods and *noisy* foods. Quiet foods are those I can eat any time and as much as I want, like carrots and pretzels. They fold themselves into whatever I am doing and flow through without disturbance. They can be crunchy or creamy, settling or quickening, but are always calming and safe. Eating them, I breathe easily, for I know: *quiet foods do not mask my ability to know that I have had enough.* Quiet as they are, they allow me to stay in tune with my sense of enough.

Noisy foods, on the other hand, scream so loudly that they make it nearly impossible to find the arc of my pleasure with them. Noisy foods are almost always processed, loaded with salt and sugar and fat, designed to unleash every craving ever identified — savory corn chips or sweet, crunch-filled granola; coconut bars or butterscotch cookies.

Such foods often trick me into feeling satisfied for a moment before the feeling of satisfaction yawns into an even greater hunger. Carried by the clamor of the sensory impact, I contract and extend myself in ways that move me beyond what I can support. I grow weaker, relying on the illusions of strength these foods provide.

Knowing this, I approach noisy foods gingerly and with respect. To find my way with them I know that I need to be calm and relaxed, not too tired nor too full. I need a specific goal in mind, a place to channel the fragile, explosive energy they will unleash. Most of all, I need to be grounded in sensory awareness, breathing through a relaxed belly. If I am, I will be able to ride the intoxication without being thrown too far from myself.

Many times, a bit of noise is just the ticket to get me going. Ice cream is a case in point. Provided it contains a crunch and is not too creamy, it is a perfect food, settling and quickening. I love it. But it tends to be noisy, drawing attention away from my sense of enough. It dazzles me. So what do I do? I eat straight from the carton. If I eat it from a bowl I inevitably feel like I need to empty the bowl and then eat one bite more. I want that pleasure of knowing for myself that enough is enough. So I take it one mouthful at a time. I hit that bite of deliciousness, where stomach opens to meet the cream. Pleasure ripples through. I breathe down, open, through. *That's it.* I am free to go.

My mind has very little power in the face of noisy foods. My best guide is a breath-opened awareness of my bodily sensations. For only when I am willing and able to feel the arc of my pleasure can I find the fullness that guides me to spoon, swallow, and stop. My strength lies in love.

ೞ

It goes against all common sense. How can you say that *if I cultivate the pleasure in eating, I will find a sense of enough*?

If I am feeling the pleasure, won't I want to keep eating, to get more pleasure? Shouldn't I rather work to decrease the pleasure I feel in eating and rely instead on meal replacements and protein shakes to divert my desire?

No. If we open our senses to feel the pleasure of eating, the rhythm and arc of that pleasure, then we will also be acutely aware of the moment in which our pleasure starts to wane. And because we are, in that very moment, attending to our sensations as the source of our pleasure, we are more likely than ever to feel our fullness as a desire to stop. *I can eat again later, or tomorrow.* At that moment the pleasure of eating morphs into the pleasure of knowing when to stop and doing so. It becomes the pleasure of giving ourselves the experience of being nourished, of getting what we need, of having and being enough.

When we cultivate a sensory awareness of the movement making us, the desire to override what feels good in our bodies or stuff ourselves silly falls away.

It does not fall away because our will power establishes its dominance, but because we realize that we want something else more. We realize that the pleasure we desire is not one we will find by denying *or* indulging our desire. We want the pleasure of moving with the wisdom in our desire, and following its arc to a sense of enough.

The pleasure we seek from food is and is not keyed to a particular food or even to the feeling of fullness. It is a pleasure equally available to us at every moment along the arc of hunger and fullness, whether we are eating or not.

It is a pleasure we feel when we attend to our desires with attention and respect, and give ourselves an experience of eating that releases us to become who we are. It is the pleasure of learning to live in love.

ભ

Wait a minute. If all that matters is the process of attuning to our eating pleasure, can I concoct any diet I want? Can I eat anything so long as I feel a desire for it? What about a diet of ice cream and pretzels?

The freedom we tap when we cultivate a sensory awareness of our eating pleasure is infinite in one sense and bounded in another. While we are free to eat whatever we "want," we are not free to "want" anything.

The act of making choices demands honesty with ourselves over what food does in us, to us, and through us. And anyone who seriously engages in this process will soon discover that desires for food he thought he had evolve.

Motivations she has for eating foods that do not align with the ongoing practice of attending to her sensory awareness fall away and she discovers what she already knows: noisy and empty foods are noisy and empty. Foods that poison bodies poison the earth. That second handful is one too many. *Enough is enough.*

The freedom released in us as we cultivate our sensory awareness is a freedom to do what we *must* to nurture our health and well being.

∝

Too complicated? Perhaps. But only because it represents my experience of food and not yours. What are the qualities of food that matter to you? *What is your sense of eating?* What does your body know?

Is this approach effective in the fight against fat? I believe the fight against fat is fatally flawed. I am not offering a recipe for how to lose weight. I am honoring the potential of our desire for guiding us to our greatest health and well being. If we are to address the obesity epidemic and the myriad issues surrounding it, we need to think beyond a temporary restriction of calories toward cultivating a relationship to ourselves that allows us to follow the arc of our pleasure to a sense of enough.

A luxury? Certainly. Many, though not all, in the modern world are surrounded by unprecedented abundance. The options are dizzying. For this reason, it is even *more* important than it has ever been for us to learn how to exercise our bodily wisdom in discerning what, when, and how to eat. For only if we do so will we ensure that our economies of food production evolve in ways that will provide all of us, wherever we live, with the options we need in order to nourish ourselves.

CR

What I have written is true. It is also false. While it is true, as I write, the sheer fact of writing down this list of what I eat, how, when, and why, changes me. By making the list I ensure it will change, for in making it I call my attention, once again, to lingering pockets of dissatisfaction that are yearning to unfold a greater pleasure. I open the possibility for having new experiences of food, not just because the foods are new, but because, in making my list, I am making myself into someone who is exercising her freedom and creativity in relation to food, someone who is attentive to her changing experiences of food and ready to respond.

Does admitting this invalidate everything I have written? No. It highlights how it matters.

For if it seems like I am telling you what and how to eat, look again. I am sharing with you what and how *I* eat. The difference is crucial.

The pleasure we seek in our desire for food is a pleasure that we must find for ourselves by tuning into the arcing, rhythmic character of our desire for food, and learning to move with it. Our lists will be different and they will change. For the pleasure we seek lies in the act of making the list itself—in the willingness to feel and honor our sense of enough.

CR

I can find scientific data to justify the foods I choose in following the arc of my pleasure to a sense of enough. I usually eat what at least some nutritionists say I should. Noting this I smile, but I don't dwell on it. If I shift my attention towards formulas and away from my own sense of nourishment, I will lose degrees of the freedom I have worked hard to discover.

No. I want to sense and respond to my desires for food in ways that create me into someone who is committed to doing the work day to day that the satisfaction of her desires requires. I want to eat to know when enough is enough.

7

Shifting Desire

'To sense that what is harmful is harmful, to be *able* to forbid
oneself something harmful, is a sign of youth and vitality.'
— *Case of Wagner*, 165

So here we are. We can understand, theoretically at least, that we
can move to breathe and breathe to move. We can cultivate a
sensory awareness of our relationship to food and learn to follow
the arc of our pleasure to a sense of enough. All well and good.
But how do we actually field the wisdom that will guide us? Can
practicing the cycle of breaths really help? Yes.

As we practice the cycle of breaths, breathing to move and
moving to breathe, our experience of our desire for food shifts.
Desire is movement. It is movement in us that moves us toward
whatever we believe will give us the pleasure we seek. So too, as
we are ever getting new information about what works for us, our
desires have the potential to evolve.

Moving through the cycle of breaths catalyzes this process.
The different perspectives provided by each turn in the cycle help
us release the potential of our desire to grow in line with our
rolling revelations of what brings us the pleasure we seek. Our
practice, breathing to move and moving to breathe, opens a space
and time within ourselves where we create and become new
shapes of our desire for food that *express the love for ourselves we
are practicing.*

When we engage ourselves in this way, more and more
we find ourselves *wanting* to eat what nourishes us, and wanting
to do so as the condition for our greatest pleasure and health.

We move with the wisdom in desire.
Really?

 og

Imagine yourself consuming a package of Oreos. Imagine how delightful it will be. You will let yourself do it, release into your desire, and get the sweet satisfaction you crave. All of it. You will become an Oreo-eater, someone who nourishes himself this way.

With that tenth cookie, however, you begin to feel too full. Your stomach aches. You deny the ache. You want the satisfaction of eating the entire package. You begin to feel nauseous. A headache crops up. Your mind starts to blink. *Listen.*

What is happening? You want the pleasure of eating. Your desire has taken shape in the form of an ideal of what you need to do to get that pleasure: eat the Oreos. More Oreos equals more pleasure. It is an ideal that coordinates the impulse in you (for eating pleasure) and the options available in your world (Oreos).

As you eat, however, you meet resistance in your sensory awareness to satisfying your desire. *Pain!* Discomfort. If you experience this discomfort through a sense of yourself as mind over body, you may be tempted to interpret this pain as an obstacle to your full satisfaction. A nuisance. You will want to eat another Oreo just to prove that you are master of your body and can get what you desire. Yet every time you override your own resistance, in the name of greater pleasure, you dull your ability to sense what will give you the pleasure you say you want.

There is another way. If, in the moment, you can release into your sensory awareness, your experience of discomfort will shift and the resistance will make sense to you as something to trust. You will know that your discomfort is expressing the wisdom in your desire. It is telling you that the ideal you have (more Oreos) is out of sync with what will actually produce pleasure (stopping).

The movements you are making to satisfy your desire are making you sick! Your wisdom is crying out for you to stop.

Even so, it is not that easy. Even though you *know* that eating another Oreo will make you ill, and you can feel it, you may still *want* to eat it. The sensation of displeasure you anticipate cannot compete with your desire to taste it now. What then?

If we rely on coercion and denial, regardless of how fine our intentions, we will inevitably crack, gobble up what we have denied ourselves, and then eat more to compensate for our sense of deprivation. If we make our relationship with our self into a battle, we always lose, whether we eat or not.

Alternately, you can call on the cycle of breaths to enhance your sensory awareness of the movements making you. *Breathe to move and move to breathe.*

Breathe and release the tension in your wanting into the earth. Let it go. Let it settle. Feel yourself sitting, standing, from inside yourself. Connected. *Where are you? What are you feeling?*

Breathe again, and open up a space traced by the edges where skin meets air. Fill the space with oxygen and invite the reach and roots of your sensations to appear. *Why is this feeling so strong? Where is it coming from? What does it mean? Where is it going?*

Breathe again and plug the energy of your desire into your fiery core. *What is it you really want? Where does your greatest pleasure lie?*

Breathe again and kindle that fire into fluid, flowing through you. Bring your senses back to the arc of your pleasure. *What can you do right now to move towards what will give you the pleasure you seek?*

When you engage the cycle of breaths in this way, the feeling of fullness will grow stronger in your awareness than the watering in your mouth. Practicing the cycle of breaths heightens your vulnerability to the persuasive power of your own sensations. It helps tilt the balance towards that pleasure that comes with a sense of enough.

As you breathe some more, remembering and recreating your connections with the elements, your desire will spread out and gather again along the trajectory of respect-full attention you are practicing as you breathe. It will move in line with the sensations of fertile, free, fiery flow you are awakening in yourself. With every breath you are more able to sense and respond to the discomfort you feel as moving you to make it stop... to stop eating.

Do you really want that Oreo? In the time-space of breathing you will realize that it is not the Oreo itself that you want—what you want is for the Oreo to taste good. But the Oreo won't taste good if you are overriding your own sensation of fullness. It won't give you the pleasure you want. The taste in your mouth deteriorates. *It will only be the Oreo I want if I am hungry.*

A decision forms: *I won't eat it. Not now.* The move away from the Oreo may be tinged with sadness, it is true. *I am missing out!* But that edge of sadness will be followed immediately by a gush of relief.

You avoided the violence of overriding your bodily sensations and the inevitable pain that would follow. You lived through the moment in a way that nourished and nurtured you, creating the possibility in you for greater future pleasure than you would have had now. Honoring your sensations in this way, you create yourself as someone who can do so, wants to do so, and knows she can do so, for her own health.

The relief is delicious.

ೞ

We have learned to suspect our desire for food and so misinterpret what our desires are teaching us about how to get the satisfaction we want. We imagine a simple equation: *more food equals more pleasure.* It seems only logical.

Our bodies know a different logic. *Food plus desire equals pleasure.* The cycle of breaths allows us to experience our desire for food as a desire *not* to eat in a given moment. What we most want from food is the opportunity to make the movements in thinking, feeling, and acting that will create in us the pleasure of being nourished. *I have had enough. There is enough. I am enough.*

◌⃯

Step back again. What if, when you breathe to move and move to breathe, you feel rumbling? Your belly is empty; your head is light. Will you decide to eat the Oreo?

Often in such cases, the chances are that as you attune to the hunger, you will feel even then that it is not really an Oreo that you want. You want something that will meet that hunger, something that will land in your stomach with stable, strong energy. You want a deep touch, not a titillating scratch. Some cheese. A banana. A handful of peanuts. You *know* that the Oreo will give you a bright sugar rush, leaving brittle irritation in its wake, but that knowledge is not enough. It is only when you *feel* your hunger to the point that your desire shifts in line with what will nourish you that you will find yourself able to make a different choice.

Once you take the edge off your hunger, then maybe you will want something sweet, one Oreo. A bite, just enough to fill the crack between the sense of being nourished and the feeling of fullness. In that bite, you will get all that is available to you, as the bodily self you are, of that skin-rippling delight.

In either of these cases, then, whether hungry or full, the dynamic is the same. By doing what you need to do to open fully to the pleasure of eating, you release the wisdom of that desire. You feel your hunger; you feel your fullness; and you free your desire for food to move along these rhythms. You are able to follow the arc of pleasure to a sense of enough.

◌⃯

As we breathe to move and move to breathe, our desires evolve into sure and trustworthy guides. Following their, that is our, lead, we will find ourselves moved to eat in ways that coordinate our eating pleasure with our greatest health.

This process takes time. Desire evolves, but slowly. Even so, the process of participating in that movement is not itself arduous. For it does not require that we defer satisfaction to some later date. The practice of breathing to move and moving to breath involves tuning in to the pleasure that eating has to offer us *right now*. It involves finding ways to eat in this moment that exercise our capacity to *love*.

Practice, in this sense, is not a matter of imposing a formula upon our wayward bodies. It is a matter of cultivating a relationship to ourselves that allows us to honor and follow the arc of our own pleasure to a sense of enough.

8

Group Eat

'Ultimately, nobody can get more out of things, including books, than he already knows. For what one lacks access to from experience one will have no ear.'
— *Ecce Homo*, 261

The afternoon lengthens. Shadows creep across the kitchen. Tired and hungry, I crunch on a carrot to keep me going. Cook the pasta, sauté the vegetables, cut the tofu, grate the cheese, slice the bread, put it all on the table, call the troops, get drinks, load on the condiments, sit. Sing a song. A moment of quiet. The conversation begins.

"Montpelier," Jessica cries out. She and Jordan are practicing state capitals.

"I don't like rice or bread or tofu," whines Kyra. "I don't like anything in the salad. I just want ice cream."

I put dressing on my salad.

"Can I have another plate," Jordan asks.

I crunch a broccoli stalk and get the plate.

"So how was your day, Jessica?" I sit down.

Kai starts to squeal, he is tired of his green bean. I hand him a carrot.

"Good," she says.

"Jessica did you have music?" Jordan asks.

"I want some apple juice. I didn't get any apple juice," says Kyra.

I get up for the apple juice.

"What songs are you learning?" Geoff asks.

Kai drops his carrot and wails.

Jessica: "Mom, I need more milk."

Jordan: "Is there anymore pasta?"

Kai needs to nurse. I have another bite of salad and pick him up. Geoff gets the milk and pasta. Kai begins to suck and I feel the drain. I reach for my water. Liquid streaming in, streaming out. I dissolve.

"I saw the foal today!" Kyra pipes up.

"May I be excused?" asks Jessica.

The kids are done. I haven't finished my salad. I hand Kai to Geoff. Dinner for two. I breathe into a sensory awareness of my hunger. The pace slows down a bit. In the quiet, I will follow the arc of pleasure to a sense of enough, bite by bite. Soft warm bread, chunks of cheese and tempeh, vegetable after vegetable, I believe in this food. I open to meet it.

I am almost full. I don't want to stop. The table is a mess. The counters littered with dirty utensils, half empty pots, plastic bags, cheese wrappers, and vegetable scraps. If I just keep eating, I imagine, I will have the energy for it all. But I know I won't. So I breathe and release everything that I am carrying into the earth.

I feel my fullness, and stop. I lie down on the floor, put Kai on my belly, and make faces at him. I stretch through my toes. There it comes, finally. Small waves of vitality. Broccoli, bread, cheese, becoming me, moving me, returning me to life.

CR

We never eat alone. We eat in communities, large and small. Even when we are physically alone, the food we consume has come to us from the lands and through the hands of others. Everything that makes it to our (chaotic) tables begins in the earth, its soil and waters. All means of cultivating, harvesting, processing, distributing, cooking, and consuming that food in turn affect the ongoing fertility of the earth. Our every bite feeds these systems of production and distribution that have enabled its journey to us. Our every swallow supports the relationship to the earth that these systems of production and distribution enact. The sheer presence of our food before us and our ability to derive pleasure from it depend upon the existence of these networks.

When we cultivate a sensory awareness of our eating experience, we open ourselves to feeling the truth of this connectivity. We become vulnerable as we may never have been before to accounts of where our food comes from, how it gets here, and where it goes. We know that the pleasure we seek in nourishing ourselves hinges on the health and well being of those who are enabling us to enjoy it.

The movements we are making as we eat are not only making us; they are also making the concentric worlds in which we live, small circles of family and friends, to communities, cities, counties, countries, and organism earth.

Eating, we create the world.

How are we to navigate the contesting forces that shape our choices of what to eat? How can we find the way to eat responsibly, aware that we are creating the world in which we live? Here as well, it is the wisdom in our desire — and the sensory awareness we cultivate in order to discern it — that remains our surest guide.

ॐ

Food is in the news. We learn daily from journalists, scientists, and philosophers about how practices of industrial agriculture and agribusiness are depleting the topsoil, destroying our farming communities, and polluting our water and air.

We learn that processing food removes its vital nutrients; and how techniques designed to preserve shelf life or render a plant resistant to disease involve soaking the earth with chemicals that alter the genetic makeup of what we consume. We learn that so many of the agricultural practices we have lauded as models of technological progress are making the earth ill. We learn about the people and communities whose labor is undervalued in the process.

This information is loud and clear. It shocks. In response, our ideas of what is right and good to eat waver. We may respond by mobilizing a mind over body strategy to implement a change in our eating habits. We espouse new values, naming foods once dear to us as "bad." We endeavor to curtail our desire for these bad foods and redirect it to "good" foods. We feel guilty when we don't. Our buying and eating habits shift, as least for a time. However, unless change happens at the level of our desire itself, such efforts will be short-lived. In times of stress or play, we will tend to fall back on what is familiar.

More is needed. When we cultivate a sensory awareness of how the movements we are making are making us, something different happens as we sense and respond to such information. The details land with a thud in our hearts and in our stomachs. Our desire lurches sideways. Knowing that the production of those foods is exploiting the workers who harvest it, or polluting the soil that grows it, we no longer feel the same sense of enjoyment in eating them. We know that in consuming such foods, we are destroying the matrix of life that sustains us. We are not nourishing ourselves. Our pleasure drains away.

CR

Supermarkets don't help this process. Take a walk through one. As an example of human mastery over food production and distribution, the supermarket is unparalleled. On the shelves we see the fruits of a global food system that allows us, in the United States at least, to have whatever we want whenever we want it, provided we are willing and able to pay the price. The imposing bulk of these full shelves, aisle after aisle, gives us the illusion that food exists apart from the cycles of the seasons or weather, climate or soil quality. We enjoy broccoli in December and corn in March, oranges in Maine and potatoes in Florida. Cereal and crackers, milk and eggs, meat and cheese: "we" are "free" to decide what we want to buy, what "we" want to put into "our bodies."

Even so, that choice is carefully controlled to privilege our minds, the minds that have been primed to override our sense of enough and consume much more than we need.

Packaged as most of the foods are, we cannot smell or taste what is being offered. We cannot predict what the experience of eating will be like. We make decisions, by necessity, based on the color of the box, the location on the shelf, the name of the manufacturer, the price, advertisements we have seen, and the promises for health and fitness blazoned on the label.

The experience encourages us to ignore the social and economic networks that a food's presence on the shelf represents. Food makers are required by law to list ingredients and nutritional components of a food, but not where it is grown, how it has been processed, and by whom.

Without our senses, we are less able to recognize that, although the options are many, the range of difference among them is miniscule. Globalized, our food is homogenized and often disguised. We may have fifty brands of cereal to choose from, but look at the labels and you will find that they are all made of the same ingredients, differently mixed, cooked, sugared, and shaped. Nor is this list of ingredients arbitrary; it represents raw materials that are cheap to buy and easy to acquire due to world trading practices and government subsidies for corn, wheat, and dairy. Food makers seek to earn profits by combining what is cheap and adding a fancy crunch, a pretty wrapper. More often than not, this involves processing the nutrition out of a food, injecting a vitamin pill, and making what is familiar seem new, and what is new seem familiar.

The sheer diversity of packaged options forces our relationship to food into a conceptual register. We are trained to rely on our minds to decide what to eat. It is nearly impossible to choose foods based on the sensory experience they provide.

When we cultivate a sensory awareness, however, breathing to move and moving to breathe, our experience of the supermarket itself can shift. What we desire from it changes. Walking the aisles, we see products designed to snag our attention, yet the sensations they provoke rattle about in our sensory spaces, provoking little pleasure.

We don't want foods that are so noisy; we want foods that will give us the pleasure we now know we want, foods that support us in finding our way to a sense of enough. We want foods that do not disguise themselves, or trick our senses, foods that are not wrapped, waxed, or pumped with chemicals.

We gravitate instead to foods that are closer to whole, closer to the ground. We find ourselves wanting to buy foods that are being produced in ways that respect the earth and the workers involved in farming it. We find ourselves looking for foods that are made or grown locally. We find ourselves walking out of the store, to shop in places that allow us more sensory access to food so that we can make more informed decisions.

We find ourselves thinking these ideas and espousing these values because they support us in getting the pleasure we seek—the experience of being nourished, of nourishing ourselves, our families, our earth. And the purchases we make as a result nurture an economy of food production and distribution that supports us as individuals in following the arcs of our pleasure to a sense of enough.

CR

Farmer Larry stops by with milk on Tuesdays and Fridays. Milk and cream, whole milk to skim, whatever has not sold at the local store. Larry has a deal with the dairy that sells its products there: when they deliver new milk to the store, they give him the old products whose sell-by date is near. He made the deal when he was raising calves. He has no calves now, so has adopted us. He provides milk in abundance, as much as we need. The rest goes to the neighbor's pigs. Sometimes we give him eggs from the chickens, or bread or cookies we have made. But basically, the milk is free.

I open the refrigerator and grab a bottle. White silky liquid pours into my coffee. There is plenty. There will be plenty. There is pleasure in this before I even take a sip —pleasure in a sense of enough. Of getting what we need. Of recycling what would otherwise be thrown away. Nursing logic in a barter economy. I drink up, and smile.

 CR

In conversations about eating, at parties or in public places, there is always someone who protests loudly against attempts at conscious eating: "I could never give up eating *that*," he or she insists, delivering the phrase with a shocked look in an incredulous tone. The implication is clear: *You, dear eater, are depriving yourself of pleasure, condemning yourself to less of it, in the name of an ideal.* You are surrendering your freedom to the "food police."

The logic is familiar to us now. It assumes that the pleasure we seek in eating comes from food itself. More food equals more pleasure. We either have it or we don't and it is up to us, our mental powers not our bodies, to decide.

When we breathe to move and move to breathe, however, we realize that this perception of desire and deprivation is a last great hurdle to our eating pleasure.

When impelled by a dawning sensory awareness, a decision not to eat a given food is *not* a matter of mind over body restraint at all. It is the very condition that enables us to *satisfy* our desire for food as far as we are capable. We are exercising our freedom, allowing ourselves to follow the arc of our pleasure to a sense of enough.

CR

I don't eat meat. I don't like how it tastes. I never did. Even as a kid all I wanted on my hamburger bun were the pickles and mustard, lettuce and tomato. Nor do I like how meat feels in my body. I don't like what happens to animals in industrial pens. And I am uncomfortable with the ethics of using acres of farmland to produce a pound of animal flesh.

In my decision not to eat meat, then, there is little "reason" and no denial, just an ongoing process of living a relationship to food that nourishes me. For me, making the decision *to* eat meat would mean overriding a bodily sensation of displeasure, and doing so just because I think I should for someone else's benefit. In my decision not to eat meat, I am naming and making real the world in which I want to live, a world in which everyone has the opportunity and ability to find their way to a sense of enough.

CR

We face massive pressures in our living and working environments: advertisements that make our mouths water; market shelves stocked to overflowing; fast food, free food, super-sized food, and vending-machine food around every corner; elevators, escalators, and labor-saving devices that sap our energy; the frenetic pace of daily life, as well as the dieting tips and body images raining down upon us. We are bombarded by messages from media and experts, family members, religion, and tradition telling us what we should and can consume.

We are too tired and too stressed, lonely and restless. The pressures to forget our sensory experience of eating, to ignore what we are eating, while seeking comfort from eating, are overwhelming and intrusive.

In the face of the pressure, using the cycle of breaths to cultivate a sensory awareness of our eating experience is a radical act. Breathing to move and moving to breathe is our best hope for finding the pleasure and nourishment, the health and well being, we seek.

Move. When we do, what we have as resources for guiding our eating choices are not arguments but practices that support us in making decisions about what to eat that will nourish the earth in us and around us.

As we practice attuning to our sensory awareness, we will continue to gather knowledge and information as well. Indeed, we must learn all we can about how our bodies work, what nutrients they need, and which foods provide them or not. We must demand to know more about how food is made, where, by whom, and how it travels to us. We must learn how tradition and history are informing our choices. Such information can help us name and refine our experience of eating. It can help us chart a course of experimentation. But in the end, it will be the sensory awareness of the experience of eating that, paradoxically, releases in us the ability to follow the arc of our pleasure to a sense of enough.

This task, though never-ending, is endlessly fruitful, and not just because we enjoy our meals. When we open to the deep touch of food, when we learn to nourish ourselves in the act of eating, we grow stronger in love for ourselves, for others, and for the world. This pleasure that we get from doing the work required to find our way to a sense of enough is an enabling condition for our creative unfolding in *whatever* else we do.

CR

I always try to leave some small space for a final snack at the end of the day. The kids are asleep. The kitchen is clean and straight; the floor swept for the fourth time in eight hours. Homework is done, backpacks packed. A load of wash is folded; the kittens are fed. I need a moment for myself, to feed myself. With cereal and a dash of vanilla yogurt, I curl up around the paper or a publisher's catalogue. The words distract me, occupying my mind, so I can open to feel the sensation of enough. A crunch, a settling, a sweetness, and a quiet. Sliding down, opening through, releasing me into whatever pools of awareness linger.

"They say" never eat before going to bed. If I don't, I can't sleep. I want to sleep.

Entwined Desires 1

Our desire for food is not just about calories and composition. Our desire for food is about our relationship to ourselves. Once we embrace this idea, the picture of how to follow the arc of our pleasure to a sense of enough grows more complicated.

The selves we are as we eat are the same selves we are as we enter into intimate relationships with others, and the same selves we are as we pursue a sense of vitality, direction, and belonging in our lives. The pleasure we feel in one realm of our life spills over into other realms, as do the currents of our anxiety and frustration. Though we can and often do separate our desires for the purposes of analysis, in action they are never so distinct. Our desires for nourishment, intimacy, and affirmation are invariably, constantly, relentlessly pulling on each other, pressing against each other, and competing with each other for our attention.

Experts warn us of this entanglement, and counsel us against it. We are advised to ferret out the emotional reasons why we eat, so that we don't eat for solace when we are lonely, or comfort when we feel depressed. Yet the tenor of this advice misses the point.

It is true. When we are tired or stressed, when we are not feeling the strength of our own burning core, we tend to think that the sheer act of putting food into our mouths will help.

However, the point is not that we shouldn't try to nurture ourselves with food, the point is that we are out of touch with the sensory awareness that would guide us in doing so.

ભ

The entwining of our desires is not a result of substituting one object of desire for another. It does not represent a failure of mental clarity, or confusion in what we want.

It is who we are. Our sensory awareness is not partitioned into discrete realms of food, sex, and spirit. In any moment, we are sensing and responding to one desire or another, and often all at once. As we do, we draw upon a reservoir of movements, patterns of sensation and response that are unique to us, our history, and our upbringing. Any pattern we mobilize in response to one desire grows stronger in us, and we are more likely to animate it in sensing and responding to other desires erupting in us.

When we acknowledge this entanglement, the task of addressing an issue in any one realm of desire may seem daunting. We realize, for example, that the experience shift we seek in relation to food cannot and will not take hold unless we are working to unlearn the mind over body patterns of sensing and responding that we activate in response to our desires for sex and spirit as well. Otherwise, even if we succeed in cultivating a sensory awareness of our desire for food, mind over body patterns of sensation and response will keep popping up in our choice of food. It is just this easy to be shifted back into a mind over body perspective.

This entanglement, however, is not only more work for us; it also works for us. Any success we have in learning to follow the arc of our pleasure to a sense of enough will ripple through our sensory responses to other desires. This rippling, in turn, will provide us with insights and resources for engaging and releasing the wisdom in these other desires as well. If we can learn to find, trust, and move with the wisdom in our desire for food, it is more likely that we will succeed in learning to find, trust, and move with the wisdom in our desires for sex and spirit as well, for we will have opened in ourselves the sensory awareness that makes such discerning possible.

Our desires flow through one another, crossing, amplifying, redirecting, and reducing one another. A troubling in one realm sends waves through the others. So too does a movement of healing. In this interplay lies hope for mutually enabling and inspiring discoveries of what our bodies can know.

ೞ

Desire
For
Sex

ೞ

Doing It for Love

'Marriage: thus I name the will of two to create the one that is
more than those who created it.'
                                        – *Zarathustra*, 182

I am driving in my car along Memorial Drive in Cambridge,
not long after marrying Geoff. Harvard University looms on my
left. The Charles River flows to my right. Large sycamore trees
gracefully arch overhead, dappling the pavement before me.

It's never over, I think to myself. *This marriage thing.*

It is different. It is not like other projects I have pursued where
there is a goal; you work hard, set your sights on the finish line,
and generate a result. There is no such end to marriage. There are
no medals or trophies or degrees to grab. No grades or profits to
earn. All there is is a relationship to inhabit and enjoy as it
unfolds over time. That's it. Until the day I die. Hopefully.

But what is it *anyway?* Venerable institution? Flowing river?
The trees between? Whatever "it" is, I have no idea how to make
it work. No experience on which to draw. No models to consult.
Who really knows what goes on between spouses?

What *do* I know? I know that I married for love, of course. But
not really. I have no idea what love is. I married because I wanted
to learn how to love, how to give and receive love with this
particular person. The draw to him was irresistible. Something
just kept saying "yes."

But what is love? What does it mean to *love* someone day after
day who is by your side, at your table, in your bed? Someone with
whom you talk, work, play, have sex and perhaps children?

Someone with whom you live, grow old, and die? And what does it mean to *be loved* by such a person? I can't even imagine. How am I supposed to figure it out?

ભ

"It's Official: To Be Married Means to Be Outnumbered" (*NYT*, Oct 15, 2006). The headline catches my eye, front billing on the Sunday paper. I flip to page twenty-two. According to the American Community Survey released by the Census Bureau, 49.7 percent of American households in 2005, that is, 55.2 of 111.1 million, were composed of married couples with or without children. The numbers represent a drastic decline from the 84 percent registered in 1930, and an incremental slide from the 52 percent recorded in 2000. For the first time in U.S. history, married couples are in the minority.

Is marriage in crisis?

The tone of the article is not alarmist. In fact, it is decidedly reassuring. After announcing these startling facts, the article is quick to note that the "number by no means suggests marriage is dead or necessarily that a tipping point has been reached. The total number of married couples is higher than ever, and most Americans eventually marry."

So, the article assures, despite its attention-grabbing headline and statistics, we need not fear after all. The article even suggests that couples are waiting longer to marry because they want to make sure that their marriages will work; they are taking the relationship for a "test drive." In the end, the numbers are merely telling us that people are spending fewer years of their lives in pursuit of an ideal that remains very much intact: an ideal of life-long passionate love.

As I look again, however, these assurances are belied by the message between the lines. For one, people are interested in taking a "test drive" for the troublesome reason that nearly half of all marriages end in divorce. Nearly half. Such cases of divorce are not the only marriages that fail to live up to the ideal that impels people to pledge themselves for life. Couples stay together for reasons other than passionate love, such as children, habit, convenience, and shared assets, as recent reports on the "sexless marriage" confirm.

The implications are sobering: most people living in the United States pursue an ideal of lifelong passionate love that far less than half are able to make real in their own relationships. No wonder couples are interested in taking a "test drive."

I read on. The article also reports that people are waiting to marry not only so that they can be sure of making the right decision but because, simply put, they *can*. As one commentator notes, the economic reasons for marrying no longer carry as much weight. There is less need for a family unit to run the farm. Women can vote, own property, open bank accounts, get an education, and enter the profession of their choice. These societal shifts are freeing women and men to marry because they *want* to, as individuals pursuing their happiness, and not because they *have* to in order to support themselves.

A second commentator points out another reason that people can wait to get married. They don't have to wait to have sex. With the advent of safe, legal forms of contraception and abortion, people can enjoy the pleasures of sex without fear of becoming pregnant.

In response, the social mores of mainstream culture have shifted, silently condoning, if not explicitly approving, that people are getting before marriage what was traditionally reserved until after. As the article relates, it is when couples decide to have children (or find themselves pregnant) that they tend to marry.

What appears between the lines of this article, then, is at odds with its calm demeanor. The ideal of marriage and the practice of marriage are changing dramatically. The ideal of marriage as the locus of lifelong passionate love is itself new. We now expect to marry because we are head over heels, hearing bells and whistles, hopelessly *in love*, and not because we want regular sex, economic viability, or to fulfill family obligations. We want intimacy and emotional fulfillment for ourselves and for the rest of our lives. We are enthralled with this ideal, yet cautious too, for we have no idea how to make it work.

Cᴙ

As I mull over the points in the article, I realize that it has led me smack into the middle of cultural debates over our desire for sex, who should have it, when, where, and why. Its reassuring tone represents only one perspective on the matter. Nearly every point in its argument finds an echo in an opposing voice that denounces its implied attitudes towards sex.

For many in the United States, this slide of married couples into the minority is indeed cause for alarm: high rates of divorce are ripping apart the fabric of our communities. According to social conservatives and traditionalists in particular, blame for this crisis lies squarely on the shoulders of our desire for sex. When people pursue sex outside of the marriage bond, these commentators aver, marriage loses its significance (as the locus of sex) and sex loses its value (as an act of procreation). From their perspective, the idea of living together as a test drive for a relationship is an anathema. We are sure to crash. The only way to make a marriage work, as an ideal of lifelong passionate love, is to abstain from sex before marrying.

There it is. For many in the US, our inability to control our desire for sex is spawning crises — social, economic, and political. Much more than the institution of marriage is at stake.

One need only look to the policies of the recent Bush administration to see how this attitude pervades our cultural moment. Tax dollars support only those sexual education programs that teach abstinence as the sole form of birth control. They fund international aid organizations provided that they do not distribute condoms. Our leaders endorse legislative initiatives around the country seeking to ban gay marriage and abortion. Such policies prevail, even when there is little proof that abstinence does more than delay sexual experience by a few months; even when there is copious research documenting that condom use prevents the spread of AIDS and other devastating diseases; even when there is no evidence that granting gay and lesbians the right to marry will erode the health or sanctity of marriages between women and men, and no indication that outlawing abortion will cause couples to refrain from sex before marriage.

What trumps the research is the deeply seated conviction that our desire for sex is to blame: controlling it is a number one priority.

ೞ

As the contours of debates over marriage and sex appear before me, the landscape looks eerily familiar. I recognize in these debates a *suspicion of desire* similar to the distrust of our desire for food that characterizes all points in the debates over obesity.

The hunch jogs me to look again. While it might appear that only one end of these debates blames our desire for sex, that suspicion is alive on the other side of the debate as well. For as much as the idea of taking a test drive before marriage might seem to oppose the idea of waiting to have sex until after marriage, both parties take for granted that our desire for sex is a problem that "we," as minds, must control if we are to get what we supposedly want, namely, lifelong passionate love.

How so? In the case of those who encourage a test drive, sex should not be what impels us to marry. Our desire for sex may cause us to make a choice that will land us in a marriage doomed to fail. It is better to have sex, relieve the tension, enjoy the pleasure, and then gather important information about the relationship so that we can make a rational, deliberate choice about whether or not our love is sufficiently strong to last a life long, or at least about whether or not to have children.

On the other hand, for those who encourage abstinence, the assumption is similar: the desire for sex clouds our judgment. However, from this perspective, it mars our vision if we have it before marrying, not when we don't. Better to corral the power and pleasure of sex in marriage as a way to bind partners together.

On the one hand, then, we marry for love *not* sex, and our marriages work when "we" make a good, rational choice and stick to our diet of fidelity. On the other hand, we marry for love *and* sex, and our marriages work because we rely on a higher power or authority, whether legal vow or religious tradition, to help us keep our desire for sex in line with our ideal of love. Both sides presume that our desire for sex pulls against the love we want, just as both sides of the obesity debates presume that our desire for food pulls against the health we prefer.

ଔ

Breathing down and out, I continue to chart the landscape. Further resemblances to the debates over the obesity epidemic leap out at me. Not only do the responses fan out in a familiar range, from more will power and better decisions at one end, to collective authority and expertise, on the other, but they do so in such a way that the discussion between the poles reinforces a common assumption: our best resource in dealing with our seemingly insatiable desire for sex and the social crises it is spawning is *to exercise the sense of ourselves as minds over bodies.*

Across the board, "we" are responsible for bringing our desire for sex in line with our commitment to lifelong love. We are responsible for managing what all parties presume is an inevitable conflict between sex and love.

That conflict may be a source for humor or a reason to weep, the focus of a talk show, social scientific research, or soap opera saga. It is always something to negotiate.

ଔ

Regardless of whether we are married or single, gay or straight, seeking sexual pleasure or trying to avoid it, these debates over the nature and value of sex cannot help but infiltrate our experiences of it.

As citizens of contemporary culture, we are as obsessed with when, why, and how our bodies should have sex as we are about what, when, why, and how our bodies should eat.

Nor is it surprising that we respond to our own concern by looking to buy whatever promises to bridge our desires for sex and love and give us the satisfaction we seek. Bombarded 24/7 by sexualized images and images of sex, we purchase visions of the sexually satisfied creatures we want to be. We hand over money for books, songs, television shows, DVDs; fragrances and real estate; luxury items and personal grooming products, believing that our desire will be met, unfolded, touched, and relieved when we own this car or wear these clothes, when we eat this food or lose these pounds.

When our pleasure with any given object wanes, the array of available choices lures us back to the market for another toy, another promise, another will power reinforcement. If we tire of objects and want sex straight up, service industries offer it to us on line or in house without the trappings of relationship.

When it comes to sex, as with food, we can't stop talking about it, regulating it, studying it, pursuing it, or purchasing it. And sometimes the two are nearly interchangeable. The sex is delicious; the food orgasmic, and we want more.

Yet this apparent abundance of available sex, as with the surfeit of food, hides a shadow side: what we are buying is not satisfying. The images of sexual pleasure prove so seductive because fulfillment in our actual relationships is proving elusive. Faced with our yawning dissatisfaction, we keep returning to the marketplace for more. As we grow dependent upon images of sex for partial and vicarious pleasure, our success in lifelong love becomes even less likely.

We don't even know where to begin.

We are not getting the experience of nourishment we desire from food; we are not getting the pleasure of physical intimacy we desire from sex. Our waistlines expand; our passion withers; our ideals of health and lifelong love go unrealized. We can't stop eating, and we can't stop trying to lose weight. We can't stop getting married (or wishing we could) and we can't stop getting out of it once we do.

So what about it?

The comparison with food is again suggestive. Something is missing from our cultural experiences of sex, love, and the marriage that is supposed to hold them together.

There is an elephant in the room.

What is missing is a sense that our desire for sex has anything to teach us about how to create a lifelong love. As we traffic in images of sex, love, and marriage that reinforce a sense of ourselves as minds in bodies, we numb ourselves to the sensory cues that would enable us to discern wisdom in our desire for sex. We convince ourselves that such wisdom does not even exist.

How did we get here?

ᘇ

I lean into the cushioned chair. It slides beneath me, rocking back and forth. I settle on a point of comfort. My head tilts, lifting my eyes to a large white rectangle. There are people around me, but we aren't looking at each other. Or if we are, we do so secretly, without being seen. We are all facing the same direction, laps loaded with cartons of popcorn, waiting. The lights dim.

My breath releases. I have been anticipating this moment. I paid for it. My body is primed to sense and respond to what I know I will see based on the advertisements, previews, and reviews. I am ready to feel the thrill and ache with the pain; to laugh and shiver, yearn and cry. Still, there are sure to be some surprises. I hope.

Luminous images flip before my eyes drawing me into an alternate space and time. Actors turn to me, faces up close, and with passionate sincerity reveal themselves to me. I feel as if I know them. I identify with them. I am them. As they move, I move. What they sense, desire, and fear, I sense, desire, and fear. Their struggles are mine, their triumphs too.

What do I see? A story in three parts.

Part 1. Desire sparks. A couple meets. Girl likes boy; boy likes girl. They fall in love at once, even if they don't admit it to themselves or each other.

Part 2. Obstacles intervene. One partner is engaged or married; uptight or indifferent; a member of a rival clan, class, ethnic group, or religion. The two are separated by war, geographical distance, age, or the ethics governing an unequal power relationship between prostitute and client, student and teacher, patient and therapist, or player and coach. Lovers struggle against the obstacles and their desire for each other grows.

Part 3. One of two outcomes occurs. A. Comedy: Lovers overcome obstacles. They get married and/or have sex. Love prevails. B. Tragedy: Lovers fail to overcome obstacles. One or both of them dies. Love prevails.

There are variants of course. Girl meets girl; boy meets boy. One partner tells the story, or the other. Obstacles pose different kinds of challenges. The story may dominate a film, or play as a subtext.

Nevertheless, if I am moved by the movie at all, I emerge having absorbed a message that film after song after story repeats: sex is a, if not the, peak experience of human life, and it is so when it is the consummate expression of love between partners. Sex plus love equals ecstatic bliss. Such sex is so good that it is worth fighting for against all odds. We want it, always more of it. It is why we marry, to do it for love. It is why we stray, to do it for love.

The lights come on again. I bump down into my chair, an empty box of popcorn in my hands. I walk out of the theater slowly, a glaze in my eye, a rush in my heart, feelings spent. I blink like a bird, madly adjusting to the light.

I think to myself. Again and again we bend ourselves to this arc of passion as it sparks, flames, consumes, and is consummated. Why?

As we watch those movies, read those romance novels, and listen to those popular songs, what are we learning about how to sense and respond to our desire for sex? What are we learning about the possibility of lifelong passionate partnerships? Will it work? Will we get the satisfaction we seek?

10

Movie Morality

'The most poisonous things against the senses have been said
not by the impotent, nor by ascetics, but by the impossible
ascetics, by those who really were in dire need of being ascetics.'
– *Twilight of Idols*, 488

I rent the film *Cold Mountain* on video. The movie disappointed
critics, but I want to see it. I am eager for more of director
Anthony Minghella's work. *The English Patient* was a love story I
could not forget, and I am endlessly fascinated by the popularity
of the film's stars, Jude Law and Nicole Kidman.

I am not disappointed. What do I see? Based on the Pulitzer
Prize winning novel, the story of two lovers takes place amidst
the Civil War in the South in and around the town of Cold
Mountain. Inman and Ada meet only a handful of times before
Inman enlists in the Confederate Army. Their last encounter
culminates in a knee-buckling kiss. During the first battle
depicted, sparing no gruesome detail, Inman's one photograph of
Ada floats through clouds of smoke, its edges singed. You fear he
will lose it, his one image of her, but he doesn't.

After sustaining injuries, in his hospital bed, he receives a
letter from Ada, begging him to stop fighting and come home to
her. Flouting the governor's new law that defectors will be shot,
he sets out for Cold Mountain.

Meanwhile Ada, left alone by the death of her father, struggles
to manage the farm. Hungry, lonely, and cold, she begins to learn,
growing more and more radiant as she masters the tasks of
gardening and livestock care. For most of the film, the two lovers

are apart, straining toward each other, Inman in every step he takes, Ada in every word of the hundreds of letters she writes. *My love, where are you. With no hope of reaching you, I write to you... as I have always done.* Each partner witnesses horrific acts of human depravity. More blood, more suffering, more violent sex—the obstacles their love must overcome.

When Inman finally makes it back to Cold Mountain, Ada has him at gunpoint. She does not recognize him at first. They are in the winter woods. White snow carpets the forest, etched with the shape and shadows of dark trees. Inman eats, sleeps, and shaves. They talk, acknowledging the time that has past, the pain of separation, and the mystery of their enduring devotion. As evening falls they retreat into a cabin suffused with golden light. He offers to wait. She says no. They take turns chanting, "I marry you," three times. In tenderness, mutuality, and respect, they consummate their love.

After two hours of tortured suspense I sigh with relief. Who cares that he is fleeing from the law; that they barely know each other; that they haven't seen each other for years; that they are not married, or that Ruby is sleeping next door? By now I want it!

The next morning, Ada and Inman are caught by local, power-thirsty authorities whose gratuitous cruelty the film has already demonstrated. Inman is shot and dies.

Nevertheless, the love of Inman and Ada lives on in the shape of the girl child Ada carries and births. Ada names her Grace. In final sun-drenched scenes of spring on the farm, years later, we hear Ada's voice talking to Inman in her mind: *If you saw us this Easter... you would know that every step of the journey was worth it.*

Winter to spring. Love resurrected.

I rewind the last twenty minutes of the film and watch it again. It is achingly gorgeous — the filming, editing, and setting. I am moved, in spite of myself. Hooked.

Thinking back to the reviews, it occurs to me. The critics, in bemoaning the lack of "sexual chemistry" between Law and

Kidman, are criticizing the movie for failing to deliver what the movie makes its viewers want: that spark that cannot be faked. The real thing.

I wonder: is this a coincidence?

ଚ୍ଚ

The arc of *Cold Mountain* trades on our desire for passionate love, it is true, and it does so by training our desire to those of Inman and Ada. We want what they want: more of that kiss. We want a real and passionate love that conquers all, even the horrors of war. Yet the movie makes us wait for a long time, drawing us into tighter spirals of uncertainty and hope. Every villain vanquished, every obstacle overcome boosts our fear that the next one may not be and our hope that it will.

When the moment of release finally arrives, we breathe freely. Their sex is *good* — moral and pleasurable — for it expresses their *love*, a love that has prevailed through temptation and hardship. In this way, *Cold Mountain*, like many Hollywood films, teaches us what might be called *movie morality*: sex can be good, sex can be bad, and the difference lies in whether or not the sex expresses love. Sex plus love equals (marital) bliss.

As I reflect on this message, a troubling contradiction pops into view. The movie sends this message (sex plus love equals bliss) by driving a wedge between our sensory experiences of sex and love, ostensibly to heighten their ultimate union. In fact, the film spends a great many more minutes training our experiences of sex and love apart than putting them back together again. Along the way to Inman and Ada's reunion, *Cold Mountain* is loaded with sex that is violent and deceitful. There are rapes, symbolic, attempted, and completed. That sex is bad. It is not what Inman and Ada want. It is not what we want. We want sex that is *good*.

In driving this wedge between sex and love, the movie is also teaching us how to think of the relationship between them. The love that makes sex good is an emotion that, while it may exceed rational calculation or control, is nonetheless capable of patience and restraint. It is a love that is willing to wait to have sex and willing to commit. It is a love that says "I marry you" whether or not an official is present.

The implication here is that the love that makes sex good is one that tempers what is otherwise an unruly physical drive. *Mind over body.* We will get the satisfaction we want when we allow our love to direct our bodily desire. If faithful love is there, the good sex will be too.

What is missing from this education in movie morality?

Bodies and their wisdom. There is no sense that Inman and Ada might need to get to know one another's bodies; that sex might be something they need to learn; or that in learning how to have sex with each other they might be learning something about how to love.

What strikes me most about this movie morality, however, is not that the pleasure it promises hinges on training our sensory experiences of love and sex apart. What strikes me is that the movie sets us up for an inevitable disappointment. The love and the sex, when they finally come together, don't stay together. They can't. The sensory connection between them is gone. In *Cold Mountain*, the consummation we have been pining for does not last. Once is enough. The love resurrected in its final moments is a love without sex. Virtual satisfaction will have to do.

ᘔ

As I think about how pervasive this movie morality is, I realize something else. It is not just a question of content. The experience of watching movies educates our senses in ways that reinforce this morality, further reducing our chances of attaining the satisfaction that the movies make us want.

As we sit back in the womb of darkness, waves of light and sound pour down upon us, drawing us into another world. We lose awareness of our own bodies. We no longer feel tired, hungry, or sick. The popcorn disappears. We may feel all kinds of intense emotions, but the sensations are stirred in us by our identification with characters on the screen. We are watching others have sex. We watching others fall in love. Pleasure is stirred in us in so far as we are willing to see ourselves in images of strangers.

As we watch a film then, we are doing more than enjoying its story. We are training ourselves to desire this experience of having our senses vicariously overwhelmed as the path to our own pleasure. We are learning to experience our desire for sex as a desire for *consuming images* of the intoxicating bliss that we come to believe our sex lives can and should have.

We want the pleasures of our sexuality to come to us, roll over and through us, be done for us, without vulnerability or risk, as we passively receive, curled up in the dark. It is better that way.

When it isn't, we buy another ticket. We try another movie. Another lover.

Beyond that, we follow with keen interest the love lives of the actors themselves. As marriages spring to life and break apart on the set, we are relieved to know that the actors really are getting it. The actors play along. In a magazine interview after the film's release Kidman (recently divorced from Tom Cruise who had fallen in love with another co-star) confirms that she yearns to find "her Inman." Speaking as "herself," the "real Nicole," Kidman gratifies and affirms our desire for what she seemed to have in the film by claiming to share in that desire. The ideal of love she projects in the film, we are comforted to learn, is real, even though we haven't gotten it. But because she has, we will keep looking to her in film after film to reveal it.

Kidman's story appears on the cover of one of those glossy magazines that greet us at the supermarket checkout, promising us the latest tips for great sex and for losing five pounds fast. Just as we are lured in by the promises of a lean physique offered by diet plans, so we will flock to movie after movie for images of the sexual satisfaction we think we want and then buy tabloids trailing their stars.

ॐ

I see it now. In criticizing *Cold Mountain* for failing to deliver the real sensory charge it makes us want, the critics themselves traffic in movie morality.

It is *because* this film and others like it *succeed* in making us want this chemical blast *and* fail to deliver that we keep going back for more. Even if a particular movie disappoints, the critics guide us to chalk it up to the shortcomings of that particular film rather than call into question the sensory education that movie watching provides—just as we blame the failures of our diet plan on its particular gimmick and set out in search of another.

In both cases, we swallow a hook along with the juicy worm. While *Cold Mountain* pays homage to our desire for sex as something that is good, that can be satisfied, and that should be satisfied in the context of love, it does so by selling us an experience of ourselves as minds over bodies, educating us to sense and respond to our own desire for sex as if *all* that is needed for our pleasure is (marital) love. Or a good movie.

In our sex-saturated culture, realizing a lifelong passionate love is about as likely as *eating 2 lose*.

ॐ

Movie morality is not confined to movies. It is endemic to modern culture. Even voices that seem to offer an alterative, by promoting abstinence or unfettered experimentation, condition us to think and feel and act as if sex were merely physical, and our desire for it at odds with our emotional, spiritual ideal of love. Everywhere we turn, we are encouraged to pursue the pleasure we seek from sex by treating our desire for it as something that "we," as hearts and minds, can and must choose to repress or indulge.

Regardless of which path we select, however, the effects are the same, and they are not what we want.

ભ

I first learn of the abstinence movements popular among conservative Christian teens, from a student of mine. She is interested in writing her thesis on one of them, True Love Waits. *Virginity pledges*? I ask.

She sketches the history I have come to appreciate as part of the larger movement among social conservatives to shore up the institution of marriage against what they perceive as the rising tides of sexual promiscuity.

The message is simple. Take your pledge, exercise your will power, (buy and) wear your ring, and, with the help of those around you, wait to have sex until you are married. God wants you to wait. If you do your sex will be *good*, holy and satisfying. Even more importantly, your marriage will hold.

I look closely at the pledge: "Believing that true love waits, I make a commitment to God, myself, my family, my friends, my future mate, and my future children to be sexually abstinent from this day until the day I enter a biblical marriage relationship." (www.lifeway.com/tlw)

Is this the path to lifelong passionate love?

What impresses me first is how familiar the logic of this pledge is. It begins by expressing a belief about what a love that is true is. Implication: there are (images of) loves that are false. We need a test to tell one from the other. That test is to wait. Love is true and not false when it can wait to have sex.

Yet, if a love that is true is one that can wait, the further implication is that sex has nothing to teach us about whether the love we share is worthy of a lifelong commitment. Or rather, what our desire for sex has to teach us is whether our love is strong enough to repress it. The love that guides a person to join his or her life together with the life of another is a love that does and can and should stand alone, independent of sexual activity, as proof of its truth.

I marvel at the likeness to *Cold Mountain* in this regard. Here we learn again that sex is a physical act whose meaning is given by the context in which it occurs. For those who take the pledge, whatever sex they have after receiving the blessing that weds them in God's eyes is *good*, both holy and satisfying. The very same acts performed outside of marriage are impure and their fruits illegitimate.

Taking the pledge then, like watching the movie, trains us to separate our desire for love from our desire for sex as the condition for bringing them together in a moment of blessed, blissful satisfaction.

The pledge goes further too. Though it does not malign sex, it does encourage pledge takers to suspect their *desire* for sex. Even though sex is good and given by God, our desire for it does not necessarily align with what God wants from us. As a result we need to guard ourselves against our desire and against anything (including movie viewing) that might stir it into sensation.

We take the pledge, then, as an act of will power over our desire in the name of our ultimate pleasure. Pleasing God and not ourselves is what will give us the satisfaction we seek.

ભ

Is it true? If we abstain from sex before marriage, will God make our sex good?

Say that two individuals in love do succeed in abstaining from sex before marriage. As they begin married life, it is likely that the newlyweds will exercise the patterns of sensation and response around their desires for love and sex that they have been practicing. They will discover in relation to one another not only that their capacity for love is separable from their capacity for sex, but that this separation is itself desirable as an enabling condition of their love (and sex).

For one piece of evidence that this may be so, take a quotation from a popular book offered in response to Christian wives who ask: "What do you do when your husband wants to have sex and you don't?"

The authors reply: "We don't know the number of sexual relationships sabotaged by a wife's poor attitude, but we know it is high. When it comes to sex, we must each answer the questions: will I selfishly demand to have my own way, or will I minister to my husband and trust that God will bless my obedience?"

This response is striking. In communities where women are often not allowed to be pastors, they are invited to "minister" by overriding their own desires.

The message is clear: a woman's power lies in her ability to deny her bodily sensations. The process of learning to trust and honor her desires, and of learning about the mysteries of her own sexuality is not of concern to God. Or rather, there are no mysteries to her sexuality. Her sexuality is simply a matter of mechanics that can and should be performed as an expression of "love." What interests God is her obedience, not her body. Marriage makes it so. If her husband is compassionate, he will thank her for allowing him to gratify his God-given need. Her desire *not* to have sex is deemed "selfish" while his desire *to* have sex is not.

But why? Isn't God as interested in a woman's sexual satisfaction as God is in a man's? Why is she blamed for "sabotaging" the relationship and not him? Why couldn't her resistance to having sex represent a *wisdom* that both partners need to respect? What if it represents a way in which she is registering what they need for their mutual fulfillment? Why isn't it his responsibility to learn what she needs in order to unfold?

This "advice" given to Christian wives promotes within the marriage context the same mind over body suspicion towards (a woman's) desire for sex as does the pledge. In the pledge, you can choose *not* to have sex, even if you want to, for His sake. In marriage, you can choose to *have* sex, even if you *don't* want to, for h/His sake.

When a woman masters her ability to separate her sexual desire (or lack of it) from her sense of love, then the couple will not break apart over disagreements about when to have sex. The marriage will be a success, and the cost of holding it together will be the sexual satisfaction of at least one partner and in most cases both.

The message of the pledge, like that of movie morality or cereal box logic, is double: we will have the satisfaction (from food or sex) we seek when we override our desire (for food or sex) in the name of an ideal (thinness or love); and this product (diet, film, or pledge) will provide us with what we need to make sure we can.

While there may be some couples who succeed in using this mind over body solution to keep their marriage solvent, it is unlikely that it will work for many. Rates of divorce among conservative Christians are as high as those for the rest of the population. Over time, as passion wanes, we lose faith that a lifelong love is even possible — except, maybe, in the movies.

❧

What about experts who endorse indulgence rather than abstinence? Are they any closer to helping us learn to derive the pleasure we think we want? Is there hope here for learning how to sustain a lifelong passionate love?

I am looking forward to *Kinsey* (2004). I had tuned into the controversy brewing over its marketing and distribution and read some previews. The film opened in a limited number of theaters, for mostly urban populations. Christian groups, Protestant and

Catholic, were calling for its boycott, decrying Kinsey as a pseudo-scientist with questionable methods intent on promoting perverse and immoral sexual acts.

I wonder what the fuss is about. Surely films with a high quotient of sexual content parade through the theaters regularly. What makes this one unique?

The morning after watching the film, I wake up depressed. Something is not quite right. *Kinsey* makes good sex seem so easy. I keep returning in my mind to a scene where a young married couple seeks out his advice. They are having trouble with sex. Kinsey responds, drawing on difficulty with his wife "Mac" that we witnessed in earlier moments of the film.

He attributes the young couple's difficulty to misinformation and a lack of experience. All that is required to fix the problem is technical advice. Touch here and there, voila! Physical intimacy. Love incarnate. Marital glue.

What is bothering me? I turn over the facts. Alfred Kinsey was a biologist, intent on studying the human animal. As a young scientist, his primary research was on the gall wasp. He was fascinated by gall wasps because each one is different. He collected a million of them to prove it. It was only after establishing his reputation as a scientist that he turned to the human animal, appalled by the level of ignorance — including his own — that surrounded human sexual practices.

As he bent his lens to sex, his approach was that of a gall wasp collector. Compile a picture of what people actually do. Gather as many first person accounts of people's sexual history as possible. Document sexual practices, as a scientist, without moralizing. His approach presumed that he could distinguish between sexual acts and the "entanglements" of romance, love, and marriage.

What Kinsey discovered sparked anger and fear among Christians in particular. He unearthed high levels of sexual activity perceived as "deviant" — same-sex sex, masturbation, extramarital sex, etc. Critics claim that his subject group was skewed towards prisoners and perverts. Critics depicted in the film fear that if we teach people what is possible, then sexual desire will run rampant, upending all manner of civil society, marriage in particular.

Kinsey countered with the reverse: if we teach people how to enjoy sex, then they will develop healthy sexual relations, experience higher degrees of sexual satisfaction, and be less inclined to seek out vicarious or covert routes to it. All that stands between us and our sexual satisfaction, Kinsey implied, is social restraint.

So which is it? Are we willful creatures needing control or repressed creatures needing release? Are we too Puritan? Or too promiscuous?

Even though I want to be cool and side with Kinsey, something inside me balks. *Can it be so easy to separate sex from love for the purposes of analysis? Or for the purposes of pleasure?*

As I think this, I see it again: the wedge between love and sex. *The sexual play depicted in the film is not really free.* The sex is not free to be *more* than physical. Its pleasure is constrained. Is physical gratification all that we want when we desire sex?

As I reflect back on the film, I realize that it raises similar questions, often unnoticed by its more vocal critics. For one, the film traces Kinsey's ability to imagine love and sex as distinct to his Christian father's fire and brimstone preaching. *Sex is a sin.* Kinsey accepts the distinction and then turns it to his advantage: because sex is distinct from love, it is accessible to the scientific method.

How liberated is he?

Further, as the movie reveals, the morals inherent in this distinction return to haunt Kinsey's project. Kinsey encourages experimentation with sex among workers on the project, and Kinsey (also known as "Prok") and then Mac each have sex with one of Kinsey's workers, Clyde. When Kinsey initially floats the idea, Mac's tears flow because she cannot imagine sex as separate from love. Yet she bravely cooperates and later in the movie, thanks Clyde for heating things up between her and her husband. Later, however, Clyde, now married to someone else, ends up in a fistfight with another of Kinsey's workers who has had sex with Clyde's wife.

Clyde confronts Kinsey. *Sex is everything*, he cries. "It can cut you wide open."

As Kinsey himself relates later in the movie, we remain ignorant of the mysteries of love, and are incapable of managing the challenges to love posed by the extramarital sex he assumes we want.

Kinsey and Mac do survive their respective extramarital affairs with Clyde, and their love thrives. Nevertheless, as the movie suggests, it does not thrive because they can separate love and sex, but because, in the end, they cannot. Their marriage thrives because they have practices of intimacy, honest and open communication, that allow them to realize this.

The strength of their intimacy is honored in a final scene. Prok and Mac are walking in an old sequoia woods. He loses sight of her. "Mac" he calls, a slight panic in his voice. Silence. She steps out from behind a tree and calls back. He relaxes visibly, slides into professorial mode, and begins to lecture her about the trees whose roots, sinking deep in the ground, bind them in one place. He turns to her and clasps her hand where it is resting on the trunk.

Speaking of the trees he notes: "I don't think they're unhappy." Neither is he in his ongoing monogamy with her. On the contrary, the moment fills him with bright energy. He turns to walk back towards their car. She waits by the tree.

"Come on Mac!" he calls.

"What's the hurry?" she replies.

"There is work to be done!"

Even so he waits for her. Reaches out his arm. They join hands and walk on together. He can't do the work without her. Being with her provides him with the energy and joy that fuel it.

CR

The movie leaves me pondering yet again. Those who argue for sexual freedom based on the idea that sex is only physical are as "puritan" in their conception of sex as those who argue that this physical force must be given its meaning by marriage. They all agree: sex has nothing to do with love.

So too, those who argue that we must reserve sex for marriage are as "promiscuous" as those who argue that we should not: in marriage anything goes.

Both sides espouse a mind over body logic that fails to deliver either the sexual pleasure or the lifelong passion they promise. *Diets don't work.*

It occurs to me that the cultural training we receive in separating our sensory experiences of love and sex, endorsed across the board as the path to our ultimate pleasure, is the most pernicious obstacle to lifelong passionate love of them all.

CR

Are we doomed, then, to partial and vicarious satisfaction of our desire for sex? To marriages that wither and fall apart? To a lack of the love we want?

No. Our feelings of frustration and disappointment, the failure of our relationships, are not telling us that our desire for sex is impossible, ill-fated, sinful, or wrong. They are telling us, rather, that the mind over body movements we are making in pursuit of satisfaction are falling short of realizing the pleasure we are capable of experiencing. They are telling us that we need to move in relation to our partners in ways that do not presume or perpetuate a conflict between love and sex. They are telling us that we need to cultivate a sensory awareness of our desire for sex, and learn to discern the wisdom in our dissatisfaction itself that is guiding us to move differently.

We want *more* from our relationships than the wedge we are driving between sex and love allows. But what? What is that more that we want? What is it that we desire when we desire "sex"?

11

Mate or Marry

'You shall not only reproduce yourself, but produce something
higher. May the garden of marriage help you in that!'
— *Zarathustra*, 181

"What's wrong with her, Mom? Something is wrong! Call the vet,
Mom! Please!" Jessica is panicking. Our cat Zelsha is crouched on
the floor, her hindquarters slightly raised, tail held aloft. She is
uttering an insistent cry, somewhere between a purr and a growl.
She looks decidedly uncomfortable. The fur on her back is
rippling. She seems ready to pounce, yet remains glued to the
floor, rigid. Her two-month-old kittens frolic around her,
unnoticed.

"Calm down, Jessica," I reply, talking to myself more than to
her. It is 5 o'clock on Friday afternoon. "We need to gather more
information. Let's watch her so that we have something to tell the
vet, some questions to ask." I am worried. Is she sick? She has
kittens to tend.

On the way to my computer to research the problem it occurs
to me: is she in heat? *Yes*.

I watch her over the next few days as her fertile time passes.
She rolls on her back, rubs up against walls and legs, paces
restlessly, hovers by the door, and returns to her crouch, fur
rippling. Her body is alive with intention. She is ready, waiting,
and responsive. If we let her out, I am sure she would travel miles
to find a male cat willing to oblige. She is that determined. We
don't want any more kittens. Eight is enough. When she isn't
crouched and moaning, she is passed out, asleep.

The next morning Jordan asks: "Do humans go into heat?"

I smile.

"Sort of. There is a time, about three to five days a month, when a human female is fertile, and can make a baby. But she doesn't show it the way Zelsha does."

Even so, I know what Zelsha feels like.

Jessica walks in. "What are you talking about?"

"How humans mate," I reply.

"Humans don't mate," she insists.

"What do they do?" I ask.

"They marry."

ʘ

It is hard to get beyond the idea that the human desire for sex is a desire to mate, pure and simple. Just as we learn to believe that our desire for food always wants more material intake, so we learn to believe that our desire for sex wants more physical release. Scientific justifications abound for why it must be so. Myth and anecdote offer confirmation. We come to sense and respond to our desires as if it were true. We make it so.

However, if we take another look at such justifications, as we did in relation to our desire for food, we can find clues to an alternative perspective: our best hope for lifelong love lies not in repressing or indulging a seemingly physical urge, but in cultivating a sensory awareness of the wisdom in it.

This perspective confounds most contemporary understanding. According to evolutionary biologists the splitting of our desires for sex and love, of mating and marrying, is not only inevitable, it is essential for our survival. There is no other option. We are animals, great apes, and our desire for sex is a tangle of instincts driving us to pass on our genes. Monogamy, in this view, is not natural. While humans may *choose* to channel their desire for sex into monogamous relationships, such attempts are inherently conflicted and doomed to fail.

Is there room in this biological account for other interpretations?

Yes there is. Until recently, the arguments just described were based on the different levels of investment required by males and females of the species in the process of reproduction. It seemed obvious. Males invest only a few minutes. Bang. Females invest a year or two at least. Thus researchers concluded: females, driven by the urge to reproduce, want to bond with males who will stick around, males who are interested in long-term commitment. Males, driven by the urge to reproduce, want sex with as many partners as possible in order to sow their seeds.

The sexes, seeking the same end, namely children, move in diametrically opposed directions. He wants sex. She wants love. Marriage is a compromise. The male agrees to marriage as a way to gain access to a womb, or as a way of asserting control over what he claims as his. The female agrees to be owned in exchange for support and protection in raising their young.

In the bargain, a male gives up the desire to have sex with multiple partners. A female gives up her desire period because she puts her children's welfare ahead of her own. She is not really interested in sex anyway.

Such theories have seeped so deeply into our cultural milieu that we take them for granted. We assume that the split between love and sex manifests as an irreconcilable conflict between female and male. Men want it; women don't. Marriage works when lovers become friends. The passion drops out so that a child-supporting bond can form. Thus the scientific case rests: for biological reasons, most persons will not realize a lifelong passionate love. They will find their satisfaction, however partial and vicarious, elsewhere. At the movies.

ᚙ

But what if these differences in investment do *not* necessitate the splitting of sex and love? What if they predict the opposite? What if the significance of this differential investment is that reproductive success requires partners to develop a mutually satisfying *physical intimacy*?

Recent theorists are mounting arguments along these lines by factoring other differences between females and males (besides calories and time) into the reproductive question. Estrus, for one. Human females, unlike other primate species, do not advertise when they are fertile. Women don't crouch and moan. Women's rear ends don't turn red. At the same time, there are only a few days a month when a male can achieve success in finding a nesting place for his genes. As a result, a man cannot tell when those few days will be unless he sticks around *and* unless she opens to share that information with him. If he rotates through multiple partners every month, he is actually less likely of finding fertile ground than if he stays with one partner, wins her trust, and attends to her cycle.

Second, there is an organ in women—the clitoris—whose sole function seems to be providing pleasure. Physiologically, the clitoris represents the same cluster of nerves that make up the tip of the penis, but there are more nerves and they are closer together. In addition, the clitoris, unlike the penis, can experience orgasm after orgasm. This difference suggests that it is the woman who is wired to desire multiple partners. She wants to encourage competition and ensure that the male who sows in her has the strongest seed. She may engage multiple partners—male or female – to ensure protection for her young from at least one of them.

Third, a female human does not need to have an orgasm to ovulate or conceive, in contrast to the male human who must ejaculate. While this difference has been interpreted to mean that female orgasm is not necessary for reproduction, the reverse is as arguable. The man who helps a woman experience the most pleasure will be the one with whom she shares the secrets of her fertility. He will be the one whose seed she opens to receive.

Learning to help her experience this pleasure is not simple. There is no on/off lever that rises and falls. There are at least three distinct triggers for orgasm—the G-spot and the back of the vaginal wall, in addition to the clitoris. Learning how to coordinate the array of sensations takes time, creativity, and freedom from internal and external constraints. It requires experimenting, exploring, and discovering what is possible. Again, this physiological difference suggests that a woman will seek experiences with a person who is willing to attend to *her*. Her sexual pleasure is the proof she wants of his (or her) commitment to her.

Lastly, humans, among the great apes are the only mammals who can and often do mate face to face and who can do so with either partner on top. In the majority of mammals, the male mounts the female from behind. In humans, the female can be on top and often derives the most internal sensation in that position. Even when the male is on top, however, the position need not be read as a "missionary" pose. In this position *she* is the Woman on whose surfaces he wanders, to whom he owes his pleasure, his nourishment, his life.

Adding these previously discounted pieces to the picture of differential investment in reproduction alters the scene. Here, women and men must *make love*, and do so frequently, multiple times, face to face. Women and men maximize their chances of reproductive success by getting to know one other, attending to one another, and in particular, from the man learning how to unfold and maximize the woman's capacity for pleasure.

Our desire to mate, in this view, is a desire to create a relationship within which we can, over time, learn to give and receive a *life enabling* pleasure. Our desire for sex is in fact impelling us and guiding us to learn how to love from the act of having sex itself. Intimacy not periodic release is what will guarantee us both sexual pleasure and lifelong love. Seen in this light, it is evident that the bonding effects of sex extend beyond male-female couples to include other life enabling pair possibilities too.

CR

Could it be true? How do we know?

What we know is that we *can* learn to perceive our desire for love as distinct from and opposed to our desire for sex; we *can* learn to perceive this difference as a conflict between female and male, and we *can* amass a list of reasons why this must be so.

However, once we realize that we are *learning* to sense and respond to our desire for sex in these ways, we can also ask whether it is possible to learn to sense and respond to our desiring selves in other ways. It is our responsibility to ask ourselves: what possibilities for human relating are we creating or denying when we sense and respond to our desires as if we were minds living in and over bodies?

What if our greatest sexual pleasure as humans lies not in the physical punch of orgasm, but in the process of learning to discern and move with a wisdom in our desire for that blast?

What if the key to our survival as humans lies in developing our capacity to *make love*, where that love is not just a feeling, a commitment, or an ideal, but patterns of full-bodied sensory responsiveness expressed in feelings, intentions, and actions?

What would it mean to think of marriage as a context within which two persons do this work with each other, unlearning the felt oppositions between mind and body, male and female, love and sex, and learning to trust the wisdom in their desires for one another?

CR

No one less than Sigmund Freud lends support to this interpretation. I love his work. Not only are his own accounts of human sexuality provocative, his notions of conscious and unconscious, of ego, superego and id, have so thoroughly permeated our cultural experience of sex that it is impossible not to consider his perspective on the splitting of our desires for sex and love. He too, not surprisingly, gives a scientific account of why this splitting marks a necessary stage in a human being's psychological development. Nevertheless, there is play in his claims, and room for drawing conclusions that he himself does not articulate.

According to Freud, the crucial player in the development of our desires for sex and love is the mother. As was the case in the Victorian societies of Vienna where he lived, married, and raised six children, a woman occupied the private sphere of the home, playing the role of primary care giver, while her husband, the father of her children, ventured out in the public sphere to earn a living. The mother was the one who fed the infant, wiped his bottom, rocked him to sleep. She was his first love — the object of his desire for food and touch, nourishment and intimacy. He smiled and she smiled back. He believed she existed solely for him.

In Freud's narrative, however, the infant boy's joy is short-lived. He quickly learns that his mother is an independent person with needs of her own who loves someone else — most notably his father. This awareness dawns between the ages of three and six, about the time he grows physically conscious of sensation in his genital organs. During these years, he comes to experience his desire for his mother's touch as bad because it puts him in competition with his father whom he also loves.

Torn between his love for his mother and his love for his father, between his desire for her touch and his desire for his protection, a child must learn to say "no" to himself. The boy splits his desire for touch into pieces, physical and emotional;

he becomes someone who desires his mother's love but not the pleasure of her touch. He trains himself to sense and respond to the fullness pooling in his genitals as a problem to master, and he engages in such mastery as an expression of *love for* his parents. Said otherwise, he drives a wedge between his love for his mother and his desire for her touch in order to manage the conflict he experiences in himself between competing loves.

If he cannot manage such an internal splitting, Freud predicts, a boy will be forever susceptible to all kinds of neuroses and compulsions. He will idolize objects that stand for his mother, engage in repetitive acts that recreate a womb-like experience, and grow addicted to partial satisfactions—food, film, and flings.

It is harder to piece together the girl's story, but a similar logic is there. The structure of the Victorian family forces a splitting of sex and love in her as well. She must relinquish her primary love object, the mother, but not for the same reasons as the boy. She must transfer her desire for sex to men, but not her desire for love. In fact, the love she has for her mother is crucial for her to maintain as she develops her identity as a woman. In this way, the girl splits her desire for touch along the same gender lines as the male — sex from love — though for different reasons. She wants to be like her mother and have a baby.

When Freud gets to marriage, the implications of his theory fall in line with the theories of evolutionary biology described above. In so far as boy and girl pass "successfully" through this psycho-physical stage, by learning to split their desires for love and sex, then conflict between spouses is inevitable. For Freud, this conflict between male and female is inevitable because of the conflict within each one of them between their desire for sex and the requirements of love. Their respective acts of self-splitting arrest the flow of desire through their own bodies. The two pieces of each partner's shattered desires come together awkwardly, if at all.

At best each hopes that a blast of spontaneous feeling will wash over the sexual act, transforming it into an expression of love. *Maybe marriage will make the sex good.*

∝

Yet there is more play in Freud's account than he would care to admit. His insistence that the splitting of desire is necessary for our psycho-physical health rests on two assumptions — one open to interpretation, and the other to critique.

For one, Freud assumes that desire is fluid and *teachable*. When we are born, he observes, our desire is "polymorphous perverse." It can take nearly any shape. Desire is the life of a body, the energy that a body is. It is not attached to specific objects or actions, whether food or sex, ideals or body images. Infants don't have an experience of *things* as such — not even of bodies. Their desire flows via patterns of sensation and response activated by their time in the womb, where they are wrapped in a *life enabling touch*.

The implication of this view is that the split in our desire between sex and love is *not* innate; it is not present at birth. It is a split that we, as bodies, create in ourselves as a strategic response to the challenges of family life. It is a response that we create by mobilizing the sense of ourselves as minds over bodies that we are, at that time, learning to master. Since we must train ourselves to this split — or *be* trained to it — it follows that there is always hope of being trained from it.

It is Freud's second assumption that lends necessity to his account of the split between sex and love. Freud takes the gender arrangements of the Victorian family (working father, stay-at-home mother), and the public/private split of social and political life for granted as the context within which humans mature. The boy raised by his mother in his father's absence develops the pattern of self-splitting that will enable him to venture out into the public realm, identify with his mind and spirit, and leave heart and body to his wife at home. The girl, in this same situation, develops the pattern of self-splitting that will enable her to stay home, providing her children and husband with emotional and moral support. In the context of the Victorian family, children learn to experience as true the logic on which societal cohesion depends. The split between private and public, female and male, love and sex seems normal and desirable.

However, once we admit that Victorian society is neither natural nor universal, and once we are willing to take issue with the sense of ourselves as minds over bodies, then our understanding of Freud's point shifts. What he is documenting is not the *necessity* of the split, but how such a split, once established, *reproduces* itself across generations. He is documenting how the splitting of our desire for life enabling touch into a desire for sex and a desire for love serves to reproduce not *humans* per se but the *gender roles* upon which the *structure* of Victorian society rests — the male set loose in the public sphere and the female kept at home.

Of course, children do not have sex with their parents, so some splitting of our desires for sex and love is inevitable as a child matures. But once the child is ready to choose his or her own partner, the splitting is no longer necessary. In fact, perhaps partnerships are the sites where humans can and should and even must learn how to have what their relationship with their parents made them want: a relationship in which we give and receive the touch that releases us into a seamless web of sensual, emotional, and even spiritual pleasures.

Once released from its Victorian paradigms, Freud's argument offers hope and direction.

If desire is teachable, then there are possibilities for teaching ourselves differently, and it is our responsibility to explore what those possibilities might be. If the current splitting of our desires serves to reinforce gender roles that inhibit the development of lifelong passionate love, then it is worth considering the alternatives. And if the strategy of splitting our desires for sex and love expresses and reinforces the mind over body education we receive, then that fact suggests that our best hope for finding lifelong passionate love lies in cultivating a sensory awareness of the movements making us, and from this shifted sense of ourselves, learning to discern the wisdom in our desire for sex.

The implications are revolutionary, and in ways other than usually attributed to biology or Freud.

The pleasure we seek from sex is the pleasure of learning *how* to have sex in a way that enables us to experience and express the love we also want. Our desire for sex is a desire for the *relationship* in which such learning and unfolding is possible.

Our desire for sex is a desire to *give and receive a life enabling touch*.

12

Life Enabling Touch

'Desire — this means to me to have lost myself.'
– *Zarathustra*, 274

Before we hear sounds, see light, or sense touch, we are moving. We are movement, the movement of creating and becoming ourselves.

Cells copy, split, and double themselves, twist, turn, and bend over themselves. Clumps of flesh form and differentiate, sensing and resisting, pressing and being impressed, realizing the potential of extending in space. Flesh on flesh. Sensations morph and evolve. The gentle pulse of amniotic fluids, the supple resistance of uterine walls, the pounding of duel hearts, the rhythms of blood flowing.

Surfaces open into depths. The silky skin of arms and legs, curled up, rubs gently. Soon enough mouth sucks fingers, lips purse, a diaphragm pumps.

Here, in the womb, there is no space between desire and object, no hunger or thirst, no discomfort or fatigue to fight. There is only the push and pulling pressure of touch, a life enabling touch that nurtures us in making the movements that are making us into whom we have the potential to be.

Our bodies, moving, create themselves, create us, fluid forms suffused with living rhythms.

Then comes the crushing squeeze. Passage through the birth canal reshapes skull into a cone and pumps fluid from lungs. Falling into air, rough hands grab us, coax, and pull us out. Falling into arms, onto a belly, onto a breast.

The touch breaks up. It is now uneven, strong in places and weak in others. Bright lights penetrate our eyes; loud sounds pierce our ears. *Swaddle him. Wrap him tight.*

CR

We are born with patterns of sensing and responding to touch that have been created in us by our own movement in the womb and out of the womb. These patterns guide us from birth, serving as instruments of discernment. They guide us in moving towards whatever will recreate in us the experience of life enabling touch.

An open sucking swallowing mouth welcomes the breast. A curve of the neck invites a hug. An outstretched hand gets squeezed. We feel pleasure. We remember the experience and seek to move in ways that will recreate this touch. And when we lose the fluid, luminous, squeezed sense of touching and being touched, we express that dissatisfaction. We learn to cry.

Scientists are amassing evidence. How we are touched as infants plays an even greater role than was previously imagined in how humans develop, physically and neurologically, as well as emotionally. Touching releases endorphins, chemicals that induce a state of pleasure in the one who touches as well as in the one who is touched. These chemicals promote growth in our bodily tissues, nurturing our own potential for health and strength. The chemical release takes hold in our flesh as desire, a yearning that impels us towards what will give us more of that pleasure.

Researchers are now going so far as to say that how we are touched as infants may predict our ability to enter into long-term relationships, make commitments, establish intimacy, and in a word, *love.*

As we mature, we keep learning more about how to touch. We learn to touch ourselves; we learn to touch others. We learn what kinds of touching and being touched release us into the movement of our own becoming. We can unlearn such patterns of sensation and response, and create new ones. Nevertheless, throughout our lives, one constant holds: the bodies we are ever becoming exist *in* relationship with those who touch and are touched by us. We exist *because* of relationships, by the *grace* of relationships.

ભ

What interests me most about these discoveries is the importance they give, without realizing it, to bodily *movement*.

To touch is to move. To be touched is to be moved. When we touch, we move toward, we reach out and connect. When we are touched, we respond, creating ourselves as persons who do. Either way, we animate patterns of movement, of sensing and responding, that we are creating and becoming at once. We are these movements of touching and being touched.

As we touch and are touched we not only move in ways that create ourselves, we also move in ways that create the relationship with whomever or whatever touches and is touched by us. In the moment of touch, energy moves through the point of contact in two directions, impacting both parties.

A touch, in this sense, is not a coming together of two entities that momentarily crash and then separate. A touch is a moment in which we *change*, in which we make movements of reach and return, clasp and squeeze, that create us into people whose very living is enabled by our relationship to others. We are ever-becoming, and irreducibly relational.

ભ

To acknowledge the importance of touch to our ability to love is radical in a way other than specified by common chemical coordinates. Touch is important to physical health and to commitment-readiness because touch *moves* us to create and become new patterns of sensation and response. It catalyzes our bodily becoming, inspiring and impelling us to recreate that touch. It stirs our desire. *We want more.* More of ourselves. More of our own creative engagement with what is.

How we are touched may predict our ability to bond in love because it predicts our willingness to develop a sensory awareness of our bodily becoming. How we touch and are touched primes us to create new patterns of sensation and response, to move and be moved by people we have not yet met.

The logic is compelling. Whenever we are touched as infants with hostility, greed, or indifference, we respond by learning to ignore our sensations and the discomfort they breed. We may grow patterns of moving in the world that separate us from our sensory presence, and distance us from others whom we fear may hurt us again.

Those who respond to their pain in this way may be more likely to warm quickly to the ideas that we are minds over bodies, that sex and love are at odds with one another, that male and female are locked in an eternal contest, and that marriage is a nearly impossible proposition. Such ideas reinforce our protections against further touch.

On the other hand, if we are touched with care and tenderness, empathy and tact, we may be more likely, as we grow, to remain open to what we feel. We may be more inclined to cultivate our sensory awareness as a guide to our health and well being. We may be more willing and able to breathe into our emotions with a respect that allows us to discern wisdom in the fiery heart of our desires for food, sex, and spirit, and move with it.

CR

By the time we are old enough to welcome a partner, we are already formed by layers of movements we have made in touching and being touched. We have learned to welcome what we expect will please and avoid what we fear will not.

Erupting amidst these layers, our desire for a partner is a desire for a touch we believe will please — a touch that we recognize, at some level, as being like the touch that has enabled our own bodily becoming, and to a degree that we have not experienced before.

This touch awakens in us the desire to make new shapes of sensing and responding *with this person*. In this sense, our desire for sex appears within us as a desire to unfold the potential of the first touch, the potential to grow and become beyond where we have been. What we want from and with our partners is the *pleasure* of giving and receiving a touch that stirs our own creative, desiring self into action. *A life enabling touch.*

ɔઢ

A life enabling touch brings our senses to life. It awakens us to a sense of our bodily selves in time and space, with a wonder at who we are and how we are becoming. It is a touch that supports us in the work of cultivating a sensory awareness and of learning to discern, trust, and move with the wisdom in our desires.

This touch is not, strictly speaking, physical. It is as likely to take the form of words as it is a caress. It may transpire in light, rhythms, or sounds; as an image, a phrase, or a dramatic pause; as an expression, a gaze, or a movement with. The touch may be emotional, verbal, or gestural.

What marks it as "life enabling" is not how it is delivered, nor its point of application within the registers of sensory awareness. What characterizes it as enabling *life* are its effects.

A touch is life enabling when it breathes. When it releases us into the movements of our own breathing. It invites us to breathe with relief, with delight, with affirmation of ourselves and the other person. It calls into view the thoughts and feelings, hopes and fears, that are holding us in place. We feel what we were not feeling a moment before and are able to affirm, in this space of caring, careful touch, that these feelings are who we are.

In this way, a life enabling touch restores our freedom, our capacity to move one way and not another. It puts us in touch with our creativity, our ability to make patterns of sensing and responding that please us. It bursts us open; we want to *play* in the moment.

So too it does so in ways that invite us, compel us, to unfold who we are as individuals.

What appear in our sensory awareness when we give and receive a life enabling touch are the trajectories of becoming in us — the sensations of yearning and hope, depression and despair, anxiety and stress that define our being in the world. We gain an acute sense of the movements we are making to produce those emotional shapes, and may even receive impulses of wisdom guiding us to move in ways that align more fully with our own becoming. The responses that arise in us, inevitably guide us towards more of this connection — more of the touch — that is enabling us to feel present to ourselves in this sensory way.

愇

When we imagine that all our desire for sex wants is a physical event, we are never satisfied. Our desire for sex wants more.

Our desire for sex is a desire for a relationship in which our sexual pleasure is a rhythmic, ever-evolving event. It is a desire as spiritual as it is physical, as relational as it is self-oriented, as aligned with the *quality* of our lives as it is with the conditions needed for our sheer survival. It is a desire whose satisfaction requires that we learn what we need to learn about ourselves and each other in order to unfold in each other our capacities for pleasure and love.

Our desire for sex is a desire for the *pleasure of learning to live in love*.

ଓ

It is the first night of the weekend workshop called "Love Dancing." Friends who are giving the workshop have asked Geoff and me to participate. The exercise we are about to begin is "Unfolding." We are going to take turns unfolding and being unfolded by the other.

The instructions are as follows. One partner curls into the fetal position. The other unfolds the folded one by touching him or her gently, guiding his or her movements, until the folded one is opened into a standing position. No words allowed.

The room is dim, the music soothing. We begin. It is my turn to be unfolded. I curl up tight. Instantly, I feel comfortable, safe. I love the position. All my soft surfaces are guarded.

Geoff begins. He slips his finger under my fingers and begins to pull. My fingers? Why is he beginning there, I wonder. We are in love. Married. I am weeks pregnant with our first child. Still, I don't want to unfold from there.

He lets go of the fingers. I pull them back in. He tries again, going for the fingers. I let them lift slightly, but I don't want to. I pull them in again. I don't want to unfold until I know I am safe. I want a hand down my back, a firm grasp. I want to be touched in a way that releases in me a will to unfold. I want him to find it. No amount of his prying my fingers apart will do it. I will remain, internally at least, knotted in a small ball. Like the bean in my belly.

ଓ

We think of ourselves as civilized creatures, standing tall, whose need to touch and be touched is something we outgrow. *Mind over body*. It is not.

We think that we can narrow the band of acceptable touch and define its limits in terms of what we must do in order to procreate. We cannot.

We think that we determine ourselves, from within, through the use of our own reason. We do not.

We *learn* to imagine and think these things about ourselves. We need not.

If we are able to welcome a partner, then we know: we are not too far gone to remember and relearn. A potential partner awakens our desire for touch, shocking us back open through layers of accumulated memories to the patterns of touch that have enabled our lives.

Just as we can learn to follow the arc of our eating pleasure to a sense of being and having enough, so too we can learn to ask for what will release us to give and receive a life enabling touch. A partner relationship may be the perfect place to practice.

13

Recreating Passion

*'Learning better to feel joy, we learn best not to hurt others
or to plan hurts for them.'*
– Zarathustra, 200

He is standing on the stage. I am sitting on the floor, stretching. The director is making introductions. "I want you all to meet Geoff."

I look up. I could swear there is a golden halo of light emanating from him.

I hear my voice ring out, loud and clear, "Hi Geoff."

He is joining the group of musicians who are to accompany our dance performance. It is dress rehearsal.

Over the next few days, I watch him. I watch him eat a blueberry muffin. I watch him work on the score for the show. I watch him pray (a Buddhist chant, I later learn). I watch him play. I watch him watch me.

I say to myself: "If this works out, I'll know that I knew."

ॐ

Desire. An onrush of sensation flares through us, flooding all registers of awareness. It may be warm and liquid, hot and bubbly, crisp and light, or dazzling. Our blood flows, our feelings flow, our thoughts flow, and all in one direction. *Who is she? Where is he from? What is happening here?*

We may think we are drawn in by the shape of a face, the curve of a back, the length of a leg; or by intellectual acumen, business success, or athletic style. We may imagine that our desire is merely for sex or for love. But when that surge blasts through us, such distinctions mean little.

The eruption of vitality disturbs our carefully tended sense of ourselves as minds in bodies, and dislodges the wedge we drive between love and sex. It draws us into and out of ourselves, beyond ourselves, to think and feel and act in ways that we have not before. We find ourselves impelled to take risks, bear secrets, and blurt out crazy ideas. We allow ourselves to be seen by another. We feel joy that unfolds us in generosity.

We feel welling within us a love for a life that loves us. *The world is good, beautiful even.* And we come as close as perhaps we ever do to awakening and recreating the experience of life enabling touch traced deeply in our womb-born bodies.

In the wake of this desire, we are changed. We want more. We are newly conscious, in a sensory way, not just of ourselves or the other, but of our potential for becoming a person who lives in this space of radical openness, who feels this delight.

We fall in love with the full-bodied experience of being in love. We want to live in this world that opens in us, for us, and around us, when we are with the one who stirs this desire in us. We want to make this world *real*. So we do it for love. We may even want to marry.

ભ

Passion is energizing, life enabling, and we want it. It is also terrifying. We are exposed by our passion, made vulnerable to the one who can give us what we want — or not. And it is not surprising that in moments of doubt or distraction we may respond to our own vulnerability by animating the sense of ourselves we are trained to believe is our best resource in getting the satisfaction we want: mind over body.

We pull back, close off just a bit, and slowly narrow the band of ourselves we are willing to reveal. The surge of our desire no longer passes through sensory spaces blast open in early encounters. We may begin to feel our desire as an interruption, an itch to scratch, or one more task to accomplish in the course of a day or week or month. While we may open briefly to one another in a particularly ardent session of love making, when it is over, we smooth over the cracks, turn away, and fall asleep.

We drive a familiar wedge between our commitment to love and the exposure of sex. We want the physical rush that will convince us that we are okay without the radical openness needed to sustain it. We may want sex more than ever (though not necessarily from our partners), or not at all. Sex may become something we do "for love," even if we don't want to; or for physical release, even if we don't feel particularly loving. We may have sex hopefully, looking towards physical contact to reopen the flow of love. Or we may have sex efficiently, denying the experience any more significance than that of animal need.

As we become good friends, comfortable operating in the realms of exchange where we are sure of ourselves, we convince ourselves that such a development is inevitable and even expedient. We are, after all, loving hearts trapped in sex-hungry bodies. Passion inevitably wanes.

◌

It is easy at first, short and sweet. A bright, clear pop, releasing tingling waves of happiness in me. In that release I am always born again, into the present, with a shock of insight. Everything I have been thinking or feeling, all the tension and anxiety, troubles or fear gather into the present, round into a small ball, and dissolve. The experience is reliable, nearly constant, and a complete mystery, all at once. *How is it that my body can do this?*

Then come the dark times. It stops working. I stop working. I can't make it happen. We can't unfold each other. He blames me for not letting him touch me. I blame him for not knowing how.

We fight against each other, in the name of our pleasure. But really, we are fighting against our primal fears. *I will disappoint her. He could never really love me.*

For a long while it is bewildering. Sometimes I feel tremendous love. Sometimes not. The feelings ebb and flow. I thought it was my job, as a partner in life, to endure the ebbs and enjoy the flows. I work hard to rid myself of any patterns of past hurt or fear that might obstruct the flow. It isn't enough. It is then that I learn.

Living as a partner can't be about a mind over body binding of desire in the name of an elusive ideal. I want more. I want to adore and be adored. I want to live in the feeling of cell-softening passion — ever more and always. I want to sense and respond to my partner from that place, making it real day in and day out as the context of our togetherness. But how, I wonder? How do I keep a life enabling passion alive in me? In my partner? How can I learn to give and receive a touch that will?

⚭

At first, the shapes of passion recreate themselves in us without our conscious participation. We hear a partner's approaching step, feel the squeeze of a hand, the curve of an embrace, and the sensation floods us once again, quickly, easily, with the flowing wonder of life enabling touch. In the middle of an argument, we can look each other straight in the eye, and together burst out laughing. *How important could this disagreement be?* The impress of passion is still so strong that the sting of conflict pales in comparison.

Moreover, every time we allow ourselves to feel this passion as the ground of our sensing and responding, we strengthen and reinforce it. *Our movement makes us.* We create ourselves into partners whose passion for one another lives inside us as a possibility for responding to our partner with empathy, kindness, and patience. It is not that we suddenly acquire tremendous will power over our feelings of frustration and pain. We don't.

It is rather that the act of stirring the passion to life frees us from competing patterns of sensation and response — those patterns of fear, anxiety, doubt, or hurt collected from past encounters. It releases our creativity in imagining responses that will align with what we most want. It frees us to explore the potential for a relationship that the blast of passion is. *Could this passion be the seed of a lifelong love*?

Yet, the spiral can work in reverse as well. When we respond to our partners by animating our mind over body sense of ourselves, as described above, we weaken our ability to recreate our passion anew.

Our movement makes us. We know that we are, theoretically, still in love, but we aren't *feeling* it. Pulled into ourselves, we fail to touch our partners. They fail to touch us.

We blame desire. *The problem is you — your desire, or your lack of desire. You should like this. If you loved me you would like this. I love you and I want to do this so it should work.*

The blame is often guiltily reflected in the one who resists. *If I loved you I should like this. Why don't I like this? Something must be wrong with me.*

Both partners curl into themselves. We shut down sensory spaces even further. *I don't feel like it anyway. I don't want to do it.*

We decide not to say anything next time. *I'll just pretend I like it, for your sake. I'll just be over and done with, for your sake.* Sex, when it happens, is less satisfying. Partners seek out times for being alone together less frequently.

We mentally resign ourselves to the situation and rationalize its necessity. *We are just not fully compatible here. But that's OK. We have a great house. We have great kids. We are good friends. What yearns for greener pastures is only my desire for sex, a desire whose dissatisfaction is inevitable for, as we all know, passion fades.*

As opportunities for touching one another dwindle, occasions when it does happen erupt with a kind of blind intensity required to override the feelings of unease. Dissatisfaction lingers, a simmering frustration that makes the next eruption more necessary and less likely to succeed.

It is at such moments, when such a spiral of increasingly closed mind over body patterns of sensation and response begins to take hold, that we need an intervention. In the moment when we realize that we are separating our sense of self from the flow of our desires — blaming, deflecting, repressing, or rationalizing — we need to stop, breathe, drop into our bodies, and consciously invite the patterns of sensation and response formed in the blast of passion to recreate themselves in us, as us.

When we do so, our experience of the moment shifts. We begin to feel how the frustrated urgency of our desire, as prickly as it may feel, is actually pulling us toward our partner, calling us to *unfold* a potential for touch that remains tightly closed. We realize that the movements we are making are producing the knotted shapes of our desire. We realize that we have been relying on a mind over body sense of ourselves to protect us from the fear of losing ourselves to desire — and we are losing desire.

Too often, our desire for sex is calling us — even screaming at us — to discern the wisdom in its dissatisfaction and move towards deeper intimacy, more vulnerability, and more pleasure, not less. It is what our bodies can know: that this relationship may have the potential to become one in which the kind of touching we knew before learning to perceive ourselves as minds over bodies is possible.

Our path is clear, though not easy. We need to move in ways that will recreate the life enabling passion we share with our partners. But how?

❧

Everything is just fine. We are happy enough in married life, enjoying each other's company, clear about our love, and loving our children.

Suddenly, things shift. I am knocked off balance and jolted sideways by a desire I have never felt before — for someone else. I was not expecting it. I am not prepared for it. I don't know what to think about it. I frankly can't *think* about it. Sheets of white lightening are blinding, searing, burning me. It feels more real than anything else.

I can't move. I am torn in two and shredded by the effort to hold myself together. I am clinging to a rock amidst a torrential ocean storm, waiting for the wind and waves to subside. When the storm passes, I think, then I will be able to see my way through.

I chant to myself: *may whatever happens be for the well being of all*. May whatever happens be an occasion to deepen the bond between me and my love.

The storm begins to settle. I breathe again. My desire is neither as focused nor as physical as I hoped. It is easy to think that I am experiencing the eruption of some animal urge attaching itself to a worthy specimen. I *want* to think so, for then I can imagine that simply having sex will take care of everything. *Just one long afternoon*.

But I begin to see this illusion for what it is. This wayward desire *is* what I am creating with my partner. It is an expression of the movements we are making in relation to one another. I am not getting what I need, and this desire is a desire for *me*, for more of me, for more of what I can experience and more of what I have to give. It is a desire for what I want with my partner — a radical openness that I have not yet learned to create.

My desire is expressing what my body knows is possible.

We talk and talk. I learn. This desire is impelling me to *ask* for what I need in order to give and receive a life enabling touch. This desire is impelling me to *trust* in its patterns of frustration and resistance to tell me what that is, and to *have faith* that the challenges of asking and trusting are what I need to unfold what I have to offer the world.

Will it work?

14

Asking, Trusting, and Having Faith

'One could perhaps describe pleasure in general as a rhythm
of little unpleasurable stimuli.'
— *Will to Power*, #697, 370

ଜ *Asking* ଜ
Ask for what you need, and you will have more to give.

Lifelong passion may be about learning to love, yet it is not about learning to love in general, as honorable an activity as that may be. It is about learning to love and be loved by a particular person and doing it well.

It is about learning to express love in ways that allow the other to feel that love as a force releasing him or her into freedom and creativity, pleasure and joy. It is about learning to give and receive a touch that is, in this sense, life enabling.

For this journey, there is no formula, map, or destination, only an ever-unfolding process of tuning in to what we and our partners need in order to be released into the flow of the love we share—the flow of our own becoming.

Most of us, however, are not mind readers, or body readers. We don't know how our partners want and need to be touched. We barely know how we want to be touched. And rather than find out for ourselves, our tendency, given our cultural mind over body training, is to rely on the images of love and sex plied to us. We imagine that touching and being touched is a matter of identifying the right spots and applying pressure as needed. It is a technical matter.

For our part, we *want* to think of touch as merely physical, for if it is then we can be sure that we will get the satisfaction we desire, even if we are not on the best of terms with our partners. Better yet, we know that we will be able to give it to the other whether or not we feel like it. *Satisfaction guaranteed.*

However, in attaching to such images, we are not only training ourselves not to ask for what we need, we are training ourselves not to be able to ask for what we need. We cannot imagine that there is work to be done in bringing our sensory awareness to life. We cannot imagine that our tenacious sensations of physical yearning might be pointing towards kinds of touching that are not physical — the gentle question, the inquiring glance, the encouraging comment. Even if we have a small inkling of the need for such work, we are likely to ignore it. For it is easier *not* to ask than to risk opening ourselves to the disappointment that we, or our partners, will not or cannot touch us as we need to be touched.

No asking, no friction, no fear. So we lose registers of discernment, and the sensory cues that would help us recognize in ourselves what would release us into pleasure. It remains a mystery.

When we don't know what we need and don't ask for what we need, even when we think we are doing so for the sake of holding the relationship together, we create pockets of silence in ourselves and in the relationship. Dead spaces. The relationship shrinks; the sensory space it occupies in us shrinks. We are less satisfied with the relationship as it grows less able to provide us with cell opening blasts of life enabling touch. And so is our partner.

When I ask for what I need, I have more to give.

It is a paradox.

When I ask for the touch I need, just ask, without expectation, as a way of being present to myself and with you, I give you the greatest gift. I give you what you need to succeed in doing what you want to do: love me. I give you the pleasure of releasing me into ever-greater love for you.

Intimacy deepens. Love grows, and I find in myself more capacities for responding to you when you ask of me.

This logic cuts across conventional wisdom and bears repeating. When we do not ask for what we need in order to rekindle our experience of cell-opening passion, we *prevent* our partner from getting what he or she desires. When we ask for the kind of touch that will enable us, and when we open to explore what that might be, we give the gift that is most desired: the gift of ourselves.

G&R

We are sitting at dinner, celebrating my birthday at a favorite local restaurant. It is a place we come only once in a while, for a treat. We need one. It is a troubling time. Something is not working. I feel tense, unmoved and unmovable. I have no idea what is wrong.

The conversation floats along, pleasant enough, from one child to another, from his practicing to my job. In our current five-year plan, it is his turn to spend time on his art and take care of the kids while I take responsibility for our income. I make some allusion to my writing projects, still emerging, yet unfinished, and the ever-elusive goal of getting something published.

"It is really important," he mentions casually.

I freeze. I stare. Time skips a beat.

"Really?" I ask. I want to hear him say it again. Again and again. Perhaps he has said it before, but I have never heard it before. Or I never was in a place to hear it before. To believe him before. Something moves in me in response. Something releases and opens and returns to him.

He says it again, and apologizes for not saying it more. *Your work is really important.* He is saying that he believes in my work. He is telling me that my own unfolding as a person in my life and art is important to him. He is saying that he sees me as something more than just an object of his desire for sex. I didn't even know I was so hungry to hear this. A hush falls over me, soft and warm.

We welcome our meal. We savor dessert. Everything feels new.

All the while I keep marveling. I had not even known what I was missing. And when I got what I needed, I knew and he knew that in my response to him, he got what he most wanted.

I see it as I have never before. My responsibility in this relationship is to be as open as possible in myself, for his sake. If I don't know how I want to be touched, I can't ask. I may think I am giving, by not asking, but I am not giving. I am holding back the greatest gift — the gift that is most wanted — the gift of myself.

☙

What kinds of touch reawaken in you the sensations of radical openness and vulnerability, thrill and flow, that moved you towards your partner in the first place?

Do you need a conversation or camaraderie; a firm hug or gentle squeeze, an empathetic remark or amusing comment? Do you need a romantic dinner or a hike in the mountains? Do you need to move or be still? Face each other, hold hands, or sit side by side? Engage each other or attend a shared event?

Do you need to dance?

What are the parts of your self that need to be seen, heard, honored?

What kinds of touch release you to move with your desire, acknowledging its wisdom, and exploring its potential for evolving into a mutual, lifelong, full-bodied love?

Do you know?

❧ *Trusting* ❧

Trust that the desire binding you to another is setting you free.

There is a second practice — and paradox — involved in learning to live in love, and it is entwined with the first. In order to ask for what we need, we must know what we need. In order to know what we need, we must cultivate a sensory awareness of the movements making us. Yet even that is not enough if we do not greet what we sense with the *trust* that this desire that is pulling us beyond ourselves, out of ourselves, and towards another, has something to teach us about giving and receiving a life enabling touch.

This trust then, is peculiar. It is not that we trust our partners. Nor do we trust ourselves. We do not even trust in the relationship we have created between us. Rather, we trust in *desire itself* — in the changing shapes of our pull towards each other. We trust that the movements of desire — the rhythms of frustration and displeasure, yearning and release — are guiding us to ask for the more we want. When we do, we not only are more able to sense what is moving in us, but we work ourselves free from the mind over body patterns of sensing and responding that close us off from our partners.

It is a paradox.

As we trust the desire that binds us to our partners, we find our freedom — the freedom that comes with living in sensory spaces of love.

Think of it this way. When our partner asks us to move in a particular way, it is easy to feel defensive (I already did that), or inadequate (I didn't think of it). It is easy to get wrapped up in the fear that we are letting our partners down. It is easy as well to judge our own impulses to ask as not worthy of sharing, or as too great a request. We tuck the "disturbance" away, smiling as we do so, proud of our self-control and believing that such compromises are necessary for the smooth functioning of the relationship.

However, when we respond to our desires or the desires of our partner in these ways, we are placing our *trust* in a sense of ourselves as minds over bodies. We are turning away from our desire and seeking refuge in the controlling power of our "I." When we turn away from the call to presence in this way, we imply that the relationship is not and cannot be strong enough or big enough or elastic enough to contain us both. We imply that only our mentally reinforced commitment to the *idea* of love is trustworthy.

Even if we convince ourselves that we are acting on behalf of the relationship, we are demonstrating a lack of trust in it. Such a lack of trust, when it takes hold, feeds the spiral of waning passion and shrinking sensation described above. The less we turn to a partnership to provide us with what we need, the less the partnership is able to provide us with what we need. We feel it.

On the other hand, when we breathe down and through our moments of tangled yearning and tired frustration, these sensations appear to us as gifts, opportunities to ask for the precise compassion that will release us into the flow of our love.

We can ask without fear or resentment, because we trust in desire. We can hear our partner's asking of us as evidence that he or she *trusts* in his or her desire for us. We can hear such requests not as signs of our inadequacy, but as signs of our partner's desire to move closer to us.

How can we find a way to connect right now?

To trust in our desire for the other in this way, regardless of the shape it takes, is to operate within a horizon of hope. It is to trust that we will be able to touch our partner, eventually, in ways that free him or her to love us. It is to trust that our partner will be able to touch us, eventually, in ways that free us to love him or her.

It is thus to align ourselves with the transgressive, healing power of our desire as a force that, in flowing through us, is creating us into persons who can touch and be touched in ways that make a mutually enabling physical intimacy real. A lifelong passionate love.

CR

We invent a game. We think it might help. I will take full responsibility for my own pleasure. I will tell him how I want him to touch me — where and how and when, and he will do so. And he, for his part, will absolve himself of all fear of disappointing me. Not getting it right. We will both be free — me to ask, him to respond — placing our trust in our desire to move towards each other. In the context of this trust, I will be able to figure out what I need and he will be able to know that whatever he does will be right.

It works. Better than we imagined. We find our way, step by step, to places of intimacy that neither of us ever visited. We taste the tremendous power of our desire to guide us in creating patterns of sensation and response. New passageways open between us and within us for love to increase and passion to flow through the concrete moments of our living.

CR

We may not be able to create a passionate lifelong love out of every desire, but we cannot create a passionate lifelong love out of anything else. For it is our desire that calls us to be present with each other and ourselves. The louder it is, the more vulnerable it is calling us to become. And the more free.

CR

When do you trust that it is safe to ask for what you need? When do you find you can't?

When do your feelings of frustration and irritation seem so aversive, so detrimental to the relationship, that you place your trust in your own ability to swallow them?

What is it in such moments that blocks you from trusting in your desire, and in your partner's desire for you?

What is the worst thing that could happen? What is your greatest fear? Will you be hurt? Disappointed? Rejected as too much?

Do you doubt your partner's ability to respond? Or yours to follow through? Why? Are there patterns of touching and being touched that loom inside of you as warnings? Or as beacons of hope?

೧ *Having faith* ೧

Have faith that the work of asking and trusting is what you need to become who you are.

There is a third practice involved in engendering a lifelong passionate love and it touches upon the deepest mystery of all. How, when we are people who are constantly changing, growing, and becoming, can we expect to stay with one person for the rest of our lives? How can we expect, in a world of over seven billion people, to find the one person who will be our soul mate, the other half that complements and completes us?

The answer is faith. We need faith that our practices of asking our partners for the touch we need and trusting our desire to tell us are what we will enable us to become who we are.

The feeling of passion that draws us together is one we recognize as life enabling. For it opens a world of sensations, a world in which new thoughts and feelings and actions are possible. As we practice asking and trusting, this world grows more real around us and within us. We taste love.

Yet this love is far from static. It lives, and it lives in our ongoing movement in relation to one other. As we sense, ask, trust, touch and are touched, we create patterns of sensation and response that release us into the ever-evolving present of this new world.

As a result, as we practice asking for what we need and trusting in the rhythms of desire to tell us, we not only create our relationships, *we create ourselves*. Who we are changes. We become persons for whom this love and this world are real. We create ourselves into persons who can, more and more, sense and respond to whatever challenges either of us face by drawing upon the resources of that world and deepening our love.

As we grow in these ways, the kinds of touch we need to release us will change, as will the forms of our desire itself, and our experience of the life that needs enabling.

At the same time, we are not the only ones who are changing. Our partners are as well, and they are changing because of us, because of their desire for us, as they sense and ask and trust and respond to us. In our every interaction, then, how we act, what we say, how we move are part of what will enable each of us to become the person we are.

The implications are radical. As we learn to ask and trust, and as our ability to give and receive a life enabling touch develops, we realize with our partners how, in our mutual desire for relationship, we are both becoming people for whom this relationship is necessary in becoming the singular beings we are.

Our coming together is not a merging of two individuals. It is a twofold affirmation that the world that opens when we are together is the world in which we want and need to live to unfold our potential for giving and receiving love.

The one love connecting us lives when it blooms as two.

This is the faith. It is faith that whatever I do in helping you become who you are *is* what I need to learn to do in order to become who I am. It is faith that your doing what will support me in my becoming is what you need to become who you are, and for the same reasons. It is faith that the asking and trusting I must do in relation to you is freeing me not only from whatever keeps me from moving in relationship to you, but also from what keeps me from moving in my own life, along my path.

It is not that I need your love or the security of a relationship in order to grow. It is nearly the reverse. The faith is that I need the challenges involved in learning to love you and in teaching you how to love me in order to unfold what I have to give the world.

All we have to offer the world is the work that the satisfaction of our desires demands.

This faith, once realized, extends beyond asking and trusting to the farthest horizons of our existence. It is faith that the love that draws us together, demanding our interest and trust, is a love that is *good* for us, and good for the world. It is faith that the love that is developing in and between us *is* the best of what we have to give to the world.

The wisdom in our desire for sex is guiding us to move in ways that keep this faith alive.

03

How do my partner and I practice such faith?

We move to a farm.

15

Inviting Intimacy

'Dissatisfaction, instead of making one disgusted with life,
is the great stimulus to life.'
– *Will to Power*, #697, 370

The work we encounter in partnerships is different from what is generally understood. It is not that two individuals must learn to communicate and compromise, apologize and forgive. Rather, the challenge involved in learning to ask, trust, and have faith is to *refuse to reject* the "yuck" feelings spawned by desire. The challenge is to greet these feelings not as problems to fix, but as expressions of our desire for more. It involves learning to dive straight into them and allow the cycle of breaths, or an otherwise-opened sensory awareness, to help us find guidance in such moments for recreating the passionate love we seek.

If we are willing to breathe ourselves down and open, hone in on the heart of our desire, and allow its warmth to flow through us, we find ourselves able to recreate in ourselves and with our partners the patterns of sensation and response that guide us in giving and receiving a life enabling touch. We know what incredible gifts such yuck moments are.

There is wisdom in desire.

※

Yuck feelings. You know what I mean — those feelings in relation to your partner that you aren't proud to have, that you don't really want to have, but that you can't seem to shrug off. They sink their teeth into your consciousness and shake hard, not letting go. Anger, resentment, jealousy, bitterness, suspicion, boredom, frustration. They seem to threaten the relationship. They call it into question. *How can love feel like this?*

If such feelings don't arise because of sex, they often settle around it. Questions of who wants it and who doesn't, when, where, and why, become issues of contention. You want the feelings to go away and leave you at peace with your partner. You are afraid of what they might mean. *Is this not the right relationship for me?*

Nine times out of ten, you respond by doing what your mind over body training has taught you to do. You deny the feelings and employ various stimulants and distractions to rid yourself of them (including food and movies). You make excuses to yourself about why you should override your own feelings — for love. Or you vent your feelings on your partner and in shame, turn away. Perhaps you latch on to sex itself as a drug or bargaining chip, a way to feel good despite the conflict. Or maybe you hold your partner accountable until business is put to bed. Your desire for sex lurches sideways, or buckles under itself in frustration.

Time to breathe. In such moments, the cycle of breaths can provide a crucial intervention in the spiral of increasing disaffection. When you breathe to move and move to breathe, you invite an experience shift in yourself. As in the case of your desire for food, this shift enables you to realize that the feelings you are feeling, as aversive as they may feel, are expressions of a *desire for more*—for something that you do not have in that moment that you need for your own well being. For life enabling touch.

As you breathe down into the *earth*, this ground appears. You simply would not feel upset with your partner if you didn't believe that you and your partner had more capacity to connect in that moment than you two were realizing. You would not be feeling these feelings if you did not desire from him or her a life enabling touch. These feelings are expressions of your desire for your partner.

The earth breath helps you rest the shapes of your frustration and disappointment on this knowledge and see them for what they are. Drop the weight.

As your breathing releases you into the upholding power of the earth, you gather strength to affirm that yes, this is what you are feeling. This is who you are in this moment. This is what your movements in this relationship are creating in you, and it is OK. *I want more.*

As you breathe into your heart and out through the *air* grazed surfaces of your skin, this breath invites you to uncurl the shapes of frustration or jealousy into a clearer sense of the more you want—into a clearer sense of what you need to share in that moment in order to be more present to yourself and your partner. As you breathe in this way, deeper roots of these feelings inevitably appear. Their frantic energy is drawing upon your lack of trust, the difficulty you have in trusting that your partner could and would really want to respond to you, welcome you, be with you.

As the yuck feelings fan out, you realize, *this is not just about my partner, this is about me.* You realize that parts of yourself injured in the past and now walled for protection are sounding out an alarm so loud that it overwhelms.

Yet, breathing open these feelings, you realize that they too are expressions of desire: your own desire is calling you to heal whatever would prevent you from knowing and feeling, giving and receiving more love. Your love wants to grow stronger than any fear.

As you breathe down into the pit of your belly, igniting your energetic core, the *fire* breath helps you sink beneath the hurt and reconnect with a felt sense of the desire that is fueling your dissatisfaction. You bring to life its purest, most passionate shapes. You kindle the shapes of your longing, and affirm the rightness of them. The goodness of them. Your faith in them. The cell-opening, time-tested reality of that passion in your life. *It is what you want to make real in this moment.* But how?

The realization dawns: what you want in this moment is not only more from your partner, but more of *yourself*. You want to touch and be touched in ways that *enable your life,* that unfold the potential you have to be the person that your love for your partner has helped you discover. *I have more to give.*

With the *water* breath, you open to receive impulses to move in this moment that respond to this moment—impulses that express this renewed trust. As you move with this wisdom, your experience of your own feelings shifts again. Suddenly you are ready and able to move in relation to your partner in ways that will allow you to be fully present, even if your partner is not yet there. You are able and willing to *ask* for what you need without anger or resentment, self-pity or fear, but simply and openly as an expression of your desire to give and receive a life enabling touch.

You know. The fact of sharing, the fact of presence, trumps any content, for it expresses the greatest desire—the desire to be with. Any content is mere information about how to grow, how to heal, how to do what the fact of your sharing means you can.

When you move with this faith, your asking is neither demand nor ultimatum. It emerges from you as an invitation to your partner to move with his or her desire to touch and be touched by you. It is an invitation to your partner to succeed in loving you. And your partner, sensing your faith and trust, is less likely to be defensive, combative, or critical of you for asking.

Together you are able to embrace the moment as information about what the movements that you each are making in relation to each other are creating in you. Trust pulses. Faith wells. New ways to move erupt in you — words, thoughts, feelings, and actions that enable your life with each other.

You have transformed the yuck feelings: they have become one more occasion to be healed, freed, and grown by your mutual desire to give and receive a life enabling touch.

You stand in yourself, alive to the pleasure whose potential courses through you. You know: *The movements I am making are making me into someone who is and wants to be in relationship with you for my own sake.*

❧

When we engage the cycle of breaths in this way, we dislodge our mind over body strategies for managing our desire for sex.

We *know*, in our sensory selves, that the desire that sheers off sideways, the anger that plumes, or the hurt and sadness that pool in the shadows are all guiding us to unfold a potential for pleasure in the relationship we have yet to experience.

We know, in our bodies, that moments of frustrated and buckled desire *are* what a relationship is. They *are* what the movement of any life enabling relationship is constantly creating as it enables the lives of two desiring individuals.

We know too, that learning how to sense and respond to such moments *is* what a relationship does. It is how a relationship grows. It is how *we* grow, more free, more open, more able to live in the sensory spaces opened by the flow of love in us.

A relationship that does not constantly prod partners where they are stuck does not succeed in freeing them into their love for one another.

We do get stuck. It is inevitable. By the time we meet our partners, as described above, we have amassed a large reserve of patterns guiding us how *not* to touch and be touched. Our desire will crash against these patterns of fear and self-control. When it does, we can deny such sticking points as nonsense, repress them as irrelevant, or dismiss them as tiresome, tedious, and out of place. If we do, however, as we now see, we miss out on the occasions our desire for life enabling touch is creating in us and for us for greater pleasure *and* greater love —and one because of the other.

Better to breathe and welcome such moments as *invitations to intimacy.*

ೞ

It is the end of the day. We are up at the well house taking down the old wires that connect the well pump to the barn. We are tired, having worked all day painting the house. It is getting cool and dark. The ladder propped up on the post falls just short of the wires we need to disconnect. Geoff and Jordan get another bigger ladder and crawl up the other side. Geoff pulls one wire free. The others are just out of reach.

"Can't you reach up from the top of the smaller ladder and cut them?" I ask. No response. Feels chilly. I have been saying as much already.

"I can try," says Jordan, beginning to shimmy up the pole. He does this shimmying very well and it is usually a source of pride and praise from Geoff and me.

"Sure," I say. "Try it."

"Won't work," says Geoff. His tone is negative. He is muttering under his breath. Jordan climbs up the pole, Geoff says it again. "It won't work. He can't do it."

I counter, "No harm in trying." I can't understand why Geoff isn't willing to give Jordan a chance. Geoff suggests leaning a big ladder downhill on the slanting post.

"No, no, no," I say. Way too dangerous.

Geoff scowls. Finally he climbs up the smaller ladder (as I had suggested) and begins prying out huge rusty staples, dropping them on the ground.

"Can you not drop those?" I ask. Pause. He drops another. "Geoff! Those are dangerous. People will be walking around here and could get hurt by them."

"I've been collecting hardware all day," he replies.

The wires we have hated since our first days here finally fall. I turn, pick up Kai, and walk down the hill. Halfway down I turn around. "This could have been a great victory but you took all the joy out of it."

On the outside, I am calm. On the inside, I am aching. Seething. My desire for Geoff is tangled in hard knots; sensors that usually connect with him curl under themselves for protection. I feel closed off, dismissed, resentful. Yuck feelings.

At the same time I yearn to reconnect. I trust that it will happen, but I know that it will take some work getting from this gnawing hurt back to the flow of love. I will have to ask for what I need. And who knows how he will respond.

Geoff comes into the house five minutes later and begins to explain why throwing rusty staples into the grass doesn't matter. I am incredulous and push back. Finally he admits that he agrees with me but did not know what to do with the staples at that moment.

"Fine," I say. "Hand them to me or ask what to do but don't treat me as if the suggestion is stupid!" He utters a small sorry. But things are still not right. He is still defending his behavior.

I breathe into the earth, waiting for a clear sense of what I am feeling, waiting for the next thing to say. It bubbles up.

"I need some acknowledgment that you were not treating me very well," I say. No comment. I walk out of the house to pick up a stray tool. He follows. He is trying to find the right thing to say. The effort is paralyzing him. His face is blank.

"We did a lot today," he says. I nod, but cannot say yes. I cannot meet his gaze. The yes is stuck in my throat. It is so hard to ask for what I need! And then this. I breathe through the discomfort, feeling its press and pulse. My desire for him reaches out again, in spite of me.

I reply. "I would rather have that wire still hanging than feel like I do right now."

No response. I am incredulous again. Doesn't he feel the distance between us? Isn't he aching inside? Where is his desire toward me? I was sure he would simply agree with me and we would touch each other there. I breathe again down into the fire of my own desire for him, losing myself there, burning away whatever is preventing me from connecting with him.

"What do you mean?" he asks. Face blank. It is worse than I thought.

"You don't know?" I ask.

"No." Face blank. It is as if he is a stranger.

I pause. Breathing deep, flowing through, yes. I can risk speaking from my faith in what is possible.

"At this moment we are not loving each other," I say.

It doesn't work. We go around and around. He is defiant. Chilly. My insides feel scratched, raked. My heart hurts. I don't know why I am still standing here. Yet I am.

I keep breathing down, out, in and through. I feel my discomfort and unhappiness pushing me toward him. I just want to go away and curl up in a comfortable place, yet the impulses towards him keep surfacing. I ride them, almost in spite of myself.

"This is like those other times (I list them). You are trapped inside yourself and I don't know how to break through." The intensity of the moment is burning through me.

He tries to approach me, to give me a hug. I recoil. He can't touch me like that. I can't receive it. He is not really giving it. He is still far away, pretending that he is not. I need something else. What? I pull back but stay close. Standing. Open.

Finally, and I can't remember how or when or why, his face cracks. His tears well, and he comes alive. Something inside me releases instantly in response, flooding my cells, warm and full. My relief, our relief, is palpable. We drop into the flow of our desire and move towards one another in our words.

"It just hurts me so much when you disapprove," he says. The words rush out. "Your disapproval is so painful I just want it to stop."

Yes, I understand. Words flow quickly now. I did not mean to disapprove. I just wanted the job to be finished as much as he did.

He says he is sorry. He means it. I feel it. Relief. I am sorry too. We are present to each other.

He says, "I know what is happening. I know what I am doing. I feel like I am in jail. And you are sitting there yelling at me 'You are in jail, you are in jail,' and I know it but I can't get out!"

"You know that I want to be connected with you, doesn't that help? Doesn't knowing that give you confidence?"

"Yes! But when you want to connect, I don't want to not be there for you," he replies.

It is our pattern, our self-reinforcing cycle of fear and doubt, at the growing edge of our desire for one another. The cycle triggers unexpectedly, in a moment when either one of us is tired, frustrated, or doubting ourselves. We pull back from one other — he in the fear that he cannot give me what I need; I in the fear that I am asking him for too much. He turns against me, angry at me for "making him" feel inadequate. I turn against myself, angry at myself for feeling yuck feelings that I would prefer not to feel.

But in this moment, I am not turning against myself. I am standing and asking, without blame or anger, in a sensory awareness of my yearning towards him. I am allowing the pain of my frustrated desire for connection with him to take shape in me as impulses to move toward him. It is difficult to hold myself open. It is difficult not to lash out in pain. But I know what I want. I believe in it.

We affirm the moment for what it is: an occasion to go deeper in our relationship, allowing our love for one another to grow more real in us than patterns of our past hurt.

"Don't you see," I offer, "your fear of not being able to respond to me creates the very situation you fear most?" He nods. *Yes*.

Later, crawling into bed, he offers, "I don't know what it is that prevents me from responding." He pauses. "It probably has something to do with Dad."

We settle in, limbs entwined, and hold each other tightly. The touch pours us into a realm of sensory togetherness we are still discovering years after marrying. We don't have to solve the mystery at that moment. We are in it together, asking for what we need, trusting in our desire to guide us, and having faith in the process.

That is enough.

16

Getting It Right

> 'Sex: for the free hearts, innocent and free, the garden
> happiness of the earth, the future's exuberant gratitude
> to the present.'
> – *Zarathustra*, 300

Wait! What about sex? Aren't you going to talk about the nitty-gritty details?

There is no recipe for what to eat that will enable you to find the experience of being nourished. There is no manual for how to have sex that will guarantee you a life enabling touch. There are plenty of books, videos, and media programs that can advise you what to touch when and in what sequence. They are helpful and informative as far as they go. At the same time, no one else's recommendation can make you feel someone else's touch as pleasurable, even if an expert says it should. That information represents what other people have gleaned from their own experiences, and extrapolated to yours. It can be helpful, but only in the same way that information about food composition and production can be. If folded into a relationship of mutual desire, where partners are open to learning how to give and receive a life enabling touch, such ideas and suggestions may spur new experiments and explorations.

Nevertheless, in the end, *partners must discover for themselves what will unfold the potential of the particular passionate link they share with one another*. It is only human. If we try to reduce sex to a question of technical matters, we will not unfold its life enabling potential. We will feel the pinch.

CR

Still, what about the sex? Why connect physically at all? Must we? Should we? What role does sex play in the process of giving and receiving a life enabling touch?

Within a partnership, married or not, same sex or not, sex is a unique act. Yet the reasons why may surprise. Once we have dislodged the mind over body sense of ourselves and cultivated a sensory awareness of our bodily becoming, our experience of it changes.

Sex is *play*. Sex is a time to practice, over and again, entering into the present moment with each other as fully as possible, with a willingness to sense and move with the shapes of our desire.

How so? Sex marks a time and place where partners practice bringing their senses to life. It is an activity in which we experiment with different forms of touch, physical or not, and discover what helps us release the liberating, healing potential of our desire. The possibilities are endless. We can experiment with words and gestures, thoughts and feelings. Whether blurting out frustration, venting anxiety, sharing a meal, or walking through the woods, we can explore what kinds of dynamics awaken us into a mutual experience of life enabling touch.

As we do so we slowly and attentively replace whatever patterns of mind over body response are hindering us from getting the most from our love. We learn to move with and towards our partners, as the enabling condition of our own health and well being.

Our pleasure points the way. When we succeed in making our way to the present of our togetherness, we taste the intoxicating bliss, flowing with a love that spills through all dimensions. A full-bodied love.

In this way, the time and place of sex is a time and place where we practice shifting our experience of our desire for sex itself. As we open to one another, body, heart, and mind, we can see and sense and know that "sex" is not a *goal* — as in the consummate pleasure in life. Nor is sex is a mere *means* to a healthy relationship — as in some kind of marital glue. Sex is not a physical act whose meaning is given in context. Nor is it guaranteed to be good when partners commit their lives to one another.

What counts about sex, we realize, is that we learn from it *how to move towards each other and with each other at all times and in all places, even when we are not having sex.*

Every moment in our togetherness with our partner is a point along an ongoing rhythm of our ever-evolving desire for each other. Every moment harbors a potential for tapping into the bliss of that togetherness and letting it flow into and through our words and gestures. Our desire for sex is calling us to be present to ourselves and each other.

In this regard, when a physical connection does happen, it unfolds in the moment as a way to deepen and punctuate the *experience we are already enjoying* of living in the world that opens when we are together.

ൡ

As a play-full moment in the rhythms of our togetherness, sex is exceptionally powerful. The intensity of the pleasure of it draws us to repeat the play, and such repetition is essential to its ongoing life.

Why? Because repetition is never the same. Even when we set out to recreate the very sensations we felt yesterday, we are not the same. Our partner is not the same. The movements we made yesterday have changed us and our partners. What we need today to stir similar responses will be different. What we learn from our need for repetition, then, is how different each span of time together is. What we gain is more practice in learning to drop into the moment and unfold its singular potential.

The very pleasure we seek from sex guides us to return again and again to the tasks of asking for the touch we need, trusting in our desire to tell us, and having faith that the challenges of doing so are what we need to become who we are. Once is never enough.

⊗

If the powerful play of desire is between woman and man, there is the possibility as well that the act of having sex will enable life literally, in the form of another human being.

A child gives concrete form to what the act of two individuals coming together is already accomplishing. For as we learn to move with and towards each other in sex, we are giving birth to ourselves as bodies who need a relationship, who need this particular bodily relationship, to become who we are. A child reflects this truth back to us.

Conceiving, we give birth to a moving body who needs a relationship, this relationship, to become who it is.

⊗

In conversations around conscious partnerships, as in conversations around conscious eating, metaphors of restraint and control dominate. Viewed through a mind over body lens, the act of entering into a relationship means giving up sources of pleasure. It means giving up freedom, and doing so in the name of a nearly impossible ideal, namely lifelong love. It is to wear a wedding band that signals to all that we have corralled our desire for sex within the ring of marriage. We promise our partner that we will forsake all others, from now until the day we die.

When we perceive our choices in relation to sex as restricting our desire to a limited realm of its possible pleasures, as in the case with food as well, we build an instability into those relationships that no amount of will power can overcome. Our desires grow increasingly restless and will eventually erupt. We grab that bag of cookies or jump into an easy affair. Dissatisfaction is inevitable, even expected.

When we cultivate a sensory awareness of the movements making us, however, our experience of entering into a lifelong partner relationship shifts. We are choosing, yes, to privilege a relationship with one person, but we do so as the condition that will enable us to achieve what we most want. We do so knowing that we are entering a mystery, embarking on a journey whose challenges will prime us to unfold our capacity for pleasure and for love.

What we are choosing is not to settle with someone or even to settle for someone. We are choosing *to honor our desire*—our desire to become the person who loves and is loved by *You*.

Once we understand our partner relationships in this way, we also know that the passion of our desire for the other can and will live. In fact, it is bound to grow. It must. The passion will grow as we hold open a vulnerability in relation to ourselves and each other, intent on learning, moment to moment, how to give and receive a life enabling touch.

ରେ

Eros unstrung? No. Our bodies delight in each other for sure. Our bodies are drawn to each other in all kinds of random moments and situations, regardless of commitments we have or have not made, heedless of sex or gender. In this intense erotic interest is the energy that funds human relationships of all kinds — generous acts of healing and tending, coaching and counseling, teaching and parenting. It is an energy that makes good friendships, congenial colleagues, and strong families.

Yet we are well aware, very aware, that there is a danger in desire. We see the casualties of unstrung eros all around us in cases of child abuse, sexual infidelity, rape, and incest.

Understandably we want to resist impulses of desire that would drive us to act against our better judgment, or do violence to ourselves or our commitments, values, and loved ones.

Nevertheless, when we respond to our own desires by acting harshly to preempt such eruptions in our selves or others, we make it more likely that such eruptions will occur. Even when desires arise that are clearly at odds with our intentions to love, even in such cases, *desire itself* is not the problem, as twisted or perverted as it may be. Rather, the problem lies in our unwillingness to greet this desire as what we ourselves are creating in this moment by the movements we are making.

An eruption of a desire to violate is, in most if not all cases, an expression of a movement we are making in violating ourselves. *To violate a desire is to create a violent desire.*

There is always play in desire and when we engage the cycle of breaths, we give ourselves what we need to find it. A sensory awareness of our desire for sex acts as an internal check on the shapes of that desire that arise in us.

For as our practice of sensory awareness deepens, expressions of desire that violate ourselves or others no longer register in us as desirable: the pleasure they offer falls far short of the pleasure we want. They may pop up in our imaginations in the wake of frustration or anger or hurt, or pop up before us on the cinema or television screen; but breathing into our selves, we stop buying them, and stop buying into them.

We want more.

The irrepressible physicality of our desire for each other is calling us, yes. Its wisdom is calling us, wherever we are, to ask for what we need to give and receive an ever-evolving, ongoing experience of life enabling touch.

It is calling us to live in love.

Entwined Desires 2

There is a tendency in our sexual lives to pull back from the brink of radical openness. Small nagging wants, doubt or boredom, disappointment and fatigue shut down our sensory selves. When a window of time does open up, it seems easier to fall asleep, turn on the television, or have an ice cream sundae than do the work of being vulnerable with a partner.

When we retreat from the call of our desire, however, we miss out on an opportunity to dislodge the sense of ourselves as minds over bodies that hinders us, not only in our partnerships, but in other realms of our lives as well.

Our desire to give and receive a life enabling touch moves together with our desire for the experience of being nourished, and it is never not so. As we cultivate a sensory awareness of our eating pleasure, we are more able and less willing to feel our displeasure in our partnerships. *I want more.*

As we learn to discern the wisdom in our desire for food guiding us to a sense of enough, we are more likely to ask for what we need in relation to our partners, trusting in the shapes of desire to draw us close. So too, as we learn to live in love with our partner, that love spills into our relationship with ourselves, supporting us in following the arc of our pleasure to a sense of enough. *Dinner for two.*

It is not just an increase in confidence, or even the fact of increased love that twines these desires. Rather, an experience shift in either realm provides us with a new context for sensing and responding to whatever movements are making us in the moment — whether our desire is for nourishment or life enabling touch. Whatever pleasure opens in us as a result of such a shift further impels us, guides us, and even forces us to take on both desires at once. If we try to compensate for a lack in one realm by squeezing more pleasure out of the other, eating more than we need or having sex indiscriminately, our level of overall pleasure diminishes.

Our entwined desires are guiding us to *whole health*.

As we pursue this line of thought, the entwining of these two desires with our desire for spirit appears as well. For as we find the wisdom in our desires for nourishment and physical intimacy, we bring into being a world — the matrix of relationships that our movements of eating and loving are creating. Eating and loving, we stir to life a desire for the sense of vitality, direction, and belonging we also need to thrive. *A desire for spirit*.

Just as our hunger for food is not about the material content of food, and our desire for sex is not about the technical points of stimulation and release, so our desire for spirit is not about finding the right teacher or community, ritual or belief.

Where our desire for food guides us to create a relationship to ourselves in which we are nourished, and our desire for sex guides us to create a relationship with a partner where we can give and receive a life enabling touch, so our desire for spirit, as we shall see, is guiding us to name and make real a network of relationships that will support us in discovering what we have to give—*a world we love that loves us*.

Desire
For
Spirit

17

Signs of Depression

'Alas, all this delusion and all these mistakes still dwell in our
body: they have there become body and will.'
— *Zarathustra*, 188-9

"Psychiatry by Prescription" the title blares. It is the cover story,
accompanied by a picture of a mock medicine cabinet lined with
bottles of prescription pills (*Harvard Magazine*, Jul-Aug 2006). I
look at the subtitle: "Do psychotropic drugs blur the boundaries
between illness and health?"

I flip to the article. A recent study by a professor of health
policy at Harvard Medical School estimates that nearly half
of all Americans will suffer a period of mental illness during
the course of their lives. Depression, the leading cause of suicide,
is at the top of the "Eight Most Common" list, and the ranks of
those diagnosed with the disease are growing. Besides
depression, this list includes social phobias, attention deficit
disorders, and other disorders having to do with conduct,
anxiety, oppositional-defiance, and intermittent explosive acts.
Notably, the list excludes substance abuse disorders; major
psychiatric illnesses like schizophrenia and psychosis do not even
rank.

Many of these diseases are new, or at least, the names are new.
There is disagreement over whether it is only our recognition of
them as problems that is new. Even so, there is something
troubling here: each disease represents a heightened expression
of an otherwise normal emotion or behavior: fear, anxiety,
shyness, restlessness, independence, and love. Most Americans, it

seems, have a hard time at some point fitting into the shapes of living that are expected of them.

As I read on, the article plunges into the heated controversies concerning the mental health of people living in the United States. We are as riled about mental disorders as we are by expanding waistlines and declining rates of marriage. We want to be happy — we think that we should be happy — living well-adjusted and successful lives. Yet large numbers of people seem to be falling short of ideals that we, to some extent, share.

The case in point here is depression. As the experts contest, even a mild depression can have debilitating effects. People suffering from depression lose their joy and enthusiasm in the act of living — they lose their *spirit*.

When we are depressed, our energy levels plummet; curiosity and motivation skip away. It is as if we have been pushed backwards into a pit, sapped of vital juice, and can't get out. It can be challenging to breathe. If we feel at all, it is alienation from ourselves, from other people, from ordinary life, and an accompanying despair. For there seems to be no compelling reason to be, no direction or purpose to our actions. We are not engaged or connected to ourselves or our worlds in a way that would give our life meaning. It feels as if we do not belong.

Despite relative agreement over these primary symptoms of depression, there is little agreement on grounds for diagnosis, progress of the disease, or means to a cure.

Of the types of mental disorder listed in the study that sum to half the population, depression is the largest category. As the article relates, however, the lines separating these disorders are not clear. Symptoms of depression accompany other phobias as well (not to mention substance abuse disorders).

Nor is the line obvious between a depression that warrants treatment and the normal highs and lows of living. One noted expert accuses the study of "medicalizing ordinary unhappiness." Other experts I have read insist that many cases of depression go undiagnosed. Anecdotal evidence alone suggests that people across culture look to all manner of stimuli to distract, numb, overwhelm, and otherwise mask their feelings of disappointment and despair. *Life should be better than this.*

¢¢

As I read on, I begin to recognize a conversation whose features are astonishingly similar to those characterizing debates over physical fitness and lifelong love. The debates constellate around questions of *desire*. It is a desire evident again in common, chronic, culture-wide patterns of frustration and disappointment.

The desire, in this case, is a desire for what I call *spirit* — for the *energy* we need to get up in the morning and go; the *purpose* that gives us something to do, and the *context* where we can engage that going and doing as worthwhile, whether it be as small as a twosome or as large as the universe. Our desire for spirit is a desire for the sense of vitality, direction, and belonging that allows us to *affirm* that our lives are worth living. We want something out of life—something that will in-spire us, fill us, rouse us to action—whether it be belief in god or a spiritual practice, social justice or a personal mission, the practice of art or participation in a religious community. We want to know that our existence matters.

At first glance, it might seem that this "desire for spirit" is not at all akin to our desires for food and sex. If there is such a desire, it is not bodily. It is a non-physical yearning for something that is not physical — something that transcends and empties our finite, world-bound bodies. *Right*?

By now this response should trigger flags. The fact that we so readily assume that our mental or spiritual health is distinct from our physical bodies is a function of our training in a mind over body sense of self. Thinking, feeling, and acting as if we were minds over bodies, we are all too willing to believe that "spirit" refers to something beyond our senses. Even though we feel depression in our lagging bodies and depleted energy levels, we take it for granted that the vitality, direction, and belonging we desire will come to us from a power living over and against our sensory selves — whether that power is a divine entity, an eternal soul, or our own rational mind choosing to follow a prescription for psychotropic drugs. We imagine that we will feel happy when we make the right choices in our lives about which paths and principles to obey, which traditions to uphold. When we can't decide, when we don't know what we want, when our wanting seems impossible, we despair.

Just as we tend to misread food and sex as merely material needs whose rhythms we can and should control (or not), so we tend to think of our spiritual needs as non-material, and again feel justified in prescribing for our bodies the ideals and practices we believe will secure us the affirmation we seek.

We practice overriding the sensory cues of our desires. We may even convince ourselves that such denial is itself desirable. We may come to believe that we will satisfy our desire for spirit by mastering our desires for nourishment, touch, and affirmation. *We do it for Him.*

⚮

As I ponder these developments, a sense of danger lurks, familiar from discussions of our desires for food and sex. It is not so easy. If we, as individuals, pursue our desire for spirit by paving over our bodily sensations (including our desires for food and sex), we will lose any wisdom that our patterns of dis-ease are offering us. In the words of one researcher: it is like treating kids for dysentery without cleaning up the dirty water they are drinking. The "cure" obscures the cause.

As the comparison with food and sex also suggests, our sensations of depression, anxiety, and despair—these bodily sensations of wanting more — may be the very resources we need to learn how to live our lives in ways that *will* satisfy our desire for spirit.

ℭℜ

As I set this article in the context of ongoing debates over our mental health, more parallels to the debates over our desires for nourishment and life enabling touch emerge. In a similar way, proposed solutions to the rising tides of depression fan out along a spectrum with each point and both ends sharing a common suspicion of our desire for spirit.

At one end, experts encourage people to exert more will power over their mental and spiritual health. We are urged to seize our own well being, choose our path, and stick to it. At the other end, experts advocate changing our bodies or changing our environments so that our desire for spirit will better align with what is expected of us and with the tasks we face in our jobs, families, and communities.

Here, as in the debates over health and partnerships, the variety of responses is deceptive. For the controversy among positions reinforces the same assumption seen in the article on psychotropic drugs, and evident in all three realms of societal crisis: the assumption that our greatest hope for satisfaction lies in exercising the power of our individual or collective minds over our erring desires.

Take a closer look. At the will power end of the spectrum, we find a vast and burgeoning field of *self-help* products designed to help people help themselves find whatever they think they need to make themselves happy. Such offerings teach us what will make us happy and how we can secure it — finding our purpose, making money, or achieving success, a slender body, great sex. The self-help market abounds with books, videos, workshops, and retreat centers that offer principles of positive living, strategies for finding our callings, and practices of meditation and self-reflection designed to propel us along the road to personal fulfillment and peace of mind. *Speed up. Slow down. Do this practice. Say this mantra. Pamper yourself. Test yourself. Be happy.*

The message of this genre, moreover, goes beyond the idea that we can and should help ourselves, moving right in line with the cereal box logic and movie morality we have already traced in the realms of eating and relationships. The message here is that we can help ourselves by buying and buying into a program that will give us the spirit — the sense of vitality, direction, and belonging — that our sensory selves lack.

Along the way, we are encouraged to hold our own histories, heritage, and traditions lightly, with gentle skepticism, as we reclaim our right to choose what, whether, and how to obey. Many self-help offerings demonstrate this stance, mining ancient, esoteric, and non-Western traditions for spiritual exercises or a perennial philosophy and adapting these practices to the challenges of living now. We piece together a teacher here, a class there, a workshop elsewhere, shelling out time and money along the way. We do so believing that we can make a choice, that we should make a choice, and that we have to make a choice. *My life is my responsibility.*

At the other end of the spectrum are those who believe that we cannot will ourselves into a state of emotional solvency nor choose to believe in a religion. Individual initiative is not enough. Forces beyond our control are at work.

While the arguments at this end of the spectrum are diverse, taken together they stress the lack of fit between our human desire for spirit on the one hand and the post/modern marketplace of values on the other. The affirmation we want is impossible in this world. Given this lack of fit, "we" need to rely on a collective mind to help us 1) alter our *unmet desire* so that we need not feel it in depressing or debilitating ways; or 2) alter our living *environments* by wrapping ourselves in an alternative moral universe more conducive to our spirit-desiring selves. Either way, authorities in religion and science, medicine and politics will help us.

Here, under the category of altering our *unmet desire* is where the psychotropic drugs described in the article above weigh in. The search for such drugs is at the forefront of scientific research. Paxil, Prozac, Zoloft, and other antidepressants, sleeping pills, and stimulants such as Ritalin are raking in billions of profits for their makers. Prescriptions are rising, especially among children and young adults, despite warnings of side effects and improper use. Untested cocktails are common.

Moreover, these mood-altering drugs are not only being prescribed to people who are clearly ill. They are being marketed directly to the public, on the radio, internet, and in print, as antidotes to feelings of general stress, anxiety, or sadness. Constantly surrounded by evidence that these drugs *can* offer immediate relief, we are drawn to believe that our feelings of depression and despair are mere annoyances that "we" can get rid of by popping a pill. Even if we choose not to take such drugs, the fact that they exist, the idea of them, shapes our expectations for healing. Not surprisingly, the popularity of such mood-altering drugs is rivaled only by the popularity of pills for altering our digestive systems (including medications for weight, cholesterol, stomach acid, and blood pressure) or for boosting our sexual potency.

Alongside mood-altering drugs, there is also a range of responses — religious and secular, new age and traditional — aiming to alter the *environment* to which our desire for spirit seems so mismatched.

More and more frequently, teachers and communities are marketing themselves to the public as providing alternative moral and spiritual universes to those disaffected by post/modern culture and its bankrupt promises. It makes sense, they insist, that we are disheartened and dispirited. We want to escape from the stress-inducing, value-eroding, health-depleting, purpose-poor rat race of capitalist consumerism. The post/modern world has failed to deliver the reason-based peace and harmony it promised. On the contrary. Where all values are equal, nothing matters, no one cares, and anything goes.

The alternative universes advertised to the public are varied. As sociologists detail, membership in fundamentalist, evangelical, renewalist, and conservative forms of religion, whether Christian or Jewish, Muslim or Hindu, has swelled, especially among the ranks of those born in the decades after World War II. Such movements generally encourage members to sequester themselves from at least some values of the modern, scientific world, and rely instead on teachings of the tradition to guide them in addressing their spiritual needs. Often such reliance involves strictly regulating desires for food and sex. So too, these communities may provide members with intense emotional experiences that overwhelm feelings of depression, or with religious directives whose rigor fills a need for direction and belonging. Again, the availability of such communities, selling us their visions of a different world, encourages us to believe that the existence of a community, its principles, beliefs, and practices, will provide us with the sense of vitality, direction, and belonging we are lacking.

Confronted with the range of options promoting our mental and spiritual health, spanning self-help platforms and drug remedies, new age spirituality and anti-modern religious movements, it is hard not to turn towards their bright promises, and away from our bodily sensations of malaise. We want to lean on something or someone outside of our bodily selves — whether science or religion — to tell us what is true, who we are, what we want, and how to get it. Even branches of the self-help movement that emphasize listening to "the body" tend to treat "it" as if it were an object whose "wisdom" is there for us to read. Even teachers and programs that promise us everything we desire do so by appealing to an "I" who remains above the body, choosing to care for the body, resisting the fears, insecurities, and sicknesses lodged in the body and its desires. Even those who perceive depression and related disorders as merely chemical issues tend to pit "us" against our sensations of wanting more, marking those sensations as the problems to erase. In nearly every case, it is the "I" whose wants we learn to honor, over and against what our bodies are saying.

My point here is not to judge whether such offerings are true or effective, but rather, to expose how the array of options marketed to us serves to reinforce in us a sense of ourselves as spirited minds over sensory bodies. It encourages us to sense and respond to our desire for spirit as if it were possible to choose or lose whatever we need to secure for ourselves the sense of vitality, direction, and belonging we want, and then bring our bodies in line with what we decide is right.

The fight against our sensory selves, once begun, never ends. Split against our own feelings of lack, we are constantly in need of props, products, and practices to fund our efforts. *It's not so easy.*

ʘ

This cultural attitude towards our desire for spirit pervades the capitalist marketplace. Everywhere we turn, we find spirituality for sale—religious images and images of religion available for us to buy, in books, music, films, and fashion. It is impossible not to be brushed by their color.

In the biggest publishing success to date in the twenty-first century, Dan Brown's *Da Vinci Code,* a Harvard scholar unearths a hidden history of Christianity in which Jesus marries Mary Magdalene and has children with her. Fiction by Tim LaHaye about Jesus' return on the Day of Judgment has also topped the best-seller lists. The success of Mel Gibson's R-rated *Passion* astounded critics and supporters alike. Television and cable shows feature angels and persons with paranormal powers. Industry executives are creating religion-oriented film companies to service what is perceived as an untapped audience. The purchasing power of the religion-interested is driving new strategies of marketing to churches, religious organizations, and values-oriented individuals across the board. Churches themselves are spawning marketing campaigns, complete with billboards and media advertisements, T-shirts, bumper stickers, and other forms of merchandizing; retreat centers, ashrams, spas, and resorts are selling *spirit*, selling us the sense of vitality, direction, and belonging we crave. If one option doesn't work, we drop it and move along the spectrum to find another prescription, another perspective, a different brand, a larger dose.

There are exceptions, of course. Not all concerned with our mental and spiritual health exercise a mind over body sense of self in the same way. Definitions of "mind" and "body" diverge. The degree of malaise among individuals ranges from mild to severe. Many individuals experience real relief following medical plans or joining religious communities.

Even so, in so far as this cultural milieu trains us to look outside our sensory selves for antidotes to our feelings of depression, anxiety, and despair, we practice overriding a source of wisdom within ourselves: the sensory cues in our dissatisfaction that could help us learn how to move differently.

കൃ

The movements we are making are making us.

What if our feelings of depression, anxiety, and despair are not the problem?

What if the very movements we are making as we endeavor to choose the right belief, worldview, or practice are making us sick?

What if our desire for spirit wants *more*?

18

Choose or Lose

'The creative self created respect and contempt; it created pleasure and pain. The creative body created the spirit as a hand for its will.'
– *Zarathustra*, 147

There was a time when I decided not to believe in the Christian God who had grown up with me. I knew too much. Class after class on Christian history and theology had shattered my childhood illusions about the integrity of the Bible, the seamless rise of Christian faith, and the unity of the church.

There was nothing, I realized, that all Christians share except perhaps a willingness to call themselves "Christian." Even then, at every moment in history, there have been — and are — people fighting over what "Christian" means. Someone wins. Someone loses. The winners write history as their story, and claim that their version is the truth.

I couldn't believe. On a day-to-day basis, the decision was liberating. I didn't miss the father-judge. I wrestled with my own challenges and made my way.

Then the going got rough. I did miss God. I tried shifting the focus to different Christian characters — Mary, Jesus, the Holy Spirit — then to other gods and goddesses. But it just seemed that I was making something up to cover my own weakness. Religion as band-aid or crutch.

Flat against the wall, I caved. *OK*, I cried to myself. *I just have to believe in something.* Period. *So what if all of my intellectual knowledge challenges the rationality of such an act. I need to believe— otherwise I will be severely depressed!*

Silence. I breathed a bit easier. My heart released.

This is what I have to do.

My mind was quiet for a moment. Then new questions jumped forward. What am I thinking? How can I imagine that I can simply *name* something — something in which I want to believe — and make it *real*?

☙

I taught a course at Harvard with the title: *Losing My Religion?*. The reference to the REM song was intentional, as was the allusion to the narrative of secularism. According to this narrative, we, as citizens of the modern western world, lifted up by our powers of rationality, are destined to outgrow religion. Religion is something that we, over time, will lose. In the course we read philosophers and theologians from 1600 to the present who debate the question. Are we losing our religion? Should we? Why or why not?

Are rock stars our new prophets?

Michael Stipes, lead singer of REM, denies that the title of this song has anything to do with religion; he claims that it is just an expression used in the South. Yet, as I share with my students, his denial is telling. We live in a culture so saturated with a particular perspective on religion that we barely recognize it as a perspective at all. This is what I want students to see: we learn to believe that religion is something we can choose — and lose. *Name your god. It is your fundamental human right.*

Why religion? As students soon learn, any answer to the question is complicated. To answer the question *why*, you must know *what* "religion" is. And every time you define *what* religion is, you imply *why* it is. For example, if "religion" refers to a way of providing orientation in our thinking and acting, as claimed by Immanuel Kant, then we might conclude that religion is necessary for providing this orientation. Or, if religion is a matter of cultivating certain kinds of feelings and experiences that enable us to act morally and love faithfully, as Friedrich Schleiermacher counters, then we might conclude that religion is necessary for helping us do so.

By contrast, if religion is a matter of humans projecting their own powers onto images of gods and goddesses, as Ludwig Feuerbach insists, then we might conclude that it is not necessary and that it even diminishes our living. Or if religion is a universal obsessional neurosis, as Sigmund Freud avers, a way of deluding ourselves about our impotence in the face of fate and nature, then we might conclude that it is time to grow up and out of religion into a scientific frame of mind.

Regardless of how you answer the questions, the *what* and *why* are inextricably bound, and it is always so.

Among students in my classes who sympathize with religion, the problems with this kind of circular argument are becoming obvious, though they cannot yet articulate them. As soon as we frame religion as something to choose or lose, the deck is stacked against it. By asking the question *why*, we put "religion" on the defensive. We presume that there should be a *reason* why we choose religion, and that that reason *should* be rational, or at least rationally defensible. The question, in other words, drives religion into the sphere of the Other, the spiritual, the non-rational: "it" is something that needs a rational defense.

The ensuing paradox is evident. If we can explain religion in rational terms, then why do we need it? Isn't the rational translation enough? How can we have *faith* in something if we have a rational explanation for it?

On the other hand, if what religion is about cannot be explained, then what good does it do to study it? Doesn't the *study* of religion inevitably distort and do violence to what the *practice* of religion is all about?

CR

Don't you believe in God? A student asks. Others look on eagerly. Hungrily.

"Yes," I say as my head shakes involuntarily side to side.

"No," I say as my head nods up and down.

We all laugh.

CR

I introduce a second perspective that further unsettles the students' common sense. "Religion" I remind them, is first and foremost a word, a *name*. It is a name we give to phenomena that appear to us as similar in some way to other "things" we recognize by the same name. As with many names, this one has had different meanings over the course of time. In the medieval period, for example, "religion" referred to "piety," a personal relationship to the divine. It is only in the nineteenth and twentieth century, I tell my students, in the thinkers of our course, that people begin to use the word "religion" to name *a system of beliefs and practices shared by members of a group that can be studied and evaluated via rational analysis.*

The implications are striking: there is no "it" there. When we approach "religion" as something to choose or lose, we aren't just debating what exists out there for all to see. As we name "it" we are actually creating "it," assuming it to be an object or cluster of phenomena that we *can* study via rational means and methods. We are naming and creating it as a something that we can choose or lose. Beliefs plus practices.

It is when we get to the three "masters of suspicion" that students begin to grasp what is at stake in naming religion as a thing we can choose, lose, or study. At stake is a sense of ourselves as minds living in and over our bodies. At stake is a sense that we can get what we want from life. In other words, this naming of religion presumes what we have already seen at work in the realms of food and touch as well: it presumes that our best resource for getting the satisfaction we desire is to exercise the power of our rational minds over and against our desiring bodies.

Who are these masters of suspicion? Karl Marx, Sigmund Freud, and Friedrich Nietzsche. As different as their positions are, they all come together in one regard: they take issue with the experiences people claim to have had of a spiritual presence or higher power that exists beyond the sensory reach of our bodily selves. These thinkers do not deny that such religious experiences are real — they are. However, these thinkers counter, those who claim to have had such experiences are not experiencing what they think they are experiencing.

For example, Marx suggests, we may think we experience a God who comforts us in our poverty, when we are actually experiencing the fruits of our own labor power, our bodily ability to create objects outside of ourselves that represent us to ourselves and others.

Or, for Freud, we may think that we are experiencing a heavenly Father who protects us against fate and the whims of nature, when we are actually experiencing the power of our own unconscious desires for protection and comfort.

For Nietzsche, we may think we are experiencing an eternal and unchanging God when we are actually experiencing our own bodily power to create values.

In all of these scenarios, what we are experiencing is the *power* of our own *creative, bodily movement* — a power that we have projected outside of ourselves and attributed to some other entity.

Of course, the critique leveled by these three writers against religion in general and Christianity in particular is initially devastating to students who believe. It seems as if these men are saying that religion is nothing but a figment of the human imagination, a fantasy or illusion at best, a harmful and oppressive delusion at worst. Why religion, indeed.

Yet as I guide the students deeper into the texts, we realize that these thinkers are saying something else. The writers all acknowledge that "religion" refers to a sphere of life in which we humans exercise a distinctively human, bodily power — a *power to name* our values, our ideals, our goddesses and gods, and *make them real* as the condition for our ongoing existence.

The concern of all three, moreover, is not *that* we exercise this power of our breathing bodies, but *how* we exercise it. We cannot not believe in something. Their concern is that, in the forms of religion they observe, we are exercising this power *against* ourselves, against our *bodies*. That is, we are using this bodily power to cut ourselves off from our participation in it; we are creating ideals and values that attribute our own power to some source outside of ourselves.

Most importantly, as all three contend, this way of using our power reinforces the conditions of alienation (for Marx), psychological and social neuroses (for Freud), and depression (for Nietzsche) that drive us to seek relief from "religion" in the first place. This way of seeking to satisfy our desire for spirit prevents us from knowing the pleasure of participating consciously and responsibly in the creation of ourselves, our values, our worlds. And it is this pleasure and this participation that will provide us with the sense of vitality, direction, and belonging we need to thrive.

Once students grasp this critique, they also begin to perceive the alternative directions for human living in which these three men point. What we must do, they contend, in order to satisfy our desire for spirit, is to create beliefs, rituals, and practices that *affirm* our labor-making, self-forming, value-creating *bodily* movement as the *source* of our being and becoming. We must generate ideals, values, even gods, that, in Nietzsche's words, *remain faithful to the earth* in us and around us. And we must learn to appreciate and evaluate *religion* as an activity where persons exercise and unfold the creative reach of their bodily movement, as they name and make real the world in which they want to live.

Suddenly the terrain of our conversation shifts and students see.

The questions that will help us draw closer to the human condition are not "why religion" nor "what is religion" but rather: what is it that our beliefs and practices are enabling us to become? What capacities for thinking, feeling, and acting are our movements allowing us to discover, exercise, and unfold? What relationships are coming into being because of our actions? What are the movements of our breathing, becoming bodies naming and making real?

ᛊ

Evidence from the cultural ledger suggests that our modern choose or lose approach to mental and spiritual health is not providing enough of us with the vitality, direction, and belonging we need in order to thrive. The reason, as these reflections suggest, is that we are driving a wedge between sense and spirit — between our sensory awareness of lack and what we hope will fill it. Mind over body. While many compassionate humans are doing much healing work in many fields, our efforts will not go far enough in addressing the roots of our malaise until we dislodge this wedge.

When tallied alongside earlier analyses of our desires for nourishment and life enabling touch, we can also see, in the shortcomings of this approach, hope. For if we can learn to sense and respond to our desire for spirit as if we were minds over bodies, then we can learn different patterns of sensation and response as well. Specifically, we can cultivate a sensory awareness of the *movements* that are making us, and from this shifted experiential place, learn to discern the wisdom in our feelings of depression, anxiety, and despair.

We can learn to find in these sensations the guidance we need to move in ways that will not recreate the pain, but will instead express the care-full attention to our sensory selves that we are practicing.

We must ask again: what is it we desire when we desire *spirit*? How is it that we gather within us the sense of vitality, direction, and belonging that will allow us to discover and unfold who we are?

༒

"Nooooo!" The cry rings out. I lift up my head. Am I needed? More scuffling.

"I am not attacking!" Jessica implores. "Just visiting!"

I enter the living room. Before me on the floor is a vast array of blocks and figures, big mega blocks, small mega blocks, wooden blocks, organized in squares, and buildings, populated by tiny animal figures, carefully lined, arranged, and settled in their enclosures.

"What's up?" I ask. Jessica and Kyra have set up a horse farm, in line with their dream of having 150 horses each, mostly thoroughbreds, and being jockeys. Or veterinarians. Jordan has a dairy farm featuring cows of all shapes and sizes. Jessica is trying to ride over and visit his farm. He doesn't want any visitors.

We live on a farm. They play farm. When I had first noticed this, I chuckled, especially when I had to interrupt their play *at* farm to get them to *do* farm. *Time to feed the chickens!* But I had quickly learned. This play is serious.

Several weeks earlier, Jessica had helped me understand. At that time, I had been doing yoga in the living room when she paraded down the stairs with Kyra close behind her.

"We are acting out a book," she had announced, "one that I am writing." Kyra nodded.

"Oh?" I said.

"Yes," Kyra chimed in. "It is about the farm. Jessica is Jessica and she is 12 and I am Kyra and I am eight." Four years in the future. "Will you be our mother?"

"Sure," I replied. Moving to the next posture, I suggested that they go pick some raspberries from the garden. Off they went. When they returned, they told me that it was time to take care of the horses. Off they went. Meanwhile, they told me, Jordan was down by the pond, driving his tractor.

"Yes, and Mommy is doing her yoga," I responded.

Moving into another standing posture, I had smiled. My kids were not *merely* playing. They were acting out their visions for the future, but not any future. They were *creating the world* in which they wanted to live — a world that would provide them with everything they need to unfold their interests, use their skills, and become what and who they want to be. They were creating a world in which they would be the ones with the power to *name* the animals and barns, the values and goals.

It occurred to me then and now again. In their play, the kids are not only naming and making real a world they want to be true, they are naming and making real a world where *they have the power* to name and make real.

They are creating for themselves a world where they have not only what they need, but also the *ability to secure* what they need to become who they are. It is a world they love that loves them.

I look at the spread before me. Jordan, Jessica, and Kyra, crouched together in the middle, are surrounded with manure bunkers and watering troughs. They are setting up chore schedules and gathering appropriate tools, plowing fields and planting crops. Certainly, they are not "really" doing these things — they are pretending — but don't tell them so. They *feel* as if they really are doing these tasks, and in some sense, they are right. For they are practicing the bodily patterns of thinking and feeling, planning and problem solving — the patterns of sensation and response — that they will need in order to be farmers.

Their movements are making them into people for whom this desire for a farm is real and possible; and they are testing and refining that desire at every turn. They do not want to be interrupted. For anything. This play is serious.

Seen in this light, Jordan's predicament seems obvious. He does not want visitors on his dairy farm, at least not at the moment, because his farm is not finished, and he is the only one with cows. Jessica and Kyra are quick to voice their preference for horses, and he is eager to protect his budding reality from what feels to him like a threat. It is as if their love of horses calls into question the world he is bringing to life in himself, and the self he is bringing to life in our life on the farm. Their certainty toys with his doubt.

What Jordan needs, I realize, is affirmation: he needs to know that there is room in the universe for him. He needs to know that he can name and make real the home he desires — a world in which he will enjoy the sense of vitality, direction, and belonging he needs to thrive.

I turn to Jessica. "Ask Jordan if you could please come visit his *dairy farm*. Honor his world. Help him make it real. Then he will let you come over and play."

છ

The play of these children offers clues to the more we desire from our lives. They are children, yes, entertaining themselves in an imaginary world. They are also human beings, naming and bringing into being for themselves a world in which they can thrive. They are, in this sense, exercising their power to name, and doing so in ways that remain faithful to the rhythms of their bodily becoming. Their pleasure is palpable.

Just as our desire for food is for an experience of being nourished that supports our ongoing work in nourishing ourselves; just as our desire for sex is for an experience of touching that supports our work in learning to give and receive a life enabling touch; so it is time to consider that our desire for spirit is a desire for the pleasure of *naming* and *making real* a world we love that loves us.

19

The Power to Name

'To create beyond itself. That is what [the body] would
do above all else, that is its fervent wish.'
— *Zarathustra*, 147

ଔ *In the beginning 1* ଔ

The idea that religion is about naming gods and goddesses has
long roots within religious traditions themselves. In Hindu,
Buddhist, Jain traditions, in Islam, Christianity, Judaism and
indigenous religions too, people learn about what can and cannot
be spoken about god, written about god, imaged about god.
People learn that there are many names for god and that there are
no names for god; that there are speakable names and
unspeakable ones. People learn that there is something to
name, and nothing to name. And in every case people learn
how to make these names real for themselves as they perform
concrete acts of ritual and prayer, belief and practice. *What would
Jesus do?*

In the Jewish and Christian accounts of creation, whose
readers are primarily (though not solely) responsible for defining
"religion" as an object to study, *naming* is also what God does to
make the world real. God speaks and the world, its qualities and
creatures, come into being. *Let there be light*.

In the process of naming and creating the world, God names
humans as the creatures with the power to name. This power
differentiates humans from the rest of creation as like the God
who created them all. God gives humans the responsibility

of naming and making real for themselves all that God has already named into being.

What does this human naming involve?

Modern interpreters of these texts have generally assumed that such naming represents an act of mastery or dominion. Humans assign a word to a particular object. The human words give the object its meaning. Mind over body. Naming, humans express their power over what receives the name.

Nevertheless, as ecologically-minded commentators now caution, if we interpret our naming power as proof of our rightful dominion, we breed actions that pollute the earth. We squander its non-renewable resources, reduce its biodiversity, and deplete the quality of life for all inhabitants, as we have done.

The power of naming given to Eve and Adam and exercised in religion, they counter, is not a warrant to exploit. Those with the power to name are rather called to tend the garden, to be responsible stewards of whatever appears to them as worthy of a name. *The earth is not ours to bend to our will and wiles. It is God's.*

Even in this interpretation, however, the act of naming is cast as an act of mind over body, however compassionate. Naming the earth as God's, humans act in the image of God as the mind of God ruling, if responsibly, over the body of the earth and their bodies of earth.

Is this what naming entails? Will this kind of naming satisfy our desire for spirit? What's in a name?

ରଃ

"Mom, here is your ticket. The show will begin in a few minutes." I grasp the small white square Jessica hands me. She and Jordan have spent the last ten minutes gathering props from around the house for a magic show. She hands Geoff a ticket too. Several minutes later, we are all sitting on the rug. Jessica steps behind the small table she set up for herself and begins.

"I will do six tricks," she announces. One by one she offers them. She changes temple blocks from big to small and back; shoes from empty to full and back; a dime from present to absent and back; black and white to colored and back; red to blue and green.

I am impressed. She is poised and performing well. She definitely understands how to manufacture an illusion. Still, I think, she could benefit from a few tips, and better strategies for concealing what she is doing at the moment of the switch. I am excited to share them with her.

We applaud loudly and cheer her on. As the energy wanes I offer: "Could I give you a suggestion or two?" She nods. I go around behind her table to where she stores her props.

Suddenly, she is howling. "Don't go back there! Get out! Get out! Mom!"

I freeze. "I was just going to show you…"

"Get out of there! Don't look!" she interrupts. She is beside herself. Sobbing violently, hunched over. "You are going to know how I did it!" she exclaims.

Geoff motions for me to get out from behind the table. I come slowly, not quite sure of what is happening. Surely, she must have known that we could tell how she was doing her tricks? Slowly it dawns. She wants us to think that she is actually doing magic. She wants to be magic in our eyes. She wants us to believe in her tricks — to believe in her.

I kneel down in front of her. I can't lie. I tell her yes, I do know how she did the tricks. "But Jessica," I continue, "You are magic. You do magic all the time, and I will never figure out how. You pull words out of thin air and make up stories I couldn't. You invent worlds and games and I don't know how. You transform ordinary characters you meet in books into magical persons who play with you. You change yourself into animals — a cat, a dog, a horse — with a characterization that is so real. You are magic in so many ways that will always be a mystery to me."

She calms down, but still won't let me behind her table. I don't press it.

Talking afterwards, Geoff and I realize something else. Jessica didn't just want us to believe she was magic. She wanted us to believe *so that she could show us how it was done*. She wanted to have the information we lacked and then give it to us.

The pleasure she wanted in doing her tricks was not a function of mastering objects. It was the pleasure of *creating a relationship* with us in which she could be who she wanted to be—the one with the secret, the one capable of creating something out of nothing. The one who could make her tricks real for us and for herself. She wanted the *power to name*.

ભ

Are humans made in the image of God? If so, we are made in the image of breathing. For God is breathing — *spirit* moving over the face of the deep. God is the breathing that funds the words that name what is and make it real.

Naming, God creates God as a creator. Would God be God if God had not called the universe into form? Would God be God if there were no humans to believe in God as their mover and cause?

If we read the act of naming as an act of mastery, we misread the beginning. We misunderstand the power that we share with God.

The power to name is a power to *breathe*. It is a power to create and recreate the *relationships* we need with whatever and whomever will enable us to keep creating and becoming who we are. It is a power to *move* in ways that *make* those life enabling relationships *real*.

We breathe to keep breathing. We name to keep naming. And when we exercise our power to name in ways that allow us to keep breathing and moving and naming, we feel pleasure—the kind of pleasure that gifts us with vitality, direction, and a deep affirmation of life.

It is the pleasure of unfolding the potential of our *self-creating bodily movement* and discovering what we have to give.

०॰ *In the beginning 2* ०॰

Ash pits ringed with footprints. Animal, people, and geometric figures painted on the walls. Remnants of stone tools; female figurines scattered about. Long abandoned, the traces of early human culture often found in caves leave much to the modern imagination. Who were these people? What did they see? What did they do? What did they think and feel about birth, life, and death? Did they speak? When did they begin naming their goddesses and gods?

From what scholars can discern, in the beginning humans danced. The footprints suggest that early humans engaged in rhythmic, patterned bodily movement, usually in a circle around a fire, source of heat and light. Perhaps they moved to the sound of hands clapping or sticks beating, and probably with others. Images on the walls show people in animal skins, wearing animal masks. Perhaps the movements they made invoked the movements of these animals as well. Perhaps they made the movements they practiced elsewhere too, while walking through the forest or across the plains, gathering nuts or harvesting berries, hunting prey.

Invariably, after documenting such early signs of culture, scholars ask *why* with the same suspicion they direct towards religion. The question invites a response that scholars will recognize as "rational," namely, one that serves some function in relation to human survival.

So scholars hazard conclusions. People danced to secure mastery over the animals on whom they depended for food, clothing, and shelter. They danced to prepare for the hunt, to celebrate the hunt, to worship the animals they hunted. They danced to stay warm or to affirm communal bonds. They danced to develop physical strength. They danced to make something happen. *Magic*.

Yet wresting a rational explanation from these dances produces a paradox common to studies of religious phenomena. If the dance can be explained rationally, then the *act* of dancing is not significant. Conversely, if a people believe that the act of dancing is significant, it must be because they have not yet developed the same powers of rationality that "we" have. Instead, they confuse the natural and supernatural. They believe that their dances will actually make the rain come or the animal surrender; that there actually are gods and goddesses in the trees and mountains. When the people develop words, the theory goes, they will learn to mark similarities and differences among things. They will notice and predict causal relationships; and they will learn to distinguish god from nature and name "god" properly. They will stop dancing, for they will have a more efficient means of naming and communicating with each other and their gods.

Such perspectives on "primitive" dances, and there are many, rest on an assumption that is open to debate. They presume that it is *easy* to dance an animal dance. *Just move your body*. They presume that dancing is a nascent form of symbolic representation—a kind of naming as mastery—where the gestures in a dance represent an animal much as the word "bear" calls to mind the idea of a large, furry, and threatening mammal. From this perspective, dance equals movement plus meaning. Body plus mind.

But is it so easy *to dance*? Think about it. To dance like an animal, you must learn from the animal how to make its movements. You have to observe closely for a considerable time, and allow the animal's patterns of shape and energy to register in your sensory awareness. You have to experiment and discover in yourself patterns of sensation and response that allow you to recreate in yourself the movements you observe the animal making.

Then, as you begin to make these movements, the movements make you. You change. Your movements make you into someone who can make those movements, with all the coordination, agility, grace, and strength required. These movements make you into someone who knows your own capacity for creating and becoming patterns of sensation and response. A dancer.

In this view, dancing an animal dance is not a simple act of linking movement to a thing. In dancing this dance, a dancer *is creating a relationship* to that animal—a relationship characterized by attention, surrender, and respect. In dancing this dance, a dancer is honoring the animal for challenging her to *unfold a movement-making potential* in herself that she might otherwise not have discovered. She is acknowledging, by dancing, that her relationship to this animal is *enabling her to become who she is,* not just someone who is well-fed, warm, sheltered, and successful at reproducing, but someone who *knows the pleasure* of making movement, someone who can tap the sources of her freedom and creativity in making such movements.

Dancing, we become people who can greet any animal, person, tradition, or god as offering us an opportunity to learn more about our own capacity for making movement. As life enabling. Dancing, we breathe ourselves into being.

What I want from an animal is not meat. What I want is the feeling of my own power — the strength I feel in myself when I honor what appears to me as good, worthy, and beautiful.

What I want is the pleasure of naming and making real the relationships that support me in becoming who my bodily self is and can be.

If we read animal dances as a kind of mastery, we misread the beginning again. Dancing, like naming, is a style of breathing. When we dance, we create and make real the relationships with the animals, persons, places, and things that enable us to explore and develop our own movement-making potential. We bring this network of relationships to life as the condition of our unfolding. We give what we have to give.

To name another, or to dance another, is to acknowledge our debt to that other for enabling us to become who we are.

CR

Jordan and Jessica hop off the bus and run onto the front porch.

"Where's Zelsha?" they ask. We adopted our cat the day before. That morning, Geoff and I put her outside on the porch, after all she was to be an outdoor cat. She had food, a litter box, and a bed. But when we all go to look, she isn't there.

"How could you?" Jessica screams. "How could you put her outside? Why didn't you watch her?" Her sobs are clenched with anger. She stands there in front of me, glaring, accusing.

Jordan stands right beside her. "You could have waited," he says, only a bit more quietly. "You could have waited until we got home. But you didn't. And now she's gone!"

"It's your fault!" adds Jessica. They are already so attached.

"She'll come home," I say with some conviction.

They do not believe me. Our cat is gone, and she was barely even ours. We had found her by responding to a flier posted in a shop window. The flier told of a mother cat and her four kittens. We wanted a kitten. We were too late. The kittens were all gone. Left behind was their mother, a small calico stray, no more than a year old herself. She was visibly tender, suffering from the engorged nipples her little ones had left behind. Empathy welled in me. She was beautiful, clear-eyed, and friendly even in her discomfort. Jordan, Jessica, and Kyra hovered around her, admiring her.

"She was someone's baby," the storeowner explained. "She loves to cuddle when she is not so sore."

"Can we keep her?" Kyra asked.

Geoff and I deliberated at the back of the store. Should we take the mother? Perhaps there were advantages with having a cat that was older and more mature. We needed muscle to fight our mice. Besides, the storeowner was eager to find her a good home.

"Everyone wants kittens," she said, "No one wants a cat."

We left with a cat.

When we got home, the children disappeared into the living room.

"Kids' Council!" Jordan cried. Minutes later they returned.

"We have decided upon a name," Jessica announced.

Jordan stepped up: "Zelsha." *Zelsha*? I thought.

"How did you choose that name?" I asked.

"I made it up," said Jordan. "We thought of other names, but not all of us liked them. Then I thought up this name, and everyone liked it." Zelda? Sasha? No, Zelsha. It was going to take a while.

"Sure," said Geoff, "as long as I can call her 'Zelly.'"

We named the cat. Now she was missing. We had in no way ensured our mastery over her — only our vulnerability to her.

"She is a very smart cat," Geoff affirms. "She will return."

"How can you be so positive?" Jessica yells. "You don't know! You don't know that she will come back. You can't be sure."

"You are right," I reply. "She might not come back. But she might — she probably will."

"I looked forward to seeing her all day," laments Jordan. "And now she is not here. She could be eaten by a wild animal!"

"If she doesn't come back," Jessica adds, "I am never going to school again. You can't make me go! I will stay home and watch my animals." She collects herself a bit then dissolves again. "How could you? Why didn't you wait for us? Why didn't you watch her?"

Geoff and I look at each other, feeling very low. I wanted the cat outside. My nose was itching, my eyes were watering. I do not want furry creatures in my house. I want a cat to get rid of the furry creatures in my house. But I also want my children to be happy and well, and they are not. We walk around the yard, calling her name. I think about driving up and down the street. What would I hope to find?

We finally decide to go for a walk. If the cat is not home when we return, we will go looking for her in the car.

Halfway up our hill, Jessica pipes up: "May I go home?" We let her go. Half an hour later, we return to find her on the porch, stroking Zelsha. I kneel beside them.

Jessica turns to me and smiles. "I'm sorry I got so angry with you earlier, Mom."

I smile back, deeply relieved. Jessica had been right. The cat could have decided not to stay. She had not named us.

Now, when Jessica gets off the bus and Zelsha is not there, she announces confidently, "I am not worried. Zelsha will come home."

ʘ

A cat appeared to us, and she appeared to us as more than "a cat." That more called for a name. She was something we desired. The kids invented a name — Zelsha. Zelsha is not a name for the idea of cat or for cat in general. It is a name for my children's sensation of this particular cat and their responses to her. The name they chose represents the *relationship* with this cat they desire; it represents their yearning to know her, enjoy her, take care of her, and become people who know how to take care of her. In naming her they were expressing their desire to live in a world where she would enable them to become who they want to be: cat lovers.

When Zelsha was not there that first afternoon, however, all her name represented was a huge gaping hole. Pain. Vulnerability. Zelsha was gone. Even so, what they missed most was not "her" per se. They barely knew her. What they missed was the pleasure they were planning to experience in relation to her, the pleasure of doing concrete acts, feeding her, combing her, and being what she needed to thrive.

If Zelsha had not returned to claim her name, my kids would have lost the pleasure of their own life-sustaining power that she was enabling them to experience. They needed her for that. They named her for that. They loved her for that.

ଔ

You. I name You because you matter to me. I name you because you impress me as something and not nothing. You move me.

In naming you I acknowledge my debt to you: I am indebted to you for awakening patterns of sensation and response in me that are unique to you (and me). I am indebted to you for helping me be the "me" I know and want myself to be.

You. As I name you, your name holds open a space of myself, a space of vulnerability to you, where I feel my power. That power is not one of mastery or dominion. It is a power to notice you, to be moved by you, to respond to you, and to make myself into someone who moves towards you, with you, because of you.

The power of naming is a power of *love.*

The implication here is radical. As I name *you* — person, place, animal, or god — I commit myself to act in relation to you in ways that will allow you to flourish. I do so *as* the very condition of my own ongoing well being.

You. The movements I make in naming you are the movements that allow me to become who I am. To dance my dance. To make real a world I love that loves me.

Naming you, I honor my obligation to let you live.

ଔ *In the beginning 3* ଔ

Being born, emerging from the water world, we are a mesh of movement patterns that guides us in gathering what we need — nourishment, intimacy, affirmation — as we follow the arcs of our pleasure.

New to the air world, we continue generating patterns of sensation and response, animating, refining, and rehearsing our

221

sense of touch in order to learn more. We move in response to how we are touched by sounds and visual shapes. We copy gestures, finding in ourselves patterns of movement that enable us to recreate the movements that appear to us. We return a smile, stare at our fists, mirror a wave. *We dance.*

Finally, after a year or so, we begin to generate an awareness of how to move our mouths, tongues, and lips to make sounds. Watching others and listening to them, we form words. We copy mouth shapes and ear noises. We ask for food, a hug, or a favorite toy by name instead of twisting our bodies, reaching, grabbing, or crying out. Words appear in us as new patterns of sensation and response, as refined versions of the movement patterns we have already been making. *We name.*

A few years later, as we enter more fully into the realm of words, as we learn to read and to write, we begin to forget that words are gestures too whose effect is primarily aural. We get so good at making the movement needed to produce them that the words just seem to erupt "naturally" within us, spilling into our brains and from our mouths.

Our sense of ourselves evolves. Using words we create ourselves as persons who can name, who know themselves as naming, who communicate with other people by naming, and who get great pleasure out of doing so. Over time, we come to believe that words have the power to carry information from one time and space to another, from one culture to another, between worlds. We grow convinced that words can exist apart from our bodies in a separate realm. The felt experience of using words itself encourages us to perceive the act of naming as a mental act, an act of mastery, mind over body.

When we begin to believe that words float free from particular bodies, we fall prey to the *intoxication of naming*. It is then that we imagine *we* have the power to *name* the *nature* of all things. We imagine that we *have* what we name. That it is ours — my self, my god, my religion. When cracks in our sense of "I" threaten to topple us — a hunger for food, an obsession with sex, or feelings of despair—we respond by wielding the power of words: if we can name it, we can solve it. *The problem is desire.*

It is not. We learn to name and blame desire only after learning to speak and read and write—only after the exacting physical discipline involved. We must learn first to exploit the potential of our bodily movement to create images of itself, that is of ourself. We learn to think the thought: I think, therefore I am. But the thinking is not what makes it true. The mind over body movements we have learned to make make it true.

When a word pattern seems to work we repeat it again and again, placing our faith in the words themselves rather than in our ability to create them. Our repertoire of responses slowly shrinks, our ability to create new patterns declines, and soon we are operating within a world of words, immured from the ongoing currents of our sensory life, and preferring it that way. Feeling our energies ebb, we imagine that we are getting old.

We can remember, however, that words are gestures too. We can remember that naming is a species of dancing. We can remember that the pleasure our desire for spirit seeks is a pleasure of making the movements that will bring into being the relationships we need to unfold who we are.

When we remember, we know what to do. To dislodge the mind over body pursuit of spirit that is perpetuating our depression and despair, we need to cultivate the sensory awareness that will enable us to find, in our experiences of pain, a wisdom guiding us to create these relationships—to name and make real a world we love that loves us.

જી

We are animals for whom physical survival is not enough. We desire more from life, and not because we are genetically or culturally programmed to do so. We desire more because we are bodies who can and must move in order to experience their pleasure and their power.

Our movement is making us.

Pleasure is our guide.

It is the pleasure of creating beyond ourselves, of giving birth to ourselves, that stirs in us a sense of vitality. It is the pleasure of learning from our pain how to be free from it that gives us a sense of direction. It is the pleasure of moving in ways that enable us to keep moving, growing and becoming who we are, that awakens in us a sense that life is and our lives are worth living.

The wisdom in our desire for spirit, then, is calling us to move. It is calling us to be the breathing, in-spiriting, kinetic image of god, to honor what moves us — ecosystem, tree, lover, or god — with an obligation to let live. It is calling us to *name* and *make real* a world we love that loves us.

This play is serious.

So how do we do it?

20

Time to Move

'We must reckon with the fact that dancing in itself, like every
other swift movement, brings with it a kind of intoxication of
the whole vascular, nervous, and muscular system.'
— *Will to Power* #807, 425

I can't move! I am flat on my back. The pain is intense.

It is an interesting time to be in such a position, to put it
mildly. I am five months pregnant with my fourth child. I am on
the cusp of a major transition in my life, setting out to write a
book about bodies and what they know. All I want to do is to
read, research, and write. To sit. Yet here I lie. It is very
depressing.

My thoughts roam over the months before. The pain came on
gradually. I had been perched for long hours at the computer,
keen on finishing the last project in a fifteen-year arc I had spent
studying, teaching, and publishing in the field of religious
studies.

My lower back, down around the sacroiliac joint, began to
cramp. It was a chronic trouble spot, one I have learned to
negotiate over the years in my life as a dancer. Yet none of my
guaranteed methods for relieving the ache were working. I tried
stretching, shifting chair positions, crossing and uncrossing
my legs, and varying my exercise routine. The discomfort
persisted.

Then one night, after spending much of the afternoon picking
up stray toys, I reached over in bed to turn out the light. *Spasm.*
Seizing pain radiated up and down the right side of my back. I

fell back on the bed to wait until morning, hoping for the best. Morning came and there I was. The pain was no better. I could not imagine moving. The thought of getting into a car to see a doctor was overwhelming. Geoff and I juggled schedules. Jordan (nine) and Jessica (seven) would walk Kyra (three) to daycare up the street on their way to school. The daycare provider would drop her off at home. Geoff would take care of everything else.

I can't move. My thoughts float back to the present. Everyone is gone. The house is quiet. What now? What is there to do? Nothing.

No, not nothing. I know what I have to do. I have to ride the downward pull of my emotions into the pain itself and figure out what is going on inside of me. I breathe deeply, and allow myself to feel the hurt. I breathe waves of light through the muscles, ligaments, and bones—golden, rose, purple, and green. Releasing into the sensation, I look for a way *through* it down to the health I know must lie beneath it. I breathe down into the earth. *How should I move?*

Sure enough, a realization filters through.

I have lost my body and I want it back.

Lost my body? I still have a body, of course. The pain is proof enough of that. But I know what I mean. The movements I have been making, sitting and studying, have been making me sick. I have been exercising my mind over my hurting body, exercising power *against myself*, for so long that I have walled myself in my mind, cut off from my own sensory experience.

The body I have lost is a particular experience of my body – a sensory awareness of my body's movement. I am no longer calling on this sensory awareness to *guide* me along the path of my own becoming. I am no longer in touch with how to move in ways that are good for me.

I want my body back.

The message is loud and clear. But how? My thoughts drift to the book I am planning — this one. I want to write about the wisdom in desire, and about how we find it by cultivating a sensory awareness of our own bodily movement.

The irony does not escape me. Here I am, experiencing in the flesh, the very dynamic I intend to describe in the book. I am so fixed on getting the book done, so afraid that it might not get done, that I have been ignoring any sensations that suggest I move differently. I have been hoping the pain in my back would just go away.

Frustration surges and explodes in a burst of insight. *I can't write the book I want to write if I am overriding my own sensory awareness to do so. I must write in a way that remains faithful to the bodily self that writes!*

But how? Doubt spills through me. *If I am not sitting and writing, nothing will get done!*

Lying there, I realize I have little choice. I have to risk welcoming these sensations as information guiding me to whatever it is I am to do. I inhale slowly and deeply into and through my heart.

I imagine love, trickling and cascading through me, flooding my sensory cells.

It feels awkward. The love seems clotted, disconnected from my body. It bumps up against fears, doubts, cultural mores, and the childhood lessons I thought I had already released and relearned. *How dare I listen to my body?*

I breathe deeply and release the length of my bodily self into the earth, feeling the earth's ever-present ground and support. A flare of awareness. Something lets go and something wakes up. I feel an impulse to move, small at first. I wiggle my toes and rotate my ankles.

I breathe down, finding my connection to the earth again, and then open the sensation, allowing my skin to dissolve into soft air. Another wave surges, stretching open my fingers, wrists, and arms. I follow the breathing back down into the cradle of my pelvis, and stir the embers of my own well being. Another pulse, aligning belly, shoulders, and head in an arc of intent.

Minutes turn into hours. I invite and receive impulse after impulse to move, and breathe them through. Every impulse gently traces the edges of my pain, receding at the slightest twang, opening where it can.

It is as if my bodily self is moving itself, moving me. I am finding *play* in the moment. Possibilities I couldn't think before are happening through me. It occurs to me: I am somehow tapping into a wisdom that is guiding me to move in ways that are both healing and pleasing. My feet flex and point, my hips rock back and forth, muscle patterns deep in my belly contract and release. *It doesn't hurt. I don't hurt. It feels so good to move.*

Moving, I remember. *I am a dancer.*

The thought bubbles up, as it has many times before, a name for me, an awareness that I can't seem to help ignoring. It is a desire to dance that, when it surfaces, feels as close as I have ever come to a sense of who I am. It hovers, a vague and unspecified sense of what I need to do in order to feel the vitality, direction, and belonging I seek. My desire for spirit. *I am a dancer.*

With this knowledge, pulled along by it, comes the dream that Geoff and I have nurtured for ten years: the dream of buying land, moving out of the city, and creating a place, a sanctuary, where we can create our arts and ideas, raise our family, and do so in closer proximity to the rhythms of the natural world. A place where I can dance to write and write to dance. We want to create a way of living that will nourish each member of our family in unfolding whatever we each have to offer. *Remember? Don't you remember?*

More days pass. I surrender to the rhythms of this play in movement. There is nothing else to do. Nothing else that matters. Flat on my back, following the flow of my breathing, I wander into uncharted spans of bodily awareness. I find novel connections between ankle and hip, shoulder and toe. I make movements I have never made before, unfolding brand new patterns of sensation and response in me.

As the pain subsides, I know. *The movement that my body is making is making me.* My movement *is* making me. I can feel it. The movement I am making is not only healing my back, it is making me into someone who responds to my body's pain by making such movements. Someone who finds the resources she needs to heal in the practice of moving. Someone who desires this dance; someone who wants to bring into being the matrix of relationships that will support her in becoming the dancer she is.

The movement that is making me, as limited as it is, is unraveling the sense of myself as mind over body that I perfected while sitting. It is freeing me to *name* and *make real* the world in which I can be the self I want to be. *I have to dance.*

At first I suspect that my worst fears were true. I will not write the book. My desires are pointing elsewhere, towards dance.

But slowly, as my mobility returns, I experience play in my desire to dance. It is not so either/or. It is the practice of dancing that is and has been teaching me what I need to know not only to get *my* body back, but to write the book I want to write. My practice is the research, the field work, that is allowing me to explore, develop, and eventually name a concrete approach for finding, trusting, and moving with the wisdom in desire.

A cycle of breaths.

I rise from the weeks on my back with a renewed sense of vitality and direction, and a renewed connection to my work. I will write the book I want to write, and to do so I will honor this desire to dance and move with my dream to realize it.

I have no idea how.

ɔ꙰

Nearly a month after I am up and about, Jessica calls me into the living room.

"Mom, come look at this."

Jessica, age seven at the time, is sitting at the computer, surfing the web for real estate. Jessica, a girl who has always known what she wants and has always asked, is looking for farms, preferably in Vermont. She wants animals, lots of them. A horse (or several), cats and dogs, chickens and turtles. I put her off for a while, unloading the dishwasher, cleaning up the dinner mess, and then go to take a look. She has found a farmhouse, on twenty-two acres. It is a charming house, four bedrooms and two bathrooms. An extra seventy-three acres are available. It is affordable. "Interesting," I tell her.

Off she goes to play with Jordan and Kyra. I sit down to investigate. Jessica surfs the web for real estate often, but usually lands on million dollar properties in Colorado. This farm is the first that is in line with the dream Geoff and I have for our lives. When Geoff returns home later after playing his weekly dinner set, I drowsily direct him to the site. "Take a look."

"Interesting," he replies. We fall asleep.

For the next three days I can think of nothing else. I am gripped, as if by a huge wave that is lifting me up and hurtling me forward. Ideas for the place well and crest unbidden. I move through the living room, dining room, and kitchen – the heart of the house. I pick paint colors for bedrooms I have never seen and arrange the furniture.

I imagine myself dancing and writing, working out my future, ringed with family, and wrapped in the open beauty of the land.

April 9: Two days later, Geoff and I are still talking. He encourages me to contact the real estate agent. According to the agent, the land is gorgeous. The farmhouse needs work. "When can you come see the place?" We set a date.

April 9. Later it hits me. April 9 is Grandpa Peter's birthday. Or, it would have been. He died in January, three months earlier. A generous, brilliant man, he had been separated from us by a wall built of his addiction to alcohol. Only one thing could breach the wall, and then just for a moment: to talk about his life on the farm.

Peter grew up on a dairy farm in northern Ohio with his sister and two brothers, and as long as Geoff had known him, his father yearned for that farm; for his prize winning cow, Daisy Mae; for onions and tomatoes fresh from the garden; for his mother's freshly baked bread; for a life of physical work, outdoors, taking care of animals and the land. Here it was, on what should have been his seventieth birthday, and we were thinking of buying a farm and pursuing the life he loved.

May 14: Driving out the Mass Pike, all five of us, we discuss our plans. We won't move. We are going to stay where we are. Geoff is teaching what he loves to teach, in a place he is content to be. Jordan and Jessica are happily involved in a vibrant school community; Kyra is signed up for preschool in the fall. I will write my book in the study I love, in a house I adore, along a street peopled with a diverse group of friends where we have lived for thirteen years, with family close by. I will give birth with the assistance of midwives I have met and whose professionalism I respect.

Even so, we agree, there is no harm in looking. Besides, it is a nice day for a drive.

Graffiti on a rock wall catches my eye. I turn and read: HORSE. JESSICA.

"Did you see that?!" I exclaim. The words are already gone. Did I see them?

We meet the agent at the site.

"Let's go up to the land first," he offers. We climb into his Jeep and drive down the road to another access path. Up, up, and around we go, through a lovely open meadow basin with huge round hay bales to a hill with views of the Green Mountains to the east, a pond down to the west, forest and hills all around. A higher hilltop with a large rock is straight ahead. We are breathing deeply. We walk along the crest of the hill, down a bit and up to the rock, Moon Rock. *The view!*

Jordan, who until now has vigorously opposed the idea of moving, pulls me aside and sits me down on the grass.

"Mom, this is the first place I can really see us being." I nod.

We go down to the house. Yes, it needs work, but there is a large living room with an oak floor, wooden beams, and a relatively new brick fireplace. It has the one thing we absolutely need: one room where we can have a piano and space to dance.

After the real estate agent leaves, we sit behind one of the ramshackle barns and have a family discussion. It is a lot. A lot of land, a lot of mess. A lot to take care of. *Is it ours?*

We all chime in. Jordan and Jessica have made up their minds. Kyra plays in the hay.

We drive to the agent's office and place an offer. We drive four hours home.

May 15: The phone rings. Our offer has been accepted. Jessica's farm is ours. Two weeks later, we put our house on the market and sell it the same weekend. We prepare to move at the end of June.

It is time to follow my desire to dance and write the book I want to write. Without the weeks on my back, I wouldn't have been ready. The pain that initially depressed me as an obstacle holding me back catalyzed the shift in my experience that enabled me to move forward, with clarity and courage, in pursuit of conditions that would enable me to dance.

I can hardly believe it. The pain freed me from the mind over body strategies I was leaning on to pursue my goals. It compelled me to dial down, tune in, and sense impulses to move lodged deep within my lingering dissatisfaction with what I was doing.

Breathing down, out, into, and through the knots I heard my desire for spirit. The meaning of the pain changed. It was calling me to do what I most wanted to do, and making it possible. My gratitude is boundless.

ભ

So it is that six weeks later, nine months pregnant, I am camping out in the living room of a drab, insect-infested, leaky-roofed, antiquated dwelling, with no heat or running water other than the flow from one cold tap. We are home. Not one room is habitable.

Impelled by our impending arrival, we act quickly. We hire a contractor to replace the plumbing, reinvigorate the well pump, and exchange old water heater and furnace for new. I paint the one room we all live in, and we begin to demolish the rest, the laundry room, downstairs bathroom, kitchen, den, and two of the bedrooms.

A month later, on August 3, 2005, Kai Evenson LaMothe arrives. He is born at home. We are days shy of a shower; weeks short of a working kitchen. We aren't anywhere close to finished.

In the weeks that follow, as Kai unfolds into his body, we bring the house slowly back to life, helped along by visiting family. Geoff and I purchase, assemble, and mount kitchen cabinets; install electrics for dishwasher, disposal, and range hood; we lay pine wood floors in the laundry room and kitchen; replace bathroom fixtures and tile the bathroom floor. We supervise the reshingling of the roof and the construction of a twenty-five foot shed dormer; we prep, prime, and paint wall after wall after wall.

The hardest work is reminding ourselves constantly of how far we have come in the face of all that remains. Every day, we make it outside, if only for a moment, to breathe the air, walk the property, admire the sunrise, the sunset, the stars.

We name our farm Hebron Hollow.

I begin to write.

21

The Ends of Life

'You creators... One is pregnant only with one's own child.'
— *Zarathustra*, 402

The challenge to finding the spirit we desire is not what we have learned to believe it is. It is not a matter of managing our seemingly insatiable desire for affirmation in a world that seems indifferent to our needs. It is not a matter of choosing the right principles, programs, or preachers to guide our actions.

It is a matter of tuning in to the movements that are making us—the trajectories of sensation and insight arcing through us—and cultivating relationships with the ideas, teachers, communities, nature, practices, and friends that will enable these arcs to continue growing within us.

In this process, the hardest moment is when we open to our experience of desiring itself. It is far easier not to do so. Because we desire, we feel pain. We feel the pain of wanting and not getting, the pain of searching and not finding, the pain of doubting and not knowing for sure who we are, where we are going, or why we are here.

This pain may surface as a lingering discomfort, a partial satisfaction, or an acute stab of an opportunity lost. It may percolate in regret or dismay, in feelings of injustice and revenge.

Such desire-induced pain, as physical as it is emotional, pushes us to the ends of what we can endure, and we want it to stop. *It makes no sense.* It scares us, as almost no other kind of pain can, into thinking that we are not enough, we will never be enough. We will never have the touch we want, or the affirmation.

The challenge is this: How do we open to embrace the pain we feel as an expression of our desire for spirit? How do we welcome this pain as an incredible gift? Can we find in it a wisdom that is guiding us to name and make real the matrix of relationships that will support us in becoming who we are?

Yes. It is a question of inviting the shift in experience that enables us to navigate the mouth-watering pull of an Oreo, and ride the waves of our yuck feelings in a partner relationship.

We need the sensory awareness that enables us to know, in our bodies, that the pain of this desire is a pain that is teaching us how to be free from that pain. It is not an obstacle to our desire, but an enabling condition of our forthcoming pleasure. It is a pain that is teaching us how to give birth to ourselves.

∞

Every human being is born. Every human living has the bodily experience of moving out from the womb, from water to air, when it has not yet learned to think of itself as mind over body.

In religious and spiritual traditions around the world, birth is one of the most potent metaphors used to symbolize the act of entering into a spiritual life, finding a calling, or joining a community of the faithful. We are *born again*, this time of the *spirit*, often in rituals modeled on the physical act of giving birth.

In contemporary culture, with its marketplace of spiritual and medical offerings, we learn to approach the act of being born as a bodily problem best managed by the collective mind of the medical profession. Women and men are told that the "safest" way to give birth is in a hospital, on our backs, wired to machines, letting the nurses and doctors drive. We learn that the pain of birth is irrelevant and optional, that the separation between mother and child is a merely physical concern.

On the other hand, we learn to believe that the safest way to a spiritual re-birth is in a church, synagogue, temple, or retreat center where, sitting in stillness, listening to words, we let the religious authorities, gurus, or self-help experts drive. We frame our spiritual birth as one that frees us from any need for pain at all, or justifies an endless supply of it until we pass from this world into the next.

We buy into these ways of thinking about birth because they comfort us. If they are true, we can rest assured that authorities in either the medical or clerical realm can guarantee us a safe delivery. We will not suffer unnecessary pain. *Separate from your body. Trust the experts. They know better.*

However, when we approach natural birth as a mechanical process of getting a body out, and thin our understanding of spiritual birth to a mental act of getting the right belief in, we drive an all too familiar wedge between sense and spirit. We cut ourselves off from the wisdom in our physical and emotional pain that is guiding us how to be free from it. We feel the pinch.

❦

Home birth? We aren't planning one. We are planning to deliver at a hospital under the care of midwives. After moving to the farm, however, I receive disheartening news from the midwives I meet: *We can't support you in having a vaginal birth if you have already had a cesarean section.* Jordan was delivered by cesarean section. Jessica and Kyra were born naturally. Why not this fourth child too?

"Our local hospitals don't have an anesthesiologist on the premises 24/7 as state law requires," the midwife explains. The fear behind this law is that a previously stitched uterus will rupture. A deadly, painful risk. I know.

Our options are these. I can "choose" to schedule a cesarean section a week before my due date, that is, to undergo unnecessary major surgery, complete with the risks of infection contracted in the hospital, adverse reactions of mother or infant to drugs, or detours in the healing process. Or, I can "choose" to have a vaginal birth at a city hospital an hour and a half away from my home, that is, to be in full labor during the car journey and run the risk, given this is my fourth birth, of delivering en route.

The risks of a home birth pale in comparison.

I have always wanted one.

Still, we wonder. Can we find someone who will support a pregnant woman over forty in her ninth month who had a cesarean previously and who planned to deliver in an unfinished farm house? We do. We like her instantly. Everything she says, we believe to be true. *Birth is a natural process. Your body knows what to do. Trust your bodily self. Listen to it. Follow its lead.*

❦

I gave birth in a hospital three times before I admitted how thoroughly the medical community teaches us to trust its collective mind over a woman's laboring body. There are high beds to mount that encourage a sense of helplessness; cold, concrete floors that forbid touching; monitors to check, measurements to document, a rotating roster of strangers peering into one's private parts, and a pervasive climate of authority that erodes confidence in one's own bodily self.

The sheer presence of medical technology in the room creates a default pressure to use it, even when unnecessary, and even among those who would otherwise resist it. The instruments breed fear — fear of the pain they are supposed to help avoid. That fear cements a dependence on those machines to tell us what is happening and what to do. Room, protocol, and personnel thus cooperate to create an environment where it is nearly impossible *not* to doubt whether your bodily self knows anything at all.

The evident, proven power of medicine to sustain us in the face of death makes it so difficult to have faith in what gives life: *our self-creating, self-healing bodily movement.*

This time, I vowed, will be different. In giving birth, I will place my faith in the ability of my body to sense and respond to what I am feeling in the moment as my primary guide to health and well being.

Planning a home birth, I feel the radical edge. *Am I crazy?*

જી

A month and a half after Kai was born, the chief Obstetrician/Gynecologist at a hospital where I had planned to deliver, was arrested for drunk driving on his way to perform an emergency cesarean section.

જી

August 3: We all pile in the car and drive to meet the midwife. It is the day that my small traveler is due. After the appointment we stop at a bakery for muffins and scones before driving another hour to Home Depot. We buy more tiles for the bathroom floor and drive another hour home. I am crampy, restless. It is very hot. A swim would be nice, but the bathroom is still not done.

Home again, I sit down to finish the tiles. White squares. Black squares. I love tiling. It is like doing a big puzzle and being right in the middle of it. I can sit, squat, waddle about. I laugh as I plop down and tip over.

It is 6 o'clock. Time to stop for dinner. As I am changing out of my dusty work clothes, a contraction grips my belly.

Is this it? How do I know? Will labor start? Will the contractions continue? Will they stop again? I have no idea what to think. I have been thinking such thoughts for weeks. It is a bit tiring.

Geoff insists, "Call." I don't want to be a problem. I just want to curl up and sleep. He calls the midwife and leaves a message.

By 7:20 it is still happening. We call the midwife again. She is coming. It will take her an hour and a half to get here. We leave a message for my parents.

I lie down. The contractions are manageable. I count for a while. I get up and fold laundry. It occurs to me, *I don't have to go anywhere else.* Relief cascades through me. I can just be here, at home. Trusting my body, tuning in to what I need.

The kids are having ice cream. I walk into the kitchen to be with them and their bright smiling youth. I lean over on the table. Yes, I am reminded, what I am going through is worth it. My fear eases. *Look at these beautiful creatures.* I show them my belly. "Say goodbye belly!" We laugh.

It is 8:30. Geoff is reading to the kids in a beanbag chair in the upstairs hallway outside the bathroom. I crawl into the bathtub. The contractions are more intense, but still manageable. They require a bit more concentration. I breathe. The sound of Geoff's voice comforts me. He is close. They are close. I love how he loves the children. In loving them, he is loving me. Loving us. I am happy to be in the tub. Alone. Surrounded.

I close my eyes and bow my head, yielding to the force of a contraction. The pressure is intense. I breathe down into the earth. I dive into the center of the contraction and look for currents of sensation to carry me though. I try to catch the wave and ride it. I burst forth from the contraction. It is as if my head and body are breaking through the crest of an ocean wave. In the wake of the wave, bliss rushes in. I open my eyes.

She is there, my midwife, perched beside the tub, beaming. I did not hear her enter. She is wearing turquoise blue, warm and bright.

I am still in the tub. Something breaks. My water meets bath water. Dark green clouds float around me. Meconium. Is the baby in distress?

The midwife listens with an underwater Doppler. Everything is fine. I get out. Draw a breath, draw another bath, and relax back into the warmth.

I am too hot. I have to get out. I go downstairs. It is too dry down here. Too open. I have to go to the bathroom. I go back upstairs. The contractions are coming faster now. I can't breathe through them alone.

The kids are asleep. I need Geoff. I wrap my arms around his waist and hang on tight. Oh this is intense.

The midwife pipes in: *Breathe. Breathe down and out. Sink into your body. Allow yourself to open. Open, open, open.*

The words seep in through my pores. Something shifts, my pelvis tilts and angles. I notice. Oh my. This is the position I have been trying to find for years in dance. A passage opens, for me, for my little one. I try to get back to that place. Down, open, out. The contraction squeezes consciousness away. I call for my midwife. I call for Geoff. *Help me. Speak to me. Hold me.* They do.

10 o'clock. I want to push. I try not to. I am afraid of pushing too soon, tiring myself out, slowing the process. I reach up and feel the baby's head. It is coming. Oh my god. High up. A small hard circle. *When you feel ready.* The midwife's words echo through my sensory space.

The burning – I forgot about this part – as I push, searing, stretching skin. *I am going to break apart, explode, shatter into shards of pain.* I plunge into the burning and push with every ounce I can muster, dropping into gravity, pulling on Geoff, clinging, wrapped.

He is holding me up with his arms. Knees deeply bent, my legs tremble uncontrollably. I have just enough sensory awareness to keep them under me, to keep breathing. I push again. *Oh.* The head comes out. I push again, furiously this time, not waiting for anything. *Out, out, out. Get it out!*

The contractions are all broken up and running awry, no rhyme to the rhythm. *Get it out!* It comes. Shoulders through.

A little him. The cord is around his neck, then gently unwrapped, still pulsing. My body is gibberish. Shaking, shuddering. I sit back. He is in my arms. I hold him tight against my lower belly. I did it. I did it. My baby. Our baby. *Oh! Jordan! Jessica! Kyra!*

Jordan and Jessica peek in. *Look!*

"What time is it, Jessica?" It is 10:45 pm.

I glance down. He is gray. Covered with yellow scum. A gory sight. Big and healthy. With me. With us. I am afraid he will slip away. I hold him tight. *I did it.* The kids go back to Jordan's room.

The placenta plops out. Geoff cuts the cord. He stands beside me, holding the little him as I slip back into the bath. My body barely obeys. I don't recognize it.

I struggle for a familiar sensation. Hopeless. It is all too deep. Formless. *I did it.*

I am downstairs again, lying on my bed. He is beside me. Jordan and Jessica are up again, with Geoff, surrounding us. Kyra sleeps. We all witness as he evolves, water creature to earth and air creature. Blue to pink. Wet to dry. His wide eyes watching us, watching him. Seeing. *What do you see, my little one?*

We name him with a name he gives himself: *Kai Evenson LaMothe.*

The candle in the fireplace glows, strong and clear.

∞

I feel ambivalent. How can I recommend to anyone that they go through an experience that may involve great pain? Especially when it seems that help is available. Why not dull the pain?

Isn't that true as well about life itself? Why invite a child into the world in the first place? *There is no way he will escape from pain, and his pain will be my pain.*

Is the pain of childbirth a punishment — a curse leveled against woman who ate of the tree of knowledge, by an angry god whose tree she had plucked? Is it a reminder that we are not god, despite our capacity to name animals, plants, and children? *Pain is never justified.*

Is the pain an accident of evolution, a misfit between women's bodies and conditions of abundance causing them to grow big babies? *Pain is not pointless.*

We feel pain because we want to give birth, and because we need to learn how. The pain expresses our desire to get the infant out. It guides us, if we can welcome it as such, to move in ways that get that infant out.

When we do, the experience teaches us about much more than how to give birth. It quickens our bodily, sensory capacity for welcoming the pain of any unmet desire as propelling us to do what we must to give birth to ourselves.

ᘯ

There is a time in the birth process when I reach the limits of my sensory awareness. The contractions grow too strong to handle alone. As each contraction spills over the lip of consciousness, it is increasingly difficult to release into them or relax between them. As a contraction eases, my body remembers, and I quiver in anticipation of the next. I shrink away, pulling myself up and out of my body. I hold, hold, hold, resisting the oncoming sensation. It is a time when most of us *must* lean on someone else to help us through.

It is easiest to lean on the medical community and ask for drugs. I did with Jordan, and I did because I felt as if my body was not working. *It* wasn't opening. *It* was too tense, too slow. *I* was trapped inside and had to do something. I was afraid. *Give me something to make it stop*. Take a pill. Insert an IV. Anesthetize. *My body is the problem*. Put it to sleep, manipulate it mechanically.

You need not feel the experience you are living, the experience of giving birth to a human. The experience of giving birth to yourself as a mother.

Yet the experience of Jessica's birth, Kyra's and Kai's too, taught me that there are other ways to lean.

It was Geoff, making up dreamscapes in which I soared through the air, who helped me through. It was the midwife, holding my other hand, talking in my ear, who helped me through. It was their energy, their presence, their words, their touch. I leaned and pulled and breathed through the relationships we were creating. And when I did, my experience of the pain shifted.

The pain of childbirth is a relational pain. It is not only a pain of becoming two. It is a pain that calls into being the group of people who will care for mother and child. In this moment of acute vulnerability, when all we can do is lean, our pain calls into being the network of relations that support our growing lives in that moment, and in many moments to come.

I will not forget. The pain of childbirth taught me this: *I am someone who is thoroughly and utterly dependent upon a web of relations in order to be who I am. An ever-becoming bodily self.*

∞

In the name of being born again, some teachers and traditions instruct followers to inflict pain upon themselves. Some practitioners go so far as to wound their bodies, drawing blood. Some contemplate images of pain so as to identify with pain, and find meaning for their own. Some deny their need for food, their desire for sex, and their dependence on worldly possessions, so as to speed and ensure their coming salvation.

We are taught that by inflicting pain on ourselves now, we will be born into a painless place later, a new life. *What will you give up to prove that you are worthy?*

Yet pain inflicted on our bodies in the name of an ideal is not the same as the pain of giving birth. When we consciously, willingly inflict pain on ourselves, we create and become someone who is wounded and split. We become someone for whom inner conflict is reassuring. *My pain protects me, redeems me, makes me one with the body of believers.*

What we create by inflicting pain on ourselves is a hunger we must feed with further acts of self-renunciation.

Self-inflicted pain is sick. It expresses a mind whose frustration seeks satisfaction in the only way it knows how, by watching its own body writhe. It is a pain whose sting is proof of power.

Any beauty humans manage to create in the wake of self-inflicted pain is like grass growing through cracks in broken concrete. The emergent beauty does not justify paving over sensation. It is one more argument to fetch a jackhammer.

The pain of childbirth is not self-inflicted, even if we opt not to rely on the medical profession to numb it. It is a pain that reveals, with searing intensity, our *desire to be free from pain. Our desire to give birth.* When we cultivate a sensory awareness of the pain of childbirth, we are able to use it to find ways of thinking and feeling and acting that enhance the birth process, and move us beyond the pain. Breathing into our sensory present, we find ourselves making movements that release us from the pain into the arms of those who love us.

ଔ

I know, I know. It is not always possible to give birth with or without medical intervention. The pain can be breathtaking. A matter of life or death.

Despite my best efforts, Jordan was ripped from my body, swathed in towels and tubing, and raced to the intensive care unit. He survived. I survived. For a while, we all thanked the medical establishment for saving us.

A couple of years later, however, even the specialist admitted the problem: I had been induced. The forced contractions tired my uterus. I couldn't deliver. If I had been allowed to progress without medical help from the beginning, Jordan and I may well have found our way through to a natural birth.

Medical technology did not save me until after it caused me to need it. In the case of birth, too much of the time, though not always, this is true.

॰

We are bodies born, first and foremost. From beginning to end and every moment in between. We are bodies born, and because we are born, we are never alone. We are who we are because someone loved us enough to keep us alive. We are who we are because someone loves us enough to keep us living. And no matter how much we want to think and believe that we are doing it all ourselves, responsible for ourselves by ourselves, we would not be able to move or breathe or think such a thought were it not for the relationships we create and share with those whose living enables ours.

This realization can provoke fear and even anger. It challenges our most cherished sense of agency and control. Yet again, this apparent obstacle to our satisfaction is not so. The reverse is true. When we remember that we are bodies, completely dependent on other bodies to be who we are, we discover our power. The power of our birthing breathing bodily selves is not a power to do whatever we want with our bodies, or to manage other bodies to do our bidding, even if we can to some extent. It is a power to *name* the relationships that support us, challenge us, and enable us to give birth to ourselves as the moving bodies we are. It is a power to *make* these relationships *real* as the conditions that are enabling us to become.

Our sensations of depression and despair are calling us to bring this power forth in ourselves. Now.

22

Divining Truth

'With knowledge, the body purifies itself; making experiments with knowledge, it elevates itself; in the lover of knowledge all instincts become holy.'
— *Zarathustra*, 189

We live in a time where medical technology, the market economy, and a culture of consumption converge in a worldview that interprets the shapes of our thwarted desire for spirit as problems to medicate. Drug companies, religious groups, spas, and self-help workshops broadcast a similar message: *find here the remedy you seek for the pain you feel from life in the post/modern world*. Even if we refuse to buy, the climate pressures us to anesthetize our sensations of dis/ease. Any other response is deemed irrational, as if we were choosing pain by choosing not to numb our feeling of it.

The array of offerings is not the problem. Nor is our desire for guidance in finding the sense of vitality, direction, and belonging that nourishes us. Such support is crucial. The problem lies in our tendency to believe that we can hand over money, time, and energy to someone who will tell us how to live our lives, and give us what we need in order to make our pain go away.

Here the cycle of breaths proves to be a life enabling intervention. When we practice the cycle of breaths with the aim of inviting a sensory awareness of the movements making us, our experience of our desire and of our pain shifts. We learn to recognize our desire for spirit calling us, through our pain, to exercise our ability to name and make real the matrix of relationships we need to support us in giving birth to ourselves.

CR

The drag of depression can come down on us at any time. Nagging at our edges, pulling us down. Often we are not expecting it. Clouds roll slowly in over our heads; or form suddenly, at the slightest provocation, and swarm into a massive thunderhead. The storm may build across years, or crash on us all at once.

When it does, we can't move. Nothing engages us. Things we enjoyed pale into insignificance; things we have to do weigh heavily. We may feel as if our life is falling apart, or too tightly wrapped, stifled in routine. Something is missing; something is wrong. Sometimes we are clear about what that missing link is; other times we are not. Sadness soaks in or a lackluster indifference, laced with resentment. We don't want to feel this way.

When feelings of depression engulf us, our first response is predictable. We deny what we are feeling. We push ahead, mind over body, looking for some hook to pull us along. We lurch towards something we know we enjoy, something that will make us feel good!

If that doesn't work, we reach for something to pique our sensory selves and override the feeling. It may be something noisy to eat, the thrill of sexual contact, or a deluge of light and sound that distracts us from the quiet dark. We may engage in a frenzy of activity, doing good, or making things clean. Putting order in place. If the sensation continues to haunt us, we may seek to numb it with drugs and alcohol.

In the wake of our efforts, we may feel a spasm of relief, a brief respite from the weight, but more often than not, the darkness returns, heavier and less penetrable than before. We can't move.

In such downward spirals, the cycle of breaths can help break the fall. Just as it does in relation to our desires for food and sex, the cycle of breaths provides us with a breather, the time and space we need to stay in touch with our freedom; it provides us with a paradigm for problem solving, guiding us to explore and unknot our tangled desires from four different sensory perspectives; it provides us with a concrete reminder of the elemental forces webbing us into the universe, and the resources they offer, and above all, it helps us cultivate a sensory awareness of our own bodily becoming. In all these ways, the cycle of breaths awakens in us what we need to discern the wisdom of our pain and move with it.

CR

When depression grips or anxiety wrings, you can pay attention. Even if you don't feel like doing anything, even if you can't do anything, you can breathe. You are breathing, and you can respond to your feelings by allowing your attention to fall back to your breathing.

Beginning with the earth breath, you can just let go. Breathing in through your heart, you can, with the exhale, release the effort of trying to hold yourself up. You can let down, breathing the length of your body into the floor.

As you breathe your cells toward the earth, letting your flesh slide, you can notice the earth pressing back up along the length of your contact with it.

The ground is supporting you, holding you, doing work for you, even if nothing else is. You can lean into it. You will not fall. You don't have to do anything. You are breathing.

In such moments, the cycle of breaths allows you to rest and be. It opens a small safe place for you to affirm that you are. Who you are. Where you are. *This is who I am right now.*

You stop fighting yourself. *I can only begin from where I am. I am here. Am here. Here.* The earth, pressing back on you, gives you the very sense you are lacking of solidity and weight, as you give yourself to it.

ɖ

Trained as we are to choose or lose, we tend to imagine that the sense of ground we seek lies outside of ourselves, in some idea or realm of knowledge that is certain and true. *What do you believe?*

We ask and we want to know, for we are comparison shoppers. We want to know for sure that this belief or this practice, this path or this relationship, is going to take our pain away, and give us the sense of vitality, direction, and belonging for which we long. We want to be the ones who know, the ones with the right answer, even if what we know is the particular way in which we don't know what lies beyond the ends of life.

Once we are certain that we have found this ground, we defend it mightily against all other options. "My god can kick your god's butt," says a T-shirt in a Christian fashion line.

Yet as we separate from our sensory selves, in hot pursuit of certain truth, in the effort to get it right, we build up patterns of muscular and emotional tension that inhibit us from releasing ourselves into the wisdom of our desire. We grow increasingly dependent upon the authorities to support us in what we believe.

The only ground we have is the ground within ourselves that we find by breathing open a sensory awareness of our connection with the earth. The only ground we have is a sensory awareness of the movement that is making us. Breathing. Becoming. Attending. The only certainty available to us is the certainty that wells within us as we move in ways that honor our pain, naming and making real a world we love that loves us.

ɖ

Breathe down into the earth, and breathing again, out through skin into the air. Attending, follow the breath in and out. Surfaces dissolve. Skin is porous.

As you breathe yourself light, the tight wad of your pain comes into view. You breathe around it, and slowly breathe through it, inviting it to unfold. As your sensation expands, it may grow large indeed, erupting in a cry of exasperation or despair. Breathing out, you soften the jagged edges, and sigh with relief as you allow the sensation to be what it is. Your wanting. Your yearning.

Breathing again you trace the reach and roots of the discomfort. You want something you don't have, but what? Why? Possibilities shuffle before you. Food. Touch. Affirmation. Comfort. Security. Purpose. You feel constraints holding you back. *I can't. I won't. I don't have time or money. It is inappropriate. It is wrong*. You feel your attachment to what is holding you back and still you cannot let go.

As you breathe your pain open, your sense of it shifts. *The movements I am making are making me*. My movements are making me split. Conflicted. At war with my own self. Out of control. Empty. Helpless. Feeling as if there is nothing I can do and no way out.

As this perspective opens, the sensations themselves shift. *What movements am I making that are making me into someone who is feeling this?*

You may realize how tired you are. How buried in work. How dazed by the noise and confusion of your life. How immured by the walls of dulled senses. You may also feel impulses to respond that flare with frustration at your weakness. You may want to clamp down on yourself or give up.

ଓଃ

Trained as we are to choose or lose, we also come to believe that desire is about pleasure, that satisfaction is immediate, and that what we want is the particular object we desire.

None of these things are true. Pleasure is guide not goal. We feel pleasure when we are moving in relation to the object of our desire in ways that exercise our health and well being. When we make pleasure an end-in-itself, we lose it.

The object is not the goal either. The object cannot guarantee the pleasure we seek.

The "goal" is the *transformation that occurs in us as we pursue what it is that we think we want.* When we learn from the object or person or teaching or practice how to make the movements it describes, we establish a relationship with it that will enable it to give us the pleasure of our own bodily becoming. Or not.

Desire is the energy of our wanting, an energy that takes ever-evolving shapes as we continue to learn and grow. The shapes of our desire are the shapes of ourselves—the shapes that the movements we are making as we sense and respond are making in us.

And when we breathe through our desire, and allow it to unfold, we find this creativity at its core. We become aware that the desire, or rather, the pain we feel in wanting, is calling us to unfold a dimension of our own potential for thinking, feeling, and acting. There are movements in us crying out in frustration, waiting to be born. There are capacities to give, limbs of ourselves languishing for relationships that will support their fruit. *That is why I hurt. I want to move.*

The practice of moving with our desire itself teaches us what our mind over body thinking thinks we must acquire through mastering our desires. We learn patience, humility, acceptance, honesty, and love. Other movements are possible. Our pain is guiding us to overcome ourselves and find them. *To breathe.*

☙

The fire breath sinks a deeper charge. Breathe down into the ground, out into the skin-touched light, and then into the cradle of your belly. Follow the breath deep into your sensory folds and squeeze, pumping awareness through your flesh. Activate an inner sense of movement. *I am moving, in spite of myself. I can move.*

As you squeeze and release, energy pulses through yourself, up through your vital core. It will be subtle at first. Ripples then waves. It can be terrifying too. For as energy flows, feelings of depression, anxiety, or despair may grow stronger yet again. Clearer.

Even so, along with the terror, comes another realization, an even stronger sensory awareness. *The movements I am making as I breathe like this are making me into someone who can feel my pain as a gift.* The movements you are making as you breathe are making you into someone who can ground, open, and clarify that pain, transforming it into a source of insight and inspiration. The movements you are making are making you into someone who knows, in your body, that your capacity to create and become new patterns of sensing and responding is stronger and more real than this moment.

I am giving birth to myself as someone who is more than this pain. Someone who can name this pain, and dance with it.

∞

Our mind over body training primes us to want to find the one ladder, the one calling, the one way, the one drug, the one will. We train our senses to look for the one place or path that will fit us like a glove. Fingers and toes. *If I find the one right thing, then I will be happy.* I will know who I am, why I am here, what I am supposed to do. I will know where I belong.

Happy if, happy when.

It is an illusion. The world is not already carved into a set menu of all possible paths. All paths do not yet exist. While some people may know early on in their life who they are and where they are going, for most people, the path is crooked. While some people are born with a potential that mirrors a possibility that exists already, most aren't. While the pursuit of an external prize can indeed be the challenge we need to unfold a part of who we are, the value of doing so will never lie in the prize itself. The value lies in the movements that the pursuit elicits from us, the discoveries we make about ourselves, the capacities we develop along the way, and the relationships we honor and tend as crucial to our well being.

Our desire for spirit is as richly textured and complexly knit as the web of talents and gifts we have. If we search for the one right place to fit in, we separate ourselves once again from the sensory awareness that would guide us in naming and making real the matrix of relationships that our singular person needs to be born. The pleasure our desire seeks is the pleasure of participating consciously in the rhythms of our own bodily becoming.

When we participate in these rhythms we do feel a sense of agency; we are choosing how and where to direct our attention. Yet we enjoy and exercise this sense of agency in the complete awareness that we are wholly dependent for this feeling on our relationships with those who have supported us in feeling it.

We thus know our responsibility: we must tend the sensory awareness that keeps us learning from our pleasure and our pain about how to give birth to a life enabling world.

CR

Breathing again, into the fiery core of your being, dive into the heart of your desires. What do you want? What do you feel you are lacking? What are the movements within you that are dying to be made? What are the potentials for pleasure that you have yet to explore?

At first, you may not feel anything. Your mind may drift to fears that rope you tightly. To your obsession with the one Will. To your despair at ever finding a way for yourself. You breathe again, down, out, and deep within. You let go and wait.

Soon enough, inklings appear. At first you may feel that all you want to do is eat. Stuff your feelings of malaise into the dark corners of your brain. You may want the rush of sexual pleasure to take you away. But as you breathe some more, as you press on these desires, asking for more clarification, they yield to others.

New movements appear that align with your pleasure and health. What you want is to do something that will give you a feeling of satisfaction. You want to find a place in the world where what you have to give is needed and appreciated. You want that kind of deep engagement with life that yields the deepest pleasure.

Simply feeling the ache of this desire can be overwhelming. Exhausting. It pushes you to the brink of despair. How are you ever to find what you need? Will you ever be happy?

As you breathe into the ground, and find your strength in the earth; as you breathe open and find your freedom in the air; as you breathe deep into your belly and ignite your creative fires, you begin to sense what is true.

There is no path. There is no ladder that will get you there. No prize to snag at the end; no competition to master along the way. All you have to guide you to this sense of deep connection are the many micro impulses to move that arise within your sensory self. Your singular bloom.

This thought comforts. For, stuck as you may be, you realize that the first move you make can be small, very small indeed. It can be and it must be. You are breathing. You are paying attention to your breathing. You are honoring the currents and composition of life in you. There is nothing else to do. Nothing else that matters.

Breathing again into the flames of your being, a sense of strength begins to pool, even in spite of yourself. You feel the strength of the elements—in you, of you, not you, beyond you. Breathing through your connections to earth, air, and fire, you open up a sense of your bodily self as connected, as part of a larger mass. *This is not just about me.*

As you breathe, the grounded, air-filled, fire-warmed energy begins to flow, through your limbs and into the world. You breathe the water breath, and the pull of the current through you invites impulses to move. Pain sprouts possibilities.

You remember a book that a friend recommended. You recall a performance you wanted to see that will be given next weekend. You feel a pull to walk, long and hard, into the thick of the woods. Or to try out that yoga class. You feel an impulse to write in a journal, paint a picture, or clean out the closet. You decide to talk to someone. To visit the local religious community. To bake some bread.

It doesn't matter what it is. At first, it doesn't even matter whether or not you respond in any other way but to acknowledge the impulse, to appreciate how the movements you are making in breathing, as you attend with care and respect to your elemental sensory self, are making you into someone who can feel these impulses to move.

After some time, one impulse may return, stronger than the others, calling for attention. It need not be big. It can be small indeed. But if you allow ourselves to follow it, to make the movement in relation to yourself or others that is arising, your sensibility cracks and shifts.

You are exercising your power to name. You are finding in the pain an impulse to move in ways that bring to life the relationships you need to support your ongoing unfolding.

It is not that you are creating relationships for yourself out of nothing. You are rather acknowledging what is already true for you at the level of those impulses, however tiny, and committing yourself to honor those relationships consciously as strands in the matrix that will support you in giving birth to yourself. Again and again.

CR

This is how we grow. We unfold who we are, as singular persons, by feeling the opening of a direction, the span of a challenge that we have not yet crossed. We can feel this gap as pain and turn away. We can reflect it back on ourselves as hatred or judgment for not yet having it or being there. Or, if we can cultivate a sensory awareness of this desire as what our movements are making in us, we can learn to welcome our unmet desire as a potential for pleasure that we have yet to unfold—as an incentive to reach deeper into our freedom and farther into the space of the not-yet towards what we want, trusting somehow that our desire is carrying the seeds of its fruition. This is faith.

Once begun, the journey never ends. We are constantly becoming until the moment of death. In every instant along the way, our desire for spirit is calling us to be fully present in and to that moment, to engage our abilities in ways that support our ongoing participation in the work of giving what we have to give.

Every day, if we attend to it, our desire for spirit offers a new twist, a subtle variation, a pinch of longing, a sense of some movement yet to be made. There is no once and for all point in time where we arrive at certainty and our final self.

The cycle of breaths keeps us honest. As we return again and again to our sensory awareness, we discern, trust, and move with the ever-evolving wisdom generated in our own unique engagement with the all that is.

All we have to give is the work that the ongoing satisfaction of our desire for spirit demands.

ᛕ

A month or so after Kai's birth, I begin to notice that Geoff seems depressed. His energy is low. He isn't smiling. For several days I wait and watch, letting him be. But it continues. A week goes by, and another. It isn't just the exhaustion of working on the house. Something more is going on. What? Should I bring it up?

Sitting on the grass behind the house, we begin to talk. Yes, he admits. He is overwhelmed by the list of tasks to be done. Even more, however, he is paralyzed with the uncertainty over how we will support ourselves financially. He is unsettled by the chaotic stacks of boxes piled everywhere. We spend hours looking for objects we safely stowed. Somewhere. He can't move.

Gazing up at our unfinished bedroom, he notes: "It is like carrying a large board. You are on one end and I am on the other. It is really hard work. Sometimes you just don't feel like singing."

Something within me rises in protest. "We should always feel like singing!" I cry. "And if we don't, then we should put the board down and hug each other until we do. Nothing else matters. Nothing else matters. All that matters is that we are loving each other through it!"

I had never thought this thought before. It erupts within me as a visceral response to the pain I feel in the face of my partner's pain. It seems so right. I am naming what is at stake. Understanding dawns.

"If we are loving each other through it," I repeat for myself as much as for him, "then whatever happens is OK. And if what we are doing pulls against our love, then it just is not worth it."

‹∞›

It takes another several months for me to grasp the meaning of the words that burst through me that day. I realize that Geoff and I moved to Hebron Hollow *for love*. How romantic, I muse.

It was love that brought us here, not the dream, not the book, not the deal. We moved because we loved each other enough to desire a life lived together, a life in which our love could be and would be the creative force and defining horizon manifest in every detail of our living.

Yes, we want a life where we can work side by side and together, co-parenting and co-creating. A life where the kinds of thinking and valuing we believe essential for the health of the planet can flourish. A life where we can cultivate a relationship to the natural world, honoring its seasons and rhythms as the enabling medium of our art and ideas. All of these movements contributed to leading us here.

But even more to the point: our desire to move sprang forth as an expression of how much we value the love we have for each other as a flow that gives birth to what is best in us. We moved to the farm so that we could live more and more in the world of that love.

The implication of this insight is something I had not anticipated. *By moving for love Geoff and I were creating a situation in which the love we had wasn't enough.* Our love had to grow. We felt the pinch of depression and dread because we loved enough to want more. The anxiety of taking on such a huge risk wrapped us and wrung us out, demanding that our love grow strong enough to handle it.

The pain was love calling. *Put down the board.*

In another life, I might have fled from the pain of my desire for more by retreating into a warm bath, a far corner of the house, or a crossword puzzle, and waiting for the moment to pass. Here, when the mess seemed hopelessly chaotic, our only option was to name the relationships with each other and with our children that were supporting us in giving birth to ourselves. Our only option was to find a home in love.

Hug until you feel like singing.

Here on the farm, our love must be strong enough, selfish enough, to dare to have faith in its right to thrive. The hug that brings us to the point where we feel like singing is a life enabling touch, a touch that drops us into our bodies, and reconnects us with the sources of our freedom and creativity. It is a hug that draws forth in us a sense of being supported, enlivened, and released from our pain. It is a hug that makes love real in the moment as what will enable us to pick up the board and sing.

Nothing else matters, as long as we are loving each other through it.

As the love Geoff and I have for each other grows, so does the desire we feel to live in it, and the pain we feel when the world it opens in and around us fades. It is the kind of love that grasps you hard and whispers in your ear: never enough. *There will never be enough time for me to experience this. Never enough time to enjoy it.*

We live for such moments, for making more of those moments, as many as are possible before we die. We want to leave in the full-bodied knowledge that it is a blessing to live.

Geoff says it time and again. We are creating our religion. We are naming and bringing into being a world where we are *free* to do what we *must* to find, trust, and move with the wisdom in our ever-evolving desire for spirit.

23

Moving for Love

'The spirit is then as much at home in the senses as the senses
are at home in the spirit; and whatever takes place in the spirit
must enkindle a subtle extraordinary happiness and play in the
senses. And also the other way around!'
— *Will to Power*, #1051, 540

When surfing for answers to the questions of life's meaning and
purpose, the options dazzle and overwhelm. Every worldview
tells a story about what is real and true. Every human tells a story
about what a given religion or philosophy means and why it is
right. Amidst a weave of stories, personal and communal, shapes
of culture emerge, a religion, a philosophy, a way of life.

Yet the differences among the options are less significant than
what they share. When we breathe to move and move to breathe,
we realize that every symbol, teaching, belief, or practice,
philosophy, religion, or treatment plan, itself represents a pattern
of movement — multiple patterns of mind, heart, body coordination. Each one is offering us an opportunity to discover inside
ourselves the capacity to make the movements it represents,
whether those movements involve cultivating a mind over body
sense of ourselves, engaging a daily meditation practice, or
believing in a vision of the promised land.

As we stretch to consider an idea, bend into a demonstrated
posture, or organize our senses around a ritual, we exercise
capacities for thinking and feeling and acting in ways other than we
had previously experienced. We create and become new patterns of
sensing and responding that unfold our talents and gifts.

With this perspective, we arrive at a new understanding of what it means to believe. If the effort of moving with a particular belief or practice ignites a blast of pleasure or joy or healing within us, then our immediate impression is that this symbol or teaching or practice is true, and it is. It is real and true *for us* because it has allowed us to discover something about ourselves that strikes us as who we are and want to be. Our movements are creating the network of relationships that is actually enabling our unfolding. *We believe*.

When we believe, then, we are exercising our power to name and bring into being a world we love that loves us. And by exercising this capacity, we stir in ourselves the feelings of vitality, direction, and belonging that our desire for spirit seeks as the condition for our ongoing well being. It is intoxicating.

લ

At first this observation may trouble us. Isn't there anything to believe or trust that is once and for all true? Are our beliefs and practices mere figments of imagination that we concoct for our own pleasure? Why believe or practice at all?

Breathing to move and moving to breathe, we know why we do. It is not to guarantee ourselves a certain ground or a safe delivery from pain. When we believe and when we practice, we provide ourselves with a *sensory training* that we cannot get anywhere else. As we learn to make the movements prescribed to us by a given religious platform or program, we wake up to the creative power of our bodily becoming. As we bear witness to the changes in us that our believing and practicing effect, we know our capacity to change. We become aware, as nowhere else, of a basic fact of human bodily life: we are always bodies becoming. We are never not engaged in this process of creating and becoming new patterns of sensation and response. We are never not creating our values, our ideals, our gods, and the relationships by which we live.

We find ourselves believing, and believing in whatever we perceive as enabling us to thrive. *God is true because God lives in me enabling me to be who I am.*

Once we make this shift in how we experience our will to believe, we have the best criteria available to us for navigating the dizzying array of religious and spiritual options surrounding us. For if, in making the movements we are led to make by a given authority or text or context, we find ourselves separating from the very sensory awareness that is guiding us to seek them out, then we know: the relationship is not one that will support me in giving birth to myself. *This is not true for me. I can't believe.*

On the other hand, if, in making the movements, we find ourselves enlivened, unfolded, and brimming with the pleasure of it, then we are inclined to name what is enabling us to become who we are as *our* religion, our faith, our practice. We make a commitment to let live what is ever enabling us to be. We join the community of those who are similarly moved. We proclaim its truth to all. And as we do, we make that matrix of relationships *real*: it is an enabling us to give birth to ourselves. It is real because it lives in us. We are different.

People with different sets of talents and gifts will find their self-creating powers exercised by different approaches. Those with a large capacity to reason will find more pleasure and truth when engaging perspectives that offer rational arguments for their program. Those with a strong emotional life will warm to dimensions of religious life that emphasize devotion and love. Those with a vibrant kinetic, sensory orientation will gravitate towards forms of belief and practice that allow and encourage them to exercise this capacity for movement as an instrument of discernment.

In any case, a path will be true for me when the movements I am making as I learn to move with it are allowing me to name and make real the relationships that support me in giving birth to myself.

CR

We are complicated. Our bodies are full of mystery. There are capacities for sensation and movement in us that we never even imagine possible. We may discover whole ranges of experience by accident. We may be led to explore other regions by the example of someone else's account. We may experiment for years without uncovering that trigger that releases the desired responses within us. We may exert all of our efforts in one direction only to be swept sideways into novelty or bliss.

The patterns of movement we must make to unfold who we are are more complex than any rational account can delineate. The imagination of the Universe is far greater than ours. All along the way no one else can ever know or tell us how to awaken the unique patterns of creativity that we each are. It is our desire for spirit, our sensations of pleasure and pain, that provide us with the surest guides we have.

Discerning the wisdom of our desires is a life's work. The work of a life. The work that a life is. The work that takes a life and more to complete. Yet at any moment along the way, if we are bending the power of our minds to the ongoing rhythms of our bodily becoming, we will find the vitality, the sense of direction, and the deep connection with life that satisfies our desire for spirit.

CR

The question begins to bother me about a year after moving to the farm. A nagging, unanswered question. Why am I *here*? Why has my desire to dance, my desire for spirit, led me here?

I moved to the farm to dance, to honor the practice of dancing as the source of my writing. I wanted to make dances that remain faithful to our bodies of earth and the body of the earth, dances that would express a mutually enabling relationship of human to earth as the context of our lives. That was my belief. My truth. I named it and acted on it, and moved to create the network of relationships that would enable me to realize it.

So, what is happening? Nothing. I'm not dancing. I don't feel like dancing. I am walking and doing lots of yoga but I am not dancing. Why not?

I am confused. Slightly troubled. As I think back to my most memorable experiences of dancing, most of them occurred out of doors, in nature spaces. On the beach. In the mountains. In the woods. It is not that I would decide to dance as a response to beauty. I would simply find myself moving. At such moments something surges alive within me and yearns to leap and turn, to throw my arms to the heavens, to dive and blow, tumble and disperse, fall and rise again. Only then do I begin to notice what is around me, and see what is moving me as *beautiful*. So why not *here*?

Days pass. I walk and walk with my blooming body, then my nursing body. Walking the land and loving it. Taking in the shape and texture. Witnessing the summer greens shading into autumns golds and oranges, folding into winter wind-swept blues and grays. Honoring the edges of the mountains, revealed. But I am not dancing.

On my early walks I trace a path, and repeat that path again and again. I notice changes. One day I see only horizons, the next blades of grass. A following day a view over the shoulder of a hill pops up before my eyes, surprising me. On another I catch the shadow of a haystack, mirroring a passing cloud. I stop making the grandest view my goal. I start to play, to go off the beaten path. I follow the impulse to move over the surfaces of the fields, backwards and sideways.

The land begins to teach me, soften me, open me up. I breathe down and out and in and through. Sensations breach and dive. Waves of unrecognized wakefulness course through my limbs. At the crest of a hill, my heart bursts as the curve of another hill comes into view. Following the arc of a tree trunk, I ache for the sky.

Getting to know the land, I muse, is like getting to know a human body, the body of a beloved. Every curve of its expanse is an infinity to explore. I revel in the play, but I am not dancing. I run and skip. I cavort and lung. Yet the space seems too vast, too complicated, too strange to comprehend in movement. Only once did I come down the mountain saying to Geoff, yes, I danced.

One Sunday I am so troubled that I am not dancing, that I have to do something. I decide to begin again, to try to reawaken my passion for dance. I put on *Concert at Lowell Hall* – the CD of Geoff's that had inspired me to make my own movement years earlier. I lead myself through old exercises, familiar friends. I lean on them to move me, and open me up to myself. I breathe through the routines, breathing to move and moving to breathe. Down, out, in, and through. Warmed, I begin to improvise, inviting and following impulses to move as they arise in me.

As I am doing so, the horizon of the room suddenly shifts. The land I have been walking comes alive in me. It is startling. I feel the shape of the rolling hills, the view across to Farmer Larry's. Clouds fleck the sky, floating overhead in me. The grass stretches before me, softly blowing in me. I can't see this view, but it is as if I am there, on the meadow. I am seeing and not seeing, and not just seeing. I am part of what I am seeing inside myself.

Other senses perk to life, a sense of touch, of skin. I am in the picture and it is alive in me. I am myself, the land, the air and sky, the relationship between.

The days of walking and witnessing begin to make sense. I have been steeping myself in the sights, sounds, and smells; the sunshine, earth, and sky; the sensibilities, thoughts, and emotions evoked in me by my movement.

My movements are making me. Earth, air, fire, water. Outside came inside and now inside is coming outside. *I guess I was dancing after all.*

It occurs to me. *I am becoming the dancer I wanted to be. Yes!* I cry inside. *I desire this. I name this. I want it to be true.*

Am I moving in a different way than moments before, when my mind was preoccupied with dinner plans, errands to do, aches and pains, and evolving nap times? It is hard to say. I feel different. I know only this: the movements I am making are expressing what it is about the land that moves me. My dancing movements are making real the relationship to nature that I need for unfolding my capacity to dance. The relationship that inspires me to move. I feel the pleasure, and it is a pleasure that obligates me to let what moves me live.

The words of Nietzsche's Zarathustra float through my mind: *I could only believe in a god who could dance.*

ॐ

Where is the line between delusion and dream? Between impractical fantasy and the creative, bodily work of naming and bringing to life new worlds, values, and gods?

There must be a time when new worlds do not exist, when they are only figments of the imagination, fragile wisps in the air, kept alive against all odds by a warm and beating heart. Such worlds may appear decidedly irrational. Why drop a good job and move to a farm? Why have a home birth? To some they may seem to contradict the way life works. They assume some kind of magic.

Yet I know for myself. I have to create beyond myself. I have to be constantly naming and making real a world in which I want my children to live. To survive without such hope, I would need a constant supply of Valium or alcohol. I would stop eating. Stop having sex. Stop loving life. A domino of denials.

Still, can we create any reality we want? No. And for the same reason that we cannot simply eat anything or have sex with anyone and expect to find the pleasure we seek.

The freedom we have to follow our desires is guided by forces internal to desire itself, to the rhythms of the desire, and the conditions necessary for its fulfillment.

In the case of our desire for spirit, too, if we are attending to the wisdom in our desire, then the shapes of the worlds we create will express the honest and care-full attention to our selves that we are practicing.

There are "spiritual" worlds I reject as humanly wrong. People starve themselves and claim they are stronger. People renounce their sexual desire and claim it is a sign of their greater love. People cut and brand themselves, inflict pain upon themselves, and claim that these actions give their lives meaning. People lie to one another and claim that they are protecting each other; people abuse one another, for their own good.

What is wrong with such worlds? They do not support those who inhabit them in honoring their bodily sensations and feelings as a source of wisdom. When we override a body's most basic means of discernment, we are not free to do what we must in order to unfold what we have to offer the world. We ignore our obligation to let live... to let our own bodily selves be born.

A body, so denied, rebels. Softly at first, then more persistently. We may try to suppress the signs, but they keep appearing in the form of erupting desires. We imagine that we must exert more will power; we buy reinforcements for our self-denial. We purchase products and processes, beliefs and practices, that promise to alter our wayward desires. We hide our transgressions and confess them in secret. Tiring of the effort, we inevitably release our grip and pursue immediate gratification, imagining that such gratification is possible, fast food, easy sex, quick judgment. Then in shame, we crack the whip even harder, herding wayward desires back into line.

What is the difference between delusion and dream?

Pursuing a delusion, we dull, numb, and overwhelm our senses. We separate ourselves from the healing wisdom of our bodily movement.

Pursuing a dream, we open ourselves to sense and respond to the movements that are making us, ever alert to whether those movements are bringing into being a world we love that loves us. We cultivate our ability to participate consciously in the rhythms of our bodily becoming, honoring our obligation to let all those on whom we depend live.

While there may be pain involved in learning to move with the wisdom of our desires, that pain is neither goal nor means. It is neither accidental nor necessary. It is not desired in itself nor pursued as a proof of merit. It emerges in us as a sign of a potential in ourselves we have to unfold for greater creativity, freedom, and love.

ଔ

Human beings exist to move. Human beings evolved to move, to find pleasure in moving. And when we are not too tired or hungry or lonely or cut off from ourselves, moving is what we want to do. When we move, we breathe. When we breathe, we feel. When we feel, we find play in the moment and experience the wisdom our desires contain. What we perceive changes. We who perceive change. And our desires themselves shift, falling more and more in line with what we need for our maximal pleasure and ultimate health.

We find our way to the experiences of nourishment, intimacy, and affirmation we seek. And we do so as the condition that enables us to unfold what we have to offer the world. We learn to live in love.

It is time to move.

Acknowledgements

This book would not have been written without the support of many people who have appeared at various points in its life to inspire, encourage, and offer constructive advice.

First to name are the readers whose responses buoyed me along at critical points in the seemingly endless process of writing and rewriting. Courtney Bickel Lamberth read an early draft in its entirety, grasping its strands of truth and pulling firmly in pages of thoughtful comments. Suzanne Evenson, Susan Franklin, Cynthia LaMothe, Jack LaMothe, Sharron Rose, Miranda Shaw, Kathleen Skerrett, Melissa Schulz, and Tony Stiker read sections of the manuscript at stages along the way, in each case mirroring moments of it back to me in ways that helped refine the whole. I appreciate their engagement with the project immensely.

Conversations with Bill Throop helped me better navigate crucial bends in my argument. I am also grateful to the inspiring work of Deborah Abel and Lee Perlman, and an opportunity to speak provided by Martin Evans-Jones that catalyzed insights along the way.

The couples I have married have contributed to this book as well. Every set of reflections on marriage I have offered, and the unique shape of each couple's relationship, have helped me unfold a new dimension in my understanding of its mysteries. I am grateful for the trust of these couples.

I am grateful to Joelle Delbourgo for her good will, enthusiasm, and perseverance in promoting this book, and for prompting me to find a clearer narrative voice.

This book was a family affair. While I was in the initial stages of planning this project, Geoff and I moved with our three children from a Boston suburb to an 1840s dairy farm in upstate New York. As described in chapter 21, our fourth child, Kai, arrived a month after the move. The experiences we had together, step by step, fed the ongoing life of this project, unfolding in uncanny sync with the themes at hand.

In the couple of years since the writing began, the children have grown far beyond the accounts of their younger days offered here. I am ever grateful to them for allowing me to share these stories of how they once were – or how I perceived them to be. The respect I feel for them is and has been immense. I learn so much from each one.

Finally, from beginning to end of this project, my life partner Geoffrey has believed in the work, supported my day to day engagement in the project, read more drafts than anyone, and insisted time and again that I tell our story.

May I never stop saying thank you.

Bibliographic Essay

What follows is a list of sources and resources. Some of these books have helped me in shaping my ideas. Others have provided me with information to support my theses. Still others offer those interested in learning more about a given topic a direction in which to move from here. In cases where the significance of a work is not evident, I have offered a brief description. The list is more provocative than exhaustive, offering points of entry to topics I cover.

Preface, Chapters 1 & 2

In writing this book, the ghost that haunts most closely is that of Friedrich Nietzsche (1844-1900). The quotation at the end of the Preface is his, from *Ecce Homo* (356), as are the quotations at the beginning of every chapter. I hear his words and his logic echoing through page after page of my own writing. Yet the Nietzsche I hear is one that not many others have heard. It is the one I discovered when studying the images of dance scattered across his corpus.

Nietzsche uses "dance" to figure an alternative to the anti-life, anti-body, anti-earth worldview he perceived among Christians of his time. To dance, for him, was to affirm life – all of it. His steadfast commitment to a radical affirmation of life, to relearning the small things, and to creating values that "remain faithful to the earth" continues to inspire me.

For the reading of Nietzsche that percolates through this work, as well as a full bibliography of his work, see the first half of my book, *Nietzsche's Dancers* (Palgrave Macmillan, 2006).

For chapter headings, I have selected quotations from:

Nietzsche, Friedrich. 1989. *On the Genealogy of Morals and Ecce Homo*. Ed. & Tr. by Walter Kaufmann. Vintage Press.

— — — — —. 1984. *Human All Too Human*. Tr. Marion Faber.

Lincoln: University of Nebraska Press.

—————. 1974. *The Gay Science with a prelude in rhymes and an appendix of songs*. Ed. & Tr. by Walter Kaufmann. Vintage Press.

—————. 1967. *Will to Power*. Trs. Walter Kaufmann & R.J. Hollingdale. Vintage Press.

—————. 1967. *The Birth of Tragedy and The Case of Wagner*. Ed. & Tr. by Walter Kaufmann. Vintage Press.

—————. 1954. *The Portable Nietzsche*, Ed. Walter Kaufmann. Penguin Press, containing "Thus Spoke Zarathustra," "Twilight of Idols," and "The Antichrist."

In developing my approach to "the body" as *movement*, I have been deeply influenced by Isadora Duncan and Martha Graham—two American modern dancers who were also inspired by Nietzsche. These two artists developed practices of dance and philosophies about the value of what they were doing that have guided my own movement investigations. In particular, both women focus on the movement of *breathing* as a kinetic key to creating works of art that affirm life in a Nietzschean sense. Extended discussions of their work appear, respectively, in parts Two and Three of *Nietzsche's Dancers*.

For a general introduction to Isadora Duncan, see:

Daly, Ann. 1995. *Done Into Dance*. Indiana University Press.

Duncan, Isadora. 1981. *Isadora Speaks*. Ed. Franklin Rosemont. San Francisco: City Lights.

—————. 1928a. *Art of the Dance*. Theatre Arts Books.

—————. 1928b. *My Life*. Liveright.

For a general introduction to Martha Graham, see:

de Mille, Agnes. 1991a. *Martha: The Life and Work of Martha Graham*. Random House.

Graham, Martha. 1991b. *Blood Memory*. Doubleday.

—————. 1973. *The Notebooks of Martha Graham*. Harcourt, Brace and Jovanovich.

Helpern, Alice. 1994. *The Technique of Martha Graham*. Dobbs Ferry,

New York: Morgan & Morgan.

Horosko, Marian, ed. 1991. *Martha Graham: The Evolution of Her Dance Theory and Training*. Chicago: A Cappella Books.

My practice of hatha yoga, stretching back twenty years, provides me with an ongoing practice of sensory awareness that complements my work in dance; as well as an arena for experimenting with the cycle of breaths, and continuing discoveries of what bodies can know when they, that is we, breathe to move and move to breathe.

Finally, recent advances in neuroscience are coming around to support the philosophy of bodily becoming advanced here. Scientists are identifying the concrete pathways by which bodily movement enables the developments of our brains – how and what we think and feel and act.

Of the many current and emerging works, the following have been particularly helpful:

Blakeslee, Sandra and Matthew Blakeslee. 2007. *The Body Has A Mind of Its Own: How Body Maps in Your Brain Help You Do (Almost) Everything Better*. Random House.

Cozolino, Louis. 2007. *The Neuroscience of Human Relationships: Attachment and the Developing Social Brain*. W.W. Norton & Company.

Damasio, Antonio. 1999. *The Feeling of What Happens*. Harcourt, Inc.

Doidge, Norman. 2007. *The Brain that Changes Itself: Stories of Personal Triumph from the Frontiers of Brain Science*. Penguin Press.

Ratey, John J., with Eric Hagerman. 2008. *Spark: The Revolutionary New Science of Exercise and the Brain*. Little, Brown & Company.

Desire for Food
Chapters 3 & 4

The obesity "crisis" or "epidemic" has been so named in a swarm of articles and books appearing over the last fifteen years. In researching this phenomenon, I consulted articles and books on the subject, beginning with cover stories in *Harvard Magazine* ("The Way We Eat Now: Ancient bodies collide with modern technology to produce a flabby, disease-ridden populace," May-Jun 2004) and *Time Magazine* ("Overcoming Obesity in America," *Special Issue*, Jun 7, 2004).

The paradox that struck me – levels of obesity rising in tandem with a burgeoning diet and drug business – is one that Michael Pollan has described as a "national eating disorder" and the "*American* paradox": we are "a notably unhealthy people obsessed by the idea of eating healthily" in "Our National Eating Disorder," (*NYT Magazine*, Oct 17, 2004, 76).
For an analysis of the role of played by obesity in increasing rates of diabetes, and of the personal and social costs of these trends, see:

Kaufman, Francine. 2005. *Diabesity: The Obesity-Diabetes Epidemic.* Bantam.

For a taste of diet culture, take a look at the phenomenal success of Weight Watchers and of the Atkins Plan, the first diet program to break through into bestseller status. Several have followed since, with the most recent being the *South Beach Diet*, visible in bookstores, internet advertising, and on the printed labels of foods themselves.

For critiques of the obesity epidemic that focus on the role played by economic, political, and social systems, see:

Brownell, Kelly. 2004. *Food Fight: The Inside Story of the Food Industry, America's Obesity Epidemic, and What We Can Do About It.* McGraw Hill.

Critser, Greg. 2003. *Fat. Land: How Americans Became the Fattest People in the World*. Houghton Mifflin.

Nestle, Marion. 2002. *Food Politics: How the Food Industry Influences Nutrition and Health*. Berkeley: University of California.

Pollan, Michael. 2006. *The Omnivore's Dilemma: A Natural History of Four Meals*. Penguin Press.

Schlosser, Eric. 2001. *Fast Food Nation: The Dark Side of the All-American Meal*. Houghton Mifflin.

Spurlock, Morgan. 2005. *Don't Eat this Book: Fast Food and the Supersizing of America*. Putnam Adult.

For evidence that commercial weight-loss programs do not work, see:
Kolata, Gina. 2007. *Rethinking Thin: The New Science of Weight Loss and the Myths and Realities of Dieting*. Farrar, Straus & Giroux.

For evidence that the obsession with body size is not just an issue for women, see:
Pope, Harrison, Roberto Olivardia, and Katharine Phillips. 2000. *Adonis Complex*. Free Press.

For interpretations of the role of Christian values in shaping American eating and dieting practices by scholars of religion, see:
Griffith, R. Marie. 1999. *Born Again Bodies: Flesh and Spirit in American Christianity* Berkeley: University of California Press.

Lelwica, Michelle. 1999. *Starving for Salvation*. Oxford University Press.

Chapters 5, 6, 7 & 8

The idea of having lost a "sense of enough" was one I initially discussed with Prof. Kathleen R. Skerrett over fifteen years ago.

A sampling of the many books that focus on providing people with information about how to eat consciously includes:
Goodall, Jane, Gary McAvoy and Gail Hudson. 2005. *Harvest for*

Hope: A Guide to Mindful Eating. Warner Books.

Kingsolver, Barbara. 2007. *Animal, Vegetable, Miracle: A Year of Food Life*. HarperCollins.

Lappe, Anna and Bryant Terry. 2006. *Grub: Ideas for an Urban Organic Kitchen*. Jeremy P. Tarcher/Penguin Press.

Nestle, Marion. 2006. *What to Eat: An Aisle by Aisle Guide to Savvy Food Choices and Good Eating*. North Point Press.

Planck, Nina. 2006. *Real Food: What to Eat and Why*. Bloomsbury.

Pollan, Michael. 2008. *In Defense of Food: An Eater's Manifesto*. Penguin Press.

Wansink, Brian. 2006. *Mindless Eating: Why We Eat More Than We Think*. Bantam.

Waters, Alice. 2007. *The Art of Simple Food: Notes, Lessons, and Recipes from a Delicious Revolution*. Clarkson Potter.

Weinstein, Jay. 2006. *The Ethical Gourmet: How to Enjoy Great Food that is Humanely Raised, Sustainable, Nonendangered, and That Replenishes the Earth*. Broadway Books.

Desire for Sex
Chapter 9, 10, 11, & 12

The relationship of sex to lifelong love is an issue that arises in debates over marriage, contraception, abortion, teen sexuality, sexual education, funding of international health agencies, as well as in the rafts of how-to guides that are flooding the self-help market.

For perspectives on physiological and emotional dimensions of love and sex, see:

Angers, Natalie. 1999. *Woman: An Intimate Geography*. Houghton Mifflin. Discusses latest research on female physiology, evolutionary biology, and its cultural interpretations.

Carey, Benedict. 2004. "Addicted to Mother's Love: It's Biology, Stupid," *NYT*, 6/29, D7.

Fisher, Helen. 2004. *Why We Love: The Nature and Chemistry of Romantic Love*. Henry Holt and Company.

Slater, Dr. Lauren. 2006. "Love: The Chemical Reaction," *National Geographic*. February, pp. 32-49.

Tiefer, Dr. Leonore. 2004. *Sex is Not a Natural Act and Other Essays*. Westview Press.

For responses to sexual dissatisfaction:

Berman, Jennifer and Laura Berman. 2005. *For Women Only: A Revolutionary Guide to Reclaiming Your Sex Life*. Times Warner Books. Discusses latest work by sex researchers and therapists on female sexuality.

Conrad, Dr. Sheree, & Dr. Michael Milburn. 2002. *Sexual Intelligence: Boost Your Sex IQ and Get Exactly What You Want in Bed*. Three Rivers Press. Offers a diagnosis of and response to American's general dissatisfaction in their sexual lives.

Harris, Gardiner. 2004. "Pfizer Gives Up Testing Viagra On Women," *NYT*, Feb 28, B1-2. For account of failure to produce impotence drug for women.

Shalit, Wendy. 2000. *A Return to Modesty: Discovering the Lost Virtue*. Free Press. For a response to the oversexualization of culture that encourages modesty among women in dress and behavior.

Tuller, David. 2004. "Gentleman, Start Your Engines?: Racing for Sales, Drugmakers Cast Erectile Dysfunction in Youthful Terms," *NYT*, Monday, June 21. E1, 10. Details how popularity of drugs for impotence is shaping experience of sexuality as phallocentric.

For history of marriage as institution and ideal, see:

Coontz, Stephanie. 2005. *Marriage, a History: From Obedience to Intimacy, Or How Love Conquered Marriage*. Penguin, Viking Press. Illuminates "marriage crisis" as a unique development in human history.

For analysis of extra-marital sex and its social and psychological implications, see:

Denizel-Lewis, Benoit. 2004. "Friends, Friends with Benefits and the Benefits of the Local Mall: Life inside the under-age sexual revolution, where casual sex is common, online ratings are scrutinized, everybody wants to be so detached—and boys still get what they want on Saturday night," *NYT Magazine.* May 30, 30-35, 54-8.

Ponton, Dr. Lynn. 2001. *The Sex Lives of Teenagers: Revealing the Secret World of Adolescent Boys and Girls.* Plume.

Rich, Frank. 2004. "The Plot Against Sex in America," *NYT.* Sunday, December 12. Section 2, 1, 24.

Chapters 14, 15, & 16

Among the myriad books on how to nurture successful partnerships, two stand out:

Hendrix, Harville. 1988. *Getting the Love You Want: A Guide for Couples.* HarperPerennial.

Schnarch, David. 1997. *Passionate Marriage: Keeping Love & Intimacy Alive in Committed Relationships.* Owl Books, Henry Holt.

Desire for Spirit
Chapters 17, 18, & 19

For a critical account of escalating levels of depression in contemporary society and the booming business in anti-depressants, see:

Healy, David. 2004. *Let Them Eat Prozac: The Unhealthy Relationship Between the Pharmaceutical Industry and Depression.* New York University.

For best-selling examples of self-help literature, see:

Chopra, Deepak. 1994. *The Seven Spiritual Laws of Success: A Practical Guide to the Fulfillment of Your Dreams.* New World Library.

Gafni, Mark. 2001. *Soul Prints: Your Path to Fulfillment.* Pocket Books.

Levoy, Gregg Michael. 1998. *Callings: Finding and Following an Authentic Life.* Three Rivers Press.

Myss, Caroline. 2003. *Sacred Contracts: Awakening Your Divine Potential.* Three Rivers Press.

Warren, Rick. 2002. *The Purpose-Driven Life: What On Earth Am I Here For?* Zondervan.

For accounts of the contemporary American landscape of religion and its new age, fundamentalist, and evangelical threads, see:

Balmer, Randall. 2000. *Mine Eyes Have Seen the Glory: A Journey into the Evangelical Subculture in America.* Oxford University Press. Chronicles various manifestations of evangelical religion.

Cox, Harvey. 2001. *Fire from Heaven: The Rise of Pentecostal Spirituality and the Reshaping of Religion in the Twenty-First Century.* De Capo Press. Examines worldwide growth of Pentacostal Christianity.

Gibbs, Eddie. 2000. *Church Next: Quantum Changes in How We Do Ministry.* Intervarsity Press. Provides example of text in evangelical church building.

Moore, Laurence. 1995. *Selling God: American Religion in the Marketplace of Culture.* Oxford University Press. Details the commodification of religion in contemporary America.

Smith, Christian. 2002. *Christian America: What Evangelicals Really Want.* University of California. Gives sociologist's account of evangelical movements.

Wolfe, Alan. 2005. *Transformation of American Religion: How We Actually Live Our Faith.* University of Chicago. Charts increasing individualism across religious spectrum.

Wuthnow, Robert. 2000. *After Heaven: Spirituality in American Since the 1950s.* Berkeley: University of California. Maps movement of people away from organized religion towards personal seeking as framework for spirituality.

The Pew Forum on Religion and Public Life claims that one in four Christians worldwide are Pentacostal or charismatic.

Chapters 18, 19, 20, 21, & 22

Close on the heels of Nietzsche are a pack of philosophers and religious thinkers whose thinking about religion continues to inform my sense of being in the world. I must name:

Descartes, René. 1996. *Discourse on Method and Meditations on First Philosophy*. Ed. David Weissman. Yale University Press. Dares to imagine that he has no body.

Freud, Sigmund. 1950. *Totem and Taboo*. Tr. James Strachey. W.W. Norton.

— — —. 1961. *The Future of an Illusion*. Tr. James Strachey. W.W. Norton.

— — —. 1961. *Civilization and Its Discontents*. Tr. James Strachey. W.W. Norton.

Hegel, G.W.F. 1988. *Lectures on the Philosophy of Religion, 1827*. Ed. Peter Hodgson. Berkeley: University of California Press.

— — —. 1977. *Phenomenology of Spirit*. Tr. A.V. Miller. Oxford University Press. Offers a vision of "spirit" as the dynamic, self-creating life of all that is.

Kant, Immanuel. 1960. *Religion within the Limits of Reason Alone*. Tr. Theodore Greene and Hoyt Hudson. Harper Torchbooks. Offers classic expression of how to mount a rational defense of religion.

Kierkegaard, Soren. 1983. *Fear and Trembling and Repetition*. Ed. & Tr. Howard V. Hong & Edna H. Hong. Princeton University Press. Offers classic expression of why religion can never be held accountable to rational thinking.

Marx, Karl. 1978. *The Marx-Engels Reader*. Ed. Robert Tucker. W.W. Norton & Co. Offers unparalleled account of alienation.

Schleiermacher, Friedrich. 1988. *On Religion: Speeches to Its Cultured Despisers*. Ed. Richard Crouter. Cambridge University Press. Characterizes religion as a unique, life enabling kind of experience.

Those who have helped me evaluate and advance western attitudes towards "the body" in religion include:

Berry, Wendell. 2002. *The Art of the Commonplace: The Agrarian Essays of Wendell Berry.* Ed. Norman Wirzba. New York: Avalon.

Daly, Mary. 1978. *Gyn/Ecology: The Metaethics of Radical Feminism.* Boston: Beacon Press. Exposes the workings of patriarchal power.

Foucault, Michel. 1980. *Power/Knowledge: Selected Interviews and Other Writings 1972-1977.* Ed./Tr. Colin Gordon. Random House, Pantheon Books.

— — —. 1977. *Discipline and Punish: The Birth of the Prison.* Tr. Alan Sheridan. Vintage Books. Understands the soul as an effect of bodily discipline.

Irigaray, Luce. 1993a [1987]. *Sexes and Genealogies [Sexes et Parentes].* Tr. Gillian C. Gill. Columbia University Press.

— — —-. 1993b [1984]. *An Ethics of Sexual Difference.* Tr. Carolyn Burke and Gillian C. Gill. Cornell University Press. Embraces "woman" as a critical tool in reading and righting philosophy.

Jantzen, Grace. 1999. *Becoming Divine: Toward a Feminist Philosophy of Religion.* Bloomington: Indiana University Press. Celebrates birth as a critical category in the philosophy of religion.

Kristeva, Julia. 1980. *Desire in Language: A Semiotic Approach to Literature and Art.* Trs. T. Gora, A. Jardine, L.S. Roudiez. Columbia University Press. Traces the relationship between word and flesh.

Leder, Drew. 1990. *The Absent Body.* University of Chicago Press. Addresses the implications of our training as readers and writers for what we can experience and think about ourselves.

Merleau-Ponty, Maurice. 1964. *The Primacy of Perception.* Ed. James M. Edie. Northwestern University.

Miles, Margaret R. 1991. *Carnal Knowing: Female Nakedness and Religious Meaning in the Christian West.* Vintage Books, Random House. Attends to the different media that shape our experience of being bodies.

Sheets-Johnstone, Maxine. 1990. *The Roots of Thinking*. Temple University Press. Documents how bodily movement enables symbol use.

For voices in the academic study of religion that have influenced my understanding of religion as an expression of the human power to name and make real a world we love that loves us, see:

Douglas, Mary. 1984. *Purity and Danger: An Analysis of the Concepts of Pollution and Taboo*. Routledge. Analyzes how distinguishing between order and disorder is a world-forming act.

Durkheim, Emile. 1995. *The Elementary Forms of Religious Life*. Tr. Karen E. Fields. Free Press. Cites collective effervescence as a spur to symbol making.

Eliade, Mircea. 1987. *The Sacred and the Profane*. Harcourt Brace. Describes the sacred as a mode of experience.

Geertz, Clifford. 1973. *The Interpretation of Culture*. Basic Books. Lays out definition of religion as a system of symbols that function as a model of and for action in the world.

Kaufman, Gordon. 1993. *In Face of Mystery: A Constructive Theology*. Harvard University Press.

Smith, Wilfred Cantwell. 1991 [1962]. *The Meaning and End of Religion*. Fortress Press. Exposes religion as a word with a history.

Sullivan, Lawrence. 1990. "'Seeking an End to the Primary Text' or 'Putting an End to the Text as Primary,'" *Beyond the Classics? Essays in Religious Studies and Liberal Education*. Eds. F.E. Reynolds, S.L. Burkhalter. Scholars Press. Attends to the role of the senses in our relationship to texts.

Taylor, Mark C. 1999. *About Religion: Economies of Faith in Virtual Culture*. Chicago University Press. Illustrates how religion is "most interesting where it is least obvious."

Turner, Victor. 1995. *The Ritual Process: Structure and Anti-Structure*. Aldine de Gruyter, Examines how the movement between activities (ordinary and ritual) serve to make the world what it is—structured.

Van der Leeuw, Gerardus. 1986. *Religion in Essence and Manifestation*. Tr. J.E. Turner. Princeton University Press. Evolves a phenomenology that privileges movement, relationship, and love.

—————. 1963. *Sacred and Profane Beauty: The Holy in Art*. tr. David Green. Henry Holt. Acknowledges the religious potency of dance.

For a critique of how children are increasingly alienated from nature and why they must learn to experience it, see:

Louv, Richard. 2005. *Last Child in the Woods: Saving Our Children from Nature-Deficit Disorder*. Algonquin Books.

For recent account of reciprocal evolution of nature and human desire, see:

Pollan, Michael. 2001. *The Botany of Desire: The Plant's View of the World*. Random House.

Index

BOOKS

O is a symbol of the world, of oneness and unity. In different cultures it also means the "eye," symbolizing knowledge and insight. We aim to publish books that are accessible, constructive and that challenge accepted opinion, both that of academia and the "moral majority."

Our books are available in all good English language bookstores worldwide. If you don't see the book on the shelves ask the bookstore to order it for you, quoting the ISBN number and title. Alternatively you can order online (all major online retail sites carry our titles) or contact the distributor in the relevant country, listed on the copyright page.

See our website **www.o-books.net** for a full list of over 500 titles, growing by 100 a year.

And tune in to myspiritradio.com for our book review radio show, hosted by June-Elleni Laine, where you can listen to the authors discussing their books.